AN IMPROBABLE
ASTRONAUT

AN IMPROBABLE ASTRONAUT

How a Georgia farmboy wound up
flying the space shuttle

ROY D. BRIDGES, JR.

Heart Ally Books, LLC
Camano Island, WA

Published by:
Heart Ally Books, LLC
26910 92nd Ave NW C6-406, Stanwood, WA 98292
Published on Camano Island, WA, USA
www.heartallybooks.com

For information about special discounts or for bulk purchases,
please contact Heart Ally Books at info@heartallybooks.com.

ISBN-13: (epub) 978-1-63107-039-6
ISBN-13: (paperback, black & white) 978-1-63107-040-2
ISBN-13: (paperback, color) 978-1-63107-041-9
ISBN-13: (hardcover) 978-1-63107-042-6
Library of Congress Control Number:
10 9 8 7 6 5 4 3 2 1

*Dedicated to explorers who strive to reach their
dreams despite obstacles.
Go for it.*

Roy salutes as he is lowered into the neutral buoyancy pool
for EVA training for STS-61F

Contents

List of Illustrations

Publisher's Notes

You hold in your hands the tale of a boy who dreamed of becoming an astronaut.

Not an unusual dream. But for this boy, it came true.

The story doesn't end with that trip to space. Wrapped in tragedy and hope, this is the story of a life spent seeking adventure and looking out for others.

Finding himself in positions of power, Roy has worked to make life better for others, focusing on dignity for those around him, from the Air Force Academy all the way to Kennedy Space Center.

Throughout the book, you will find occasional passages set aside with a border. These passages contain extra information about what is going on in the narrative. If you're caught up in the adventure and can't wait to find out what happens next, you can skip these passages and come back to them later. Or, if you're curious, you can step aside momentarily and enjoy these deep dives into the moments and technology that shaped the stories.

Out of respect to the conventions and expectations of the military and NASA readership, we have selectively adopted their traditional capitalization of many organizations, titles, and ranks.

Roy's story would not be Roy's story without Roy's family. Look carefully at the first few chapters: there you will find the people who instilled the values in the boy that shaped the man. Throughout the book, you will hear echoes of their words, their wisdom, their support, and their love. In addition to segments that offer a glimpse of the Bridges's often nomadic home life, you'll find highlights from Christmas letters and a deeper understanding of the family who were inestimable to his success.

Lisa Norman
Publisher
Heart Ally Books, LLC

Preface

From a young age, I wanted to pursue a life of adventure.

When I was five years old, I searched for buried treasure and hunted bears in the woods near our home with my cap pistol.

As a ten-year-old, I devoured library books full of other people's adventures.

When I was forty-two, I fulfilled my lifelong dream: Adventure among the stars.

In 1957, when I was in high school, the Russians put the first artificial satellite into orbit. Our first US astronauts, the Mercury Seven, were selected in 1959. Yuri Gagarin became the first human in space the year that I graduated high school: he completed one orbit of Earth on April 12, 1961. Alan Shepard followed shortly, piloting *Freedom 7* to the edge of space on May 5, 1961. Those flights began the race to the moon.

After reading and hearing about all those great adventures, I decided I wanted to pursue a path that might lead me to join the explorers in this new frontier of space. I didn't care how improbable that might be. I saw it as my great adventure.

And it was.

There were many difficult steps along the way, each requiring a lot of hard work and good luck. Some were full of danger, bringing me to death's door. Others initially proved so difficult for me to master that they seemed impossible. None were easy, and any misstep could derail my quest.

My family, including my parents, grandparents, and relatives, helped shape me into the man I became—one who could succeed despite the extreme challenges of becoming an astronautics engineer, USAF fighter pilot and test pilot, NASA astronaut, USAF Major General, and NASA Center Director. They each lived lives of love and service. I admired them and their sacrifices for me as I matured.

In this book, I share my journey with you and show how each member of my family contributed to my success.

They helped me become an improbable astronaut.

Book 1: The Quest

Section 1: Formative Years

Chapter 1: Early Memories
1943 and beyond

The year of my birth was in most ways the worst year in history. Our nation was fighting in World War II (WWII) on two fronts, in Europe and the Pacific, with no end in sight. Millions were dying, and here I was, just entering the world, my journey just beginning.

First impressions

My earliest memory is of lying on a cold, hard table in the local hospital at three years of age, looking up. I remember these old, Gothic windows that made it seem like I was in some kind of a cavern, looking way up at some light. I felt icy hands touching my chest and neck.

An infected flea had bitten me while I was playing in the sandbox in the yard, and I developed typhus fever. Typhus was a dangerous illness for young children back then, and there were no effective treatments or vaccine for it during WWII—just aspirin and cold compresses to lower my dangerously high fever. Antibiotics to treat it effectively were not commercially available until years later. At this writing in 2021, there is still no vaccine to prevent it.

I don't remember much of my stay in the hospital. I was suffering from a high fever. I don't recall any other aches and pains, but I could tell from the attention I was getting that I was in danger. Although my mother and doctors were with me, I felt alone, staring up at that high ceiling, feeling so tiny in such a large space. Like I was standing on the edge of the Grand Canyon and looking down into the abyss, or staring down at the Earth from hundreds of miles high in space.

Roy's first photo with mother, Elizabeth, in October 1943

Grandparents

Grandpappy and Granny Rose

My next memory was waking on a small cot next to my parents' bed in my Grandpappy Bridges's home and seeing a lot of get-well cards from concerned friends and relatives pinned to the wall above my cot. I had been discharged from the hospital after a week. My grandpappy—Dr. Bridges—continued to treat me while I recuperated fully over the next week. After that, I was allowed out of bed, and life returned to normal.

Until the age of five, I grew up in their home. It was a two-story house, and the front room was his office where Grandpappy met and treated patients, and my grandmother, Granny Rose, worked alongside him. I grew up watching my grandfather treat many patients. They often had nothing to give him in return except ham and chickens, which he happily took as payment.

When I was just three or four years old, Grandpappy would take me with him on house calls. I don't know why he did it, but I suspect that it was to give my grandmother a break from watching me while my mother worked. I thought riding with him was fun, and he was always kind to me. I wasn't always nice to him. He would leave his ball of chewing tobacco on the car door handle, and I delighted in knocking it off into the dirt.

Looking back on my time traveling with him and observing him treating patients in his home or during house calls, I was impressed by his work ethic and professionalism. He worked around the clock when necessary, and his work was his hobby. He cared deeply for his large family, including my parents and me. He extended his hospitality to us by inviting us to live with him until my parents could save enough money to purchase a home.

Grandpappy Bridges initially started his practice in a rural community of North Georgia, making house calls using a two-horse wagon. Because of the distance to his patients, he would have to stay with them during the most severe medical crises, resulting in many long days away from the family.

To advance in his rural practice he moved to areas with larger populations several times over the years. After suffering a bout of typhoid fever and mumps, as well as a mysterious ailment similar to sleeping disease, he gave up his rural practice and moved to East Atlanta in 1922 or 1923 when he was fifty-three or fifty-four. He practiced there for over twenty-five years, specializing in treating typhoid fever and pneumonia. He also delivered over three thousand babies and cared for them as a pediatrician until he was forced to retire in the late 1940s due to heart disease. Locating his practice in Atlanta meant that he did not have to travel so far to render care on house calls, and hospitals were readily available to treat severe illnesses.

Father, Roy Bridges, in the Army Air Corps during WWII

Great-Granny Lucy

Given how young I was, I needed some parent-like guidance. My mom was always working at the hospital, and my dad was off working in the army in my earliest years. After WWII was over and Dad was home with us again, he worked at a large wholesale hardware store. Grandpappy was out on house calls or treating patients in the office, and Granny Rose helped him. I needed to stay out of the way.

So Granny Lucy, Granny Rose's mother, would visit often, and she became my caregiver and playmate during her frequent visits. I was lonely, and I loved it when she visited. She often stayed for several days, and she made an impression on me even though I was only between three and five years old. She engaged me and kept me occupied with activities and stories.

Granny Lucy had a colorful personality, a real life force. She had an interesting background. I learned about it later in life, and it impressed me.

She was born in 1854, eloped at age fifteen, and was married at the Jug Tavern in Winder, Georgia. She and her husband traveled in a covered wagon to a campground at Stone Mountain and camped for their honeymoon.

Once, early in their marriage, her husband came home a little too tipsy after a boys' night out. She kicked him out of the house, barred the doors, and guarded them with a shotgun. He spent the night outside and never came home drunk again.

When she was sixty-three, long before I was born, she was kicking up her heels and dancing with her granddaughter when she fell and broke her hip. She refused to go to the hospital and had to use crutches and a wheelchair for the rest of her life. Although she couldn't dance anymore, she still had a high-energy personality and exuded optimism and excitement no matter what she was doing.

Granny Lucy at her 90th birthday party in 1944

One of her favorite activities was making silk quilts, which were simply beautiful works of art. She always invited me to help as she arranged colors and shapes from her large collection of scrap materials. I still have one of her masterpieces; it reminds me of what a life force she was. She lived to be 101. My dad lived to be 102, so I assume that he inherited the longevity gene from her.

One of Granny Lucy's quilts

Grandaddy and Grandmother Roberson

Holidays

My mother's parents were Edgar and Esther Roberson of Screven, Georgia. Grandaddy Edgar Roberson was a carpenter and a farmer. When he was young, he sang in a barbershop quartet. Grandmother Esther Roberson was a music teacher.

Holidays, especially Thanksgiving and Christmas, were spent with my mother's extended family at her parents' home in southern Georgia. That was a really big deal, and they made a habit of doing that all during my childhood. On Christmas Eve, my grandfather would lead us around his farm to select and harvest a Christmas tree, which we decorated in the evening. Of course, Christmas mornings were always filled with excitement as we discovered what Santa had left under the tree. Santa's presents were not wrapped; we could see everything instantly as we entered the room.

Grandmother and Mom worked all morning to prepare a feast. They were joined by an African American lady named Minnie, who lived nearby. She was part of the family for these gatherings every year.

Around noon, the relatives from Jacksonville and Savannah would arrive. Everyone brought wrapped presents that went under the tree. Some brought delicious cakes and pies. The dining table was expanded with leaves to its maximum size to accommodate the adults. We kids sat with our cousins at a card table. After a delicious meal of roast turkey and many side dishes, we delighted in the bounty of desserts. The adults' conversations were filled with laughter. We kids also had a great time catching up on each others' adventures.

After dinner, we all gathered in front of the fireplace in the living room. Presents that our relatives had brought were passed out, and we tore into them to discover what was inside.

My aunts and uncles in Mom's extended family were always generous to my sisters and me with their gifts of toys and clothing. Listening to their stories about their lives and work, I imagined that they had much richer experiences than I did living on the farm. They worked in interesting jobs and lived in big cities, yet they showed an interest in me.

Growing up in affluent urban areas, my cousins had more advantages than I had. Rather than being envious, I just liked hanging out with them and hearing about their experiences. And after all the presents had been opened, my cousins, my sisters, and I would often get into some kind of mischief in the yard or barn. Being included in a large family who gathered often and enjoyed sharing and supporting each other made me feel warm and loved.

Summers

Every year, starting after my fourth birthday, my folks left my sister Eva Mae and me with our grandparents after the July Fourth holiday for an extended visit. My grandfather's eighty-acre farm was in Screven, in south Georgia, about forty miles from the seacoast. His three brothers and their families lived on adjacent farms carved out of the homestead when their father died.

We were fortunate to have a cousin, my grandfather's niece who was my age, living on the adjacent farm and within a short walking distance. We often met to play. We delighted in playing games of kick-the-can, or board games such as Monopoly or Clue when we had to hide from the sun from 10:00 a.m. until 4:00 p.m. to avoid sunburns in those days before sunscreens.

One favorite activity was going swimming in the afternoon. Granddaddy had a "swimming hole" formed on his property when he allowed the county to excavate clay to repair the local roads. The water table was high, and the clay hole filled with fresh water. He built us a diving board. My sister, my cousin, and I spent many hours swimming and playing in that rustic swimming pool.

Once we got older, we could occasionally go to a nearby river to swim. Our great-uncles chaperoned these river trips; they had cars and my maternal grandparents did not. Some afternoons we would jump in the back of the pickup truck and they would haul us over to Jekyll Island for some beach time.

My grandparents and I developed a very special relationship. The year before I started school, when I was spending the summer in south Georgia with them, we got the letter telling us that Grandpappy Bridges had died. Grandmother took me out on the steps at the side of the house and read the letter to me. Of course I was sad to lose him; he had been part of my life. But I was so young when I knew him that I was not able to form the same degree of closeness with him as I developed with Granddaddy and Grandmother Roberson.

Given such experiences—holidays, summer vacations, spending my second-grade year with them—I was a frequent traveler with my maternal grandparents.

Chapter 2: Testing My Boundaries
Age 5–7

Our family outgrew our one-room apartment at Grand-pappy and Granny Bridges's home after my sister Eva Mae was born. My grandparents' bedroom was on the other side of the house from the great room that served as the office where they received and treated patients, separated from it by a foyer and heavy wooden sliding doors in the bedroom doorway. We had the big bedroom, which was upstairs—just one room, with a bathroom down the hallway.

When I was five years old, my folks bought a home in Lithonia, Georgia, a suburb of Atlanta. The two-bedroom house was called a garage apartment. The living quarters were upstairs. A garage and laundry room were on the first floor.

In addition to more room for our growing family, it helped my dad get a more stable and productive job than working in a hardware store. The garage apartment was next to a one-story workshop on the property; its proximity allowed him to start his own business repairing automotive parts.

Loaded for bear

Moving to our new home in Lithonia, Georgia, was exciting because I had opportunities for adventures in the area around our garage apartment home. Dad had a large workshop in a separate building where he rebuilt automobile generators and starters. To get to it, we had to go through the woods parallel to the highway, which ran in front of our house and his shop for several hundred feet.

Behind our house and the shop, the woods covered many acres. I loved to imagine hunting for bears in those woods with my cap pistol, but I wasn't allowed to do it unless accompanied by my mom or dad. They feared that I would become lost in the underbrush.

True, the underbrush *was* extremely thick. You could imagine that you heard something rustling around in there. I'd pull my cap pistol out and shoot at it, then we'd go running in there to see if we had shot a bear. Of course there was never any bear there. Just like there was never any buried treasure, although I imagined my sister could somehow clairvoyantly point me to it.

My sister, Eva Mae, who was two and a half years younger than I, was my constant companion on my adventures. She helped me search for buried treasure by playing guide and divining where I should dig. We never found any, but the hunts were fun, and we continued to believe that we would eventually uncover the mother lode.

One day I wanted to go bear hunting, but Mom was busy washing clothes and couldn't go with me. I wasn't in the mood to be denied my fun, so I quietly locked her in the garage, exited the house with my sister, and went anyway.

My mother, Elizabeth Roberson Bridges, grew up in Screven, Georgia, the middle child of five. She graduated from Piedmont Hospital Nursing School in Atlanta, Georgia, when she was

twenty-one and then worked as a Registered Nurse at the Piedmont Hospital, where she gave birth to me in 1943. Mom was
the ultimate professional nurse, and for the rest of her nursing
career she worked in a hospital and later on ran a clinic for a
textile mill, giving hearing tests and first aid for on-the-job injuries that didn't require a doctor. She was tough; I think that
anybody who met my mother would say she was sort of a lady
of steel. On this particular day, I seriously underestimated her.

I foolishly thought that I could get away with it, since she
was busy with chores. I really wanted to go hunt bears, and she
didn't have time for it. So I thought if we were really quiet and
just snuck outside of the garage, where she was doing laundry,
we could pull it off. After all, it was going to take a while; this
was back in the days where laundry wasn't just a push of a button. You had to put it through a ringer and all, so I thought, well,
she's busy. She won't notice. She didn't have any need to go
outside; she could just go back up the stairs to the living area
without finding out that the door was locked.

Except that, when I left, I made sure that the downstairs
door that led upstairs was locked as well. So the only way she
could feasibly get out was to break down that garage door. I was
sure we could go hunt bears for a while and go back home and
everything would be just fine.

We hunted and pretended to shoot at bears on the way
through the woods to Dad's shop. After we visited with him
for a while, he became suspicious; he knew that we shouldn't
be there without Mom. He insisted on escorting us back to the
house. I didn't want him to go and tried to talk him into just
letting Eva Mae and me go home on our own. He didn't buy it.

I tried my best to divert my dad by trying to get him to help
me find some bears on the way. I kept pointing out likely spots
to look that would take us off of a direct path, but he just kept
us moving forward.

I prayed that Mom had not noticed that we had locked her inside and left. After all, I told myself, she was busy, and we were quiet as we began our adventure. We had been away for less than half an hour. Maybe she just stayed busy with her chores and didn't try to get out. I knew that she could get pretty angry with me when I was naughty, so I prayed for the alternative.

As we exited the woods I saw the house and my irritated mother standing outside the garage door. The garage door had been ripped from its hinges and was lying on the ground. She had one hand mounted on her hip and a hairbrush in the other, ready to deliver a whipping.

The whipping hurt.

Playing with fire

Not long after that, we were visiting my grandparents' home in Atlanta, and I set off on another adventure with Eva Mae. We went on a fantasy camping trip in the enormous crawl space under their home, which was filled with tunnels that opened at the top, containing the various plumbing pipes. To my mind, it was a cave that needed to be explored.

It was a very large crawl space. The house was on a steeply sloping back yard that flattened out when it got to the back of the house, opening up the space as you got towards the bottom, where we could walk upright. After exploring for a while, we set up a campsite. We built a small campfire, using scrap wood and old newspapers left there by the people who built the house, and pretended to cook dinner.

I knew that building the fire was wrong, but I was just too caught up in my fantasy to worry about it. No one else ever went down there. There were very few windows in the back of the house where they could have seen smoke. It was just a little fire. A few sticks, a bit of paper. Not a bonfire. Just enough to fuel the imagination.

We eventually put out the fire and returned to civilization, but I failed to warn Eva Mae to keep her mouth shut about our adventure. As soon as she saw Mom, she excitedly told her about our camping trip. When Mom learned that we had built a fire under the house, she got her hairbrush and gave me another lesson in what not to do on my adventures.

Walk down that lonesome road

After that, I became somewhat more conscious of safety on my adventures—but I still made mistakes. I started the first grade and rode the school bus to and from school. I had to find something to do in the schoolyard for an hour as I waited for the second bus route.

One day I was standing on the corner of the schoolyard, watching the teenage crossing guard. The crossing guard thought I was waiting to cross the street, and he insisted that I do so. So I did. I didn't want to appear foolish by trying to cross back to the schoolyard, so I decided to just continue walking the several miles home. The walk was on the shoulder of a busy two-lane highway with no sidewalk. When I finally made it home and proudly announced my feat, I got another memorable whipping.

By this time her hairbrush and I were well acquainted.

Hog wild

During my summer vacation with grandparents when I was six, Eva Mae and I went with Granddaddy to feed the pigs one evening before supper. The pigpen was just across the dirt road that ran by the side of the house. I had helped Granddaddy many times with this chore before. The pigs seemed tame and unthreatening. There were a dozen or so small piglets in the pen, and I wanted to make one my pet and play with it. On that evening, I decided that I would catch one.

When Granddaddy finished feeding the pigs, he took Eva Mae's hand and started walking back to the house. I stayed by the pigpen, and they didn't notice. After they went into the house, I climbed over the fence and stalked a cute little piglet, which was all by itself about twenty feet from the rest of the larger pigs. The big pigs were busy eating and didn't notice my stealthy approach.

I pinned the piglet against the fence and caught it. My piglet wasn't pleased and started squealing loudly. I was bent over at the waist as I tried to hold the pig. I happened to look between my legs and saw a several-hundred-pound mother pig and her sisters charging me to protect her baby. The mother and her sisters knocked me to the ground and started chewing on me. Fortunately, Granddaddy heard all of the noise the pigs were making and came to my rescue before they killed me. I had to go to the hospital for stitches and a tetanus shot.

I still have the scars on my buttocks to remind me of that lesson: all farm animals can be dangerous if not treated with respect.

The shape of things to come

I liked testing my boundaries. I think it says something about why I stretched to the point of flying a rocket into space. I kept pushing those boundaries all the way up through that time period.

Testing boundaries has been part of my nature, a constant in my life. For example, on a test program on a brand-new airplane, the Stall/Post-stall/Spin program was pushing the airplane out to its most extreme boundaries to see what would happen. How else could we help other people who inadvertently got into that situation figure out how to get out of it safely?

I think that was what I was doing, even as a kid. I just needed to learn to do it safely. My mom and grandfather knew they couldn't be there every time that I stretched my boundaries and were trying to help me learn safe limits without taking away my sense of adventure.

I was a slow learner.

School days

I didn't go to preschool or kindergarten. I started first grade in Lithonia when I was six. First grade was fun and interesting. I quickly mastered reading and writing despite having no early schooling. It would have been perfect except for being bullied because of my name.

My name was Roy Dubard Bridges, Jr. My family called me by my middle name, Dubard. It was also my dad's middle name, given to him in honor of the nurse who had assisted his mother at his birthing. My family called me Dubard so that there would be no confusion when they addressed me when Dad was nearby.

But that name was a problem at school. My classmates called me "Dobug" or some other variation of my strange middle name. I didn't like the bullies who did it, and I started fights at recess to make them stop tormenting me. I demanded that my classmates call me by my first name, Roy. My family started calling me "Butch" to let me know when I was being addressed instead of my father. Fortunately, I changed schools after the first grade, which put the bullying in my past.

During the summer between my first and second grade, Dad was suffering from a serious lung disease caused by the severe pollution from coal smoke in Atlanta and smoking unfiltered Lucky Strike cigarettes. They planned to move our family to the Bridges family farm near Pendergrass, Georgia, before the start of school for my third-grade year, to get Dad as far away as possible from the polluted air in Atlanta to aid in his recovery from illness. Granny Rose had given them permission to occupy the Bridges farm and make their living from it.

Meanwhile, they didn't want to move me to another school halfway through the year. Instead of uprooting me, they arranged for me to live with my grandparents in Screven for a year and attend school there for the second grade. My sister Eva Mae was not yet in school, and Mom was pregnant with my sister Nancy. They planned to join me at my grandparents' farm after Nancy was born in February and they'd had time to sell our garage apartment home.

I was delighted to spend more time with Granddaddy and Grandmother Roberson. Having spent a lot of time with them during my many visits, I was confident that all would go well. I knew Granddaddy was a quiet, supportive "coach," and I looked forward to spending the year with him as my guardian. I would miss my parents, but I knew it would only be a few months before they moved into my grandparents' home with me.

I have good memories of that second-grade year, despite the lack of many conveniences in my grandparents' home. It wasn't connected to electricity; the Rural Electrification Administration (REA) had not arrived in that area yet. So I studied by kerosene lantern in the evenings. The main bedroom was heated by kerosene stove, but mine lacked heat. Grandmother cooked on a woodstove in the kitchen and used steel irons heated on the stove for ironing clothes. On really cold nights, she would wrap a heated iron in a towel and stick it in my bed near my feet. There was no indoor toilet or shower, so I bathed in a large tin tub that was manually filled with warm water. I helped with farm and household chores before and after school.

In the spring, Mom and Dad moved in with my two sisters. Nancy was born just before they arrived. Mom got a job as a nurse at the hospital in the nearby town of Jesup. She hired an African American woman, a relative of their friend Minnie, to help care for Nancy, which included being a wet nurse. Dad was an understudy to Granddaddy on planting and caring for crops, to prepare him to take over operating the Bridges farm the summer after my second grade.

This was my first lesson on learning to endure hardships and discovering that I wanted to do something other than farming.

Chapter 3: Living on the Farm
Age 8 until high school

Prior to the start of my third-grade school year, we moved to the family farm in Pendergrass. My Grandpappy Bridges had inherited the farm after his dad died. He settled with the other heirs so that he was sole owner. He didn't farm the land, but the sharecropper family did, and they shared in the earnings from cotton crops. When he died, Granny Rose inherited it. She offered to let my father move to the farm and operate it.

The sharecropper's extended family was living in the main farmhouse on the hill, and the sharecropper's mother and father lived in the smaller auxiliary home nearby on the property. We lived in a large canvas tent over a wooden floor during the summer and early fall. During the summer, we left the tent sides rolled up to provide better ventilation and cooling,

On one of the first nights in the tent, I noticed a strange shape in the field. It looked like a big bear. It was just the hulk of a big tree that had died, and in the twilight, it looked like a grizzly bear standing up with its arms out, but I hoped there were no real bears lurking out there. I was old enough by then to know you don't mess around with bears.

Another night I woke up to find something warm and fuzzy next to me on my cot. At first, I was so frightened that my chest tightened, making it difficult to breathe. Then I heard the purring and relaxed. It was a small kitten curled up on my chest and not the dangerous animal that I had imagined had crawled into bed with me.

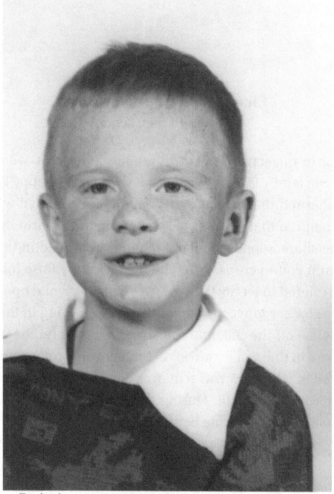

Roy's elementary school photo, probably third grade

My mother got a job as a nurse at the hospital in Winder and later at the larger Hall County Hospital in Gainesville. My father went to school on the G.I. Bill to learn more about modern farming techniques. He turned a dilapidated house on the property, an almost falling-in wreck of a house with a roof that was partially collapsed, into a weatherproof, one-room home for us before winter arrived. He braced the roof up, so it wouldn't be a danger, and installed a sort of picture window—it wasn't fancy, just a wall of regular windows, but it was big. We had electricity, a kerosene stove and oven, and a woodstove for heat, but no other amenities.

It was just one room—just kitchen and bedroom for my parents as well as us kids. It was about the size of a large tent, but it kept the cold air out, and we could have heat in the wintertime. The toilet was an outhouse—something that would continue to be true for years to come.

New school

Because of some delays in moving from South Georgia and getting our tent home set up, I was a few days late joining my third-grade classmates at the Pendergrass Elementary School, which was in a small, two-story brick building. There were two grades per classroom, a small auditorium upstairs, and a small cafeteria with picnic tables downstairs. Meals were cooked on a woodstove, and students took turns chopping wood for it. Potbellied coal stoves heated classrooms. Restrooms were in detached outhouses on the back edge of the school grounds.

I was overwhelmed on my first day at this new school. My father introduced me to the combined third- and fourth-grade class. I had become shy. I didn't like being the center of attention. Speaking in front of a group of strangers was frightening.

That morning, everyone was looking at my dad when he said my name. Thinking I was supposed to say something, I was just frozen. I let the pressure get to me and broke down, which was humiliating. To release the stress, I let out a sob or two.

Shyness was a personality trait that stayed with me until high school. It was so bad that until I was in high school, I would never ask a question in class. Ever. It was unnerving to speak out.

But apparently, there were still some risks that I was willing to take. Once while in the third grade, I stole some cigarettes from my father and took them to school with me. I had them in my book bag when I arrived at the field where we got off the bus to help my parents with chores. When I excused myself to go into the woods to relieve myself, I decided to have a smoke. To my horror, I saw my mom and dad enter the woods as I was squatting and smoking. They had seen the plume of smoke rising out of the small copse of woods and had come to investigate. After that incident, I was often referred to by the nickname "Smokey Joe."

New home

During the spring and summer of our second year on the farm, my parents constructed what was intended to become the two-car garage of our new ranch style farmhouse. The foundation was made of local stones that we harvested from around the farm. This was given a top coating of concrete for the floor.

There were three rooms in our new home. The main room was a combination eat-in kitchen and living room in one half of the house, with a big picture window in front. My parents' bedroom was in the front on the other side and also had an identical picture window. There was a large closet separating the master bedroom from the kids' bedroom, with doors leading into it from both bedrooms. We had electricity, an electric range, and a woodstove for heat at first, which was later replaced by propane gas heat. We eventually had running water in the kitchen sink from a well, but the bathroom was still an outhouse. Bathing was again in a big tin tub that we manually filled and emptied. We lived in this three-room home until I was a freshman in high school.

Using that outhouse in the winter was painful, but I didn't let it bother me or embarrass me. Growing up in this austere environment helped to make me tough and resilient.

Although my folks had grand plans to finish the house, their financial situation never permitted it.

My love/hate relationship with the sun

I don't remember being different from other kids at the time, but my red hair made me different from my friends—something one of Granny Lucy's granddaughters went out of her way to let me know years later, when I was a senior citizen. "You had so many freckles on your face and arms and such bright-red hair that you were the ugliest kid I had ever seen."

I wasn't just visually different; I sunburned easily. These were the days before sunscreen, and I loved being outside. I hated having to stay indoors during the middle of the day instead of playing outside. When I did sneak out, I was often punished with painful sunburns. Of course that didn't keep me from going swimming or hanging out with friends, but I paid a price each time that I did it in the middle of the day when the sun was most intense.

On Sundays when I lived on the farm in Pendergrass, after church I would usually go home with a friend, or my friends would go home with me, because we always went back to night church. One day, friends who had a lake invited me over. We went swimming three times—12:00, 2:00, and 4:00. I was like Batman in a cape for about a month after that, because I could not put a shirt on.

This was a lifelong hatred—my love/hate relationship between me and the sun. You know, "I love you today but I'm gonna hate you tomorrow." Later in life, I paid for it in weekly trips to the dermatologist to treat numerous spots of skin cancer—fortunately not the deadliest kind—but it's a wonder that my journey in life wasn't pre-empted by a serious skin cancer.

New skill

Dad would take Eva Mae and me with him sometimes when he went to the field to plow so my mom could have some relief. We would sit behind him on the only tractor seat. One time as we traveled down the dirt road that ran past our house, he stopped but left the tractor running and went into the house to pick up something that he had forgotten to take with him. He told us to stay put on the tractor. I slid forward on the seat and started playing with the clutch and gear shifter. When I put it into high gear, my foot slipped off the clutch. We lurched into motion.

Roy's home on the farm near Pendergrass, Georgia, from the fourth grade to halfway through ninth grade

By the time my father returned, we were fifty yards down the road. I was panicked, desperately trying to steer in the center of the road. I had no clue how to stop it. I wasn't tall enough to reach both the clutch and brake while steering. Plus, I was too focused on steering to figure a way out of the dilemma. I barely heard my dad's frantic yell, "Turn off the key!" but I did, and we slowly rolled to a surprisingly safe stop.

Dad began a dairy business to provide additional income. Milking a few cows before and after school was added to my list of daily chores. Milking cows before daylight on cold winter mornings convinced me to find a different profession.

I picked up other skills that were more fun. Once I was taller, I learned to drive our tractor correctly. Dad purchased a hay baler to provide food for our cows. To help cover the cost of the equipment, we did custom baling for other farmers for a share of the harvested crop. My father would drop me at a field to either cut or rake the hay. He would pick me up for lunch and then drop me off again for the afternoon. He would be in another field with the hay baler. I thrived on the challenge of learning to do an expert job of operating the tractor and looked forward to opportunities to operate more complex machines in the future.

I also drove the truck that we used to haul the bales of hay to the storage shed. My father and a helper would stack the bales in the truck from the field. When driving, I had to sit on a pillow to be able to see out the front windshield. Of course, I wasn't allowed to drive the truck on public roads, but I did drive the tractor on them often when going from one job to another.

Roberson farm life

Until I started high school, my sisters and I continued to spend a majority of summers in south Georgia with my grandparents.

There I learned much of what there is to know about the tobac-co-growing business.

As plants began to mature there was the manual task of re-moving blossoms and suckers. During harvest season, teenage boys picked the tobacco as the leaves ripened, from bottom to top of the plant. This was done every week or so, depending on the weather, and the salary was five dollars per day plus a hearty lunch. Younger kids took the leaves out of the sleds and "handed" them in the right amount to the stringers. "Handers" were paid two dollars per day plus lunch. Teenage girls were employed as "stringers." They would string the bundles on sticks that were about four feet long. They were also paid five dollars per day plus lunch. The sticks would be hung on poles in the multi-story tobacco-curing barns to be cured by kerosene heaters for several days. After cooling off, they were unloaded and processed by kids of all ages to remove the cured leaves from the sticks and be stacked neatly into bales that would be taken to auction. I worked in all of these jobs except "stringer" until I was in high school.

Loading and unloading the barns was particularly hazard-ous. I watched men fall from high up in the barn to the floor. Fortunately I didn't witness any serious injuries, but it was frightening. My legs were too short to stretch from pole to pole, so I would stand on a six-inch wide board stretched between the poles. I had to lean over to grab a stick being thrust up from below. Then I would lift the stick into a vertical position so the person above me could grab it. From then on, I struggled with a fear of falling.

The entire crew was fed well at lunch and allowed to rest for an hour or so during the peak heat of the afternoon. Then all would return to the field to complete the job, which typically started at around 6:00 a.m. Often, the crew was given a ride to the nearest swimming hole or river at the end of the day for a cool swim as an additional incentive. A welcome relief at the end of a long, hot day.

My great-uncle purchased a two-level motorized tobacco harvester. Pickers sat in the four seats on the bottom level and gathered several leaves at a time and placed them on a conveyor chain. The chain delivered them to the top level, where they were strung on the sticks by two stringers. When the sticks were full, the driver would store them in the back of the top level. This was a much more efficient way to harvest tobacco. It eliminated the need for a mule-powered sled, which pickers filled with the picked leaves. Sitting down to pick in the shade of the harvester was much easier than bending over in the hot sun to pick the leaves off the bottom of the big plants.

I served on the crew many times from the time I was in the sixth grade until I entered high school. It was hot, nasty work. Dew that collected on the large leaves would soak the pickers in the morning hours, while heat and humidity were brutal in the afternoons. The tar from the leaves would cover my arms and hands. I usually wore long-sleeved shirts to protect my arms from the tar and sun as well as a large broad-brimmed hat to protect my head, face, and neck from the sun in those days before sunscreen. The only really good thing about it was that we were all in it together—the handers, the pickers, the stringers—so we had a whole mess of kids there, of various ages, and we'd all go swimming afterwards. It was made tolerable, but it was gross work.

Another good reason to find an occupation other than farming!

Domestic life

I spent a lot of time helping to care for the large garden, which needed frequent weeding. Harvest days were especially memorable. We would start picking peas, lima beans, and green beans at dawn and then spend all afternoon shelling and canning them. Before they had electricity, the canning was done on the woodstove, which made the house miserably hot.

The year after I lived with them while in the second grade, my grandparents had finally had their farmhouse hooked up to the electrical grid. Getting an electric refrigerator, stove, and freezer was an immense improvement in comfort and quality of life for them and us. After that, canning was done on the electric stove. They were able to power an electric pump for their well to replace the previous manual water pump in the house. This allowed them to build an indoor bathroom with a toilet, sink, and shower. It made living with them during our extended summer visits much more enjoyable.

Grandmother Roberson had attended college after high school and learned how to be a piano teacher. She emphasized the need to take our schooling seriously and learn the subjects well. She also taught Eva Mae and me to play piano.

She regularly attended the Methodist church and always took us with her. When Eva Mae and I had reached a basic proficiency, she insisted that we play a duet on the piano on Sunday morning at church for the full congregation. That was a scary experience, but we managed to complete it without messing up. Later, when I had learned to play the trombone in the eighth grade, she insisted that I learn and play "Sweet Hour of Prayer" for the congregation during my summer visit. I did it but again hated being in the spotlight.

While Granddaddy was the real storyteller, sometimes when we were helping her prepare dinner or clean up the dishes afterwards, Grandmother would sit down and tell us stories, too.

A close call

During the summer between sixth and seventh grades, Mom took me to the doctor for an update of my typhoid vaccination. After we returned home, I felt ill and lay down on my bed. I woke up from my nap panicked. I couldn't breathe.

I stood on my bed and pounded on the wall. Mom ran into the room to see what was wrong. She quickly got her syringe and gave me a shot of epinephrine in the chest to increase my cardiac output. I started breathing again. My sister was allergic to bee stings, so we had epinephrine in the house in case she got stung.

But I developed such a high fever that she had to check me into the hospital. On the way there she cooled me down with frozen orange juice cans.

This was the only allergic reaction to a vaccine that I experienced while growing up. I soon recovered, but it was a close call.

Changes and challenges

After the seventh grade, the authorities closed our elementary school and a new building was completed near Pendergrass that would serve students through sixth grade. I had to transfer to the high school in Jefferson for the eighth grade and high school.

During my eighth-grade year, I detected a growing tension between my parents. I could overhear their conversation after I went to bed. They were at their wits' end over how to pay the bills on my mother's salary and dwindling income from the farm. She started working double shifts, a day shift as a nurse at the hospital and an evening shift as a private nurse helping sick, elderly people at their homes. This was clearly taking a toll on her, although she didn't complain. My dad had invested a lot in planting pastures and crops to support our large dairy, but a severe drought caused the crops and pastures to fail. He couldn't generate enough income to repeat the planting.

I think most people don't recognize how much capital it takes to start a farm and make it into something that can actually produce an income. It's not just buying the cows. You've got to provide feed for them, and so on. If you have a bad year or two, you can lose it all.

The banker who owned the loans on our farm equipment visited us. He propped his feet on the fence overlooking the pasture where our cows were grazing. "I see a lot of good money in those cows," he said. That was a clear threat to foreclose on the only liquid asset we possessed.

Had we owned the farm, Dad could have used that as collateral to borrow enough money to weather the crisis, but it was tied up in his mother's estate, and his older sisters wanted to be able to sell it. They resented that his mother had given Dad the opportunity to farm it. Hearing my parents' distress that they could not get family support to assist them as they approached bankruptcy moved me to tears. This soured relations between Dad and his older sisters for the rest of his life.

This situation was a heartbreaking failure for my father. He and Mom finally gave up. Dad sold the cows and farm equipment and made enough to pay off the bank loans. To provide more income, he took a job in Gainesville as the credit manager for the Hall County Hospital where my mother worked.

We continued to live on the farm while they saved money for a down payment on a home in Gainesville. Dad began taking me to Boy Scout meetings in Gainesville so that I could get a head start on making new friends. He would wait in the car while I attended evening scout meetings. I have always admired him for making that sacrifice. At the time, given that he was working pretty hard, my thought was, *I can't believe he would do this for me.*

Those scouting experiences helped me to develop my leadership capabilities, which I continued to improve in high school. They became a critical factor in succeeding with my quest.

Chapter 4: Spiritual Awakening
Age 10

From a very early age, I was drawn to being a believer. My grandmother and parents were not demonstrably religious, they just lived that way—subtly. During our summer visits, my Grandmother Roberson took us to her Methodist church every Sunday. My parents always took the family to our nearby Baptist church for Sunday morning and evening services. And, although I didn't know it at the time, my paternal great-grandfather had started this church where I made my public commitment.

So I had it in my system.

One Sunday after the evening youth class at the Baptist church when I was ten years old, I joined my family for the main service. Our young preacher, whom I knew well, was especially loud and demanding with his language as he preached about the horrible fate awaiting anyone who died before accepting Christ as savior.

He made the thought of an eternal home of fire and brimstone so real that I could see the fire, smell the smoke, and feel the excruciating pain. I had wanted to declare my beliefs earlier, but my shyness about being the center of attention paralyzed me, and I didn't overcome my fear of being in the spotlight until high school. I had successfully procrastinated at every other service. I just couldn't get up the courage to march to the altar and accept Christ.

That evening, I knew that it was time to act.

When the altar call came, I jumped out of the pew and rapidly walked to the altar. I felt the need for speed so that my shyness wouldn't gain the upper hand again. I knelt in front of the preacher and congregation and accepted Christ. I was baptized in a small lake a few days later, along with my middle sister, Eva, and my mother. I have a picture of the three of us in my "ancestor gallery."

That night was the first of many times God would guide me through terrifying situations and lead me through quick, accurate responses. Having Him with me would give me the confidence to face death without fear or hesitation and to act correctly regardless of sudden, dangerous situations that I might face in the future. Such confidence would prove to be enormously helpful in my career as a fighter pilot, test pilot, and astronaut.

Spiritual heritage

Later in life, I learned that my paternal great-grandfather, William Harrison Bridges, was the founder of the church where I accepted Christ, that he was its first preacher, and that he had written a book, *Shifting Shadows*, about his religious experience from serving in the Civil War. When I was an adult, I finally found a copy. It was like papers that get put away in the back of the closet—it had nibbles out of many of the pages. Later on, I got a better copy of it, which I have in my file now. But the copy I first read was a seriously rat-eaten version of that book. I read it and was moved by it.

But until I read it, I knew very little about him. I knew that the sharecropper house on the hill on the Bridges farm, where we were now living in our small home, had been his home. And I knew the story about him being a prisoner of war and miraculously coming from the death house back to the place of the living.

I never knew him personally. He was long dead before I came along. I didn't know his story that night when I went forward in the church he had started. But looking back on it...it just makes it more significant.

Great-Grandfather Bridges was raised as an orphan and volunteered to serve in a Georgia cavalry unit in 1862 that saw combat action in Tennessee and Kentucky. He was captured in September 1863 and spent the rest of the war in a prisoner of war camp near Indianapolis, Indiana. He came close to dying from a combination of hypothermia and malnutrition that caused a disease similar to scurvy. He wrote about the moment of his religious conversion as he lay next to men in the prison hospital who were dying.

> *I realized as I lay amid the sick and dying that God was chastising me for my disobedience by placing me on a sick-bed, rendering me impotent to help the dying men as I would otherwise have done if it was in human power. I had refused to heed the early impressions that were made upon me. I often thought of Jonah's refusal to obey the Lord, and oh! many solemn vows I made that if God would permit me to live through the war, I would serve Him the remainder of my life to the best of my ability.*

The prisoners were finally furloughed in February 1865. They were shipped on freight cars to Baltimore, Maryland. There they boarded ships for transport to a port in Virginia and eventually reached Richmond. From there he started walking home to Georgia. After a short distance he became too weak to continue and approached a lady on the porch of a house near the road, begging her for food and water. She took him in for two weeks of recuperation.

He made it home successfully weeks later only to find the area devastated from the war, with many widows in his rural community. His personal life was destroyed as well. His wife had remarried, thinking that he was dead and needing help to care for her young daughter.

As a response, he organized a group to help him build a schoolhouse that doubled as a church. He organized the Mountain Creek Baptist Church and became its first preacher. He continued as a teacher and preacher for the next forty years.

Reading his story was an inspiration to me: No matter what, never give up. Trust God to help me through whatever life brought me.

My great-grandfather had vowed to never turn away a hungry person. I have seen photographs of that house filled up with people. They're literally all over the porches and the steps in the yard. Dozens of people would show up for a Sunday afternoon meal. Many times, there were so many people who showed up for midday dinner that he had to set up tables in the yard of his farm home.

I set up my first chemistry lab in that very kitchen.

Chapter 5: Granddaddy Stories
Summers from age 5–15

My maternal grandparents, Edgar and Esther Roberson, in South Georgia, always ate their main meal at lunchtime, although it was called dinner. The evening meal would consist of cold leftovers—not actually cold, because they didn't even have a refrigerator or freezer back in the day, but not warmed over, either. They had something called a safe, basically a cabinet with screen doors on it to keep mice and bugs out, where they would keep leftover food. It also contained a small icebox cooled by a block of ice to protect food from spoiling.

Those suppers, as they called them, were very minimalist affairs. You were not expected to be very hungry at that time. Obviously cranking up a woodstove in the evening—after the hot, humid Georgia afternoons with no air-conditioning—was not a good option for warming the leftovers, but they continued the practice of cold leftovers even after getting an electric stove and refrigerator.

Storytime on the porch

After helping to clean up after dinner, one of my favorite activities was joining Granddaddy on the front porch as he rested for an hour or two before going back to the fields for an afternoon of work. We both sat in big, wooden rocking chairs. He would elevate his legs by propping his feet on one of the vertical posts holding up the porch roof to help with his varicose veins. When I worked with him in the fields, he was normally quiet. During these rest periods, he loved to share his favorite stories with me, and all I had to do was listen and enjoy.

He would just sit back in his chair, relaxing and reciting these favorite stories of his, gazing out over the fields and reminiscing. He knew I was there; it was just the two of us. And he never talked down to me. If he were reciting this story to a grown person, it would be the same; I'd heard him do that. I always felt like I was being treated as an equal as we were sitting there.

Most of his stories were about his personal experiences. Many of them emphasized dangers to avoid. One that I remember was about the danger of wild pigs native to the area, which were known as "piney woods pigs." They had black spiky fur, tusks, and a ferocious attitude. I had seen some on my trips to pick tobacco on nearby farms.

"I was crossing a split-rail fence on a shortcut across a field to the barn," Granddaddy began. "There was a lot of brush on both sides of the fence, and I couldn't see what was on the other side. That was a big mistake. I stepped over the fence into a wild-pig litter. The little pigs started squealing. The mother pig charged me, knocked me down, and started ripping off my clothes and biting my arms and legs. I managed to get to my feet and dived back across the fence. Be careful what you step into."

Since he had recently saved me from a domestic pig attack, I'm sure that he wanted to reemphasize that pigs were not playthings. They were dangerous. I got it. I never messed with pigs again.

Granddaddy had purchased a new Model T Ford when he was younger and working as a carpenter, building a military base; he needed it to get to and from work. It was now mostly junk in his tool shed. He'd repurposed the frame and wheels and turned them into the foundation for his mule-drawn wagon.

He told the story of one day when he'd been driving the Model T and developed a flat tire. He pulled over on a dry, dusty road. After jacking and getting the flat tire off the car, he felt around the tire to find the damage. A sharp pain ran through his hand as whatever it was cut into him. More carefully, he reached in and pulled out the offending sharp object—the fang of a rattlesnake! A rattlesnake had bitten the tire and caused a leak. I had seen rattlesnakes crawling across his yard. One was over six feet long and over six inches around. They could be killers. Powerful and dangerous! His hand swelled grossly and was painful for days.

One of Granddaddy's most familiar themes was the value of work ethic. "I've noticed that you are a hard worker. That is a good way to be worth something in your life. Your cousins don't like to work hard. To me, they seem weak and lazy. I fear that they will probably amount to little in life. Don't ever be like them. Whatever you do in life, remember to work hard every day."

Despite Grandaddy's concerns, one of my cousins was quite successful. He eventually earned a PhD in math education and taught math to gifted students for many years. But he never liked working on the farm or doing hard manual labor.

Gone fishin'

I occasionally went fishing with my grandfather, learning to catch catfish and other small fish that lived in the numerous streams and rivers near his farm. Eventually, his neighbor, who owned the land on the other side of a small stream that crossed their farms, built a dam and created a good-sized lake that was ideal for fishing.

Once, after catching a small fish, I dangled it in front of an alligator that was observing me while floating nearby in the lake. Granddaddy, who was watching, said nothing until after the alligator lunged and took my fish into its mouth. I was surprised by how strong the little gator was as I tried to pull him to shore.

Granddaddy spoke up. "Boy, what are you going to do now?"

The gator ended up with my fish and my fishing pole. I should have had a knife handy to cut the line. That was a great lesson: always have a backup plan in case the first one doesn't work.

Righteous protest

Granddaddy was a spiritual person but was soured on organized religion. One of his brothers had been excommunicated from the local Primitive Baptist church for being drunk in public. As a personal protest, Granddaddy quit going to church after that incident. He didn't talk about it and was generally still friendly with preachers who occasionally visited. In particular, he liked the young preacher at the Methodist church, which my grandmother regularly attended.

He disliked people who exploited people's religious beliefs for personal gain. One day we were sitting in rocking chairs on the front porch, resting after dinner. A Bible salesman parked his truck by the front gate to our yard. It was customary in the area for people to ask permission before opening the gate and approaching the house if anyone was present. He didn't. As he reached the front porch steps, he stopped and held up a large, ornate Bible and began his over-the-top sales pitch.

Granddaddy stood up and said, "Wait here a moment. I need to get something from the house."

When he returned a few minutes later, he had his double-barreled 12-gauge shotgun in his hands. "You didn't ask permission to enter my yard." As he cocked the shotgun, he continued, "I think that you should leave now."

I've never seen anyone get out of the yard faster.

Role models

Both of my maternal grandparents were no-nonsense people. They did not allow whining or complaining about anything. While they were loving, they were not often affectionate with hugs or praise. On the other hand, they were patient with us as we learned how to help with chores. Like my paternal grandparents, who led a life of unselfish service, they were great examples for me to follow.

When my sister Nancy was born, a relative of Minnie's—the African American woman who was part of the family for all of big family gatherings every year—was her caretaker and wet nurse. My grandfather would go over to the area of town where they lived—which at the time was called by a derogatory name—and visit with them on their front porch. I remember going with him and doing that and, looking back on it, I realize it was unusual. They had somewhat of a relationship there.

For example, my grandfather always had a huge garden. If he had more than he intended to can or freeze, he would go over to their house and say, "Hey, why don't you come over to the house tomorrow and finish picking the beans or the okra. I've got as much as I need, so I've got extra; come on over and you can have it." Grandaddy was always doing things like that.

There were many other stories. After I married, my wife said, "You talk more about your grandfather than about anyone else in the family."

Small wonder. I spent a lot of quality time with Granddaddy. I looked up to him and saw him as someone who was honest and pure of thought and deed. I used him as my model to guide my character development and make judgments about how to act and treat others. I would often question whether he would approve of something that I planned to do or something that I had said.

I have a picture of him in his work clothes, standing with a burlap bag of corn over his shoulder, and he's kind of looking at you. A lot of times early in my career, as I was still trying to figure out what to do and where to go, I would look at that picture and think, *Hmm. I wonder what Granddaddy would think about this.*

Granddaddy Edgar Roberson in his work clothes

Chapter 6: Developing a Love for Science and Engineering
Age 5–15

When I was five, Dad gave me my first Lionel O-gauge train set for Christmas. He set it up on a 4 x 8-foot plywood sheet in the garage workshop and installed a double circle of track. The inner track was accessed through a remote-operated electric track switch. I spent many hours re-engineering it and playing with the accessories—water tanks, coal loaders, cranes—that were electrically operated. This was my first taste of engineering.

From that day on, I was hooked.

While visiting with grandparents in south Georgia for the July Fourth holiday when I was six, my Florida cousin would bring fireworks since they were legally sold in that state. It is a wonder that no one was injured, but at the time I was having too much fun blowing things up with cherry bombs and seeing how high we could get the rockets before they exploded to worry about the consequences. This was just my first experience with rockets. There would be many more.

Fun with chemistry

For Christmas when I was in the sixth grade, my parents gave me a chemistry set. They never told me why, but I adored it. The sharecropper's family had moved on, and the main farmhouse on the Bridges farm in Pendergrass was now vacant, so I set up a complete chemistry lab in the kitchen where my great-grandfather used to cook for dozens of people. It was an amazing lab, too. A catalogue came with the set, so when I had any money, I ordered more experiments and supplies. We were pretty poor. But every cent I ever made for doing chores in the summer went to my chemistry lab. I would mail order until I had everything the company offered in their catalogue. I spent many hours conducting experiments.

My other favorite activities were building model airplanes out of balsa wood and constructing complex things with my erector set, such as a fully functioning Ferris wheel. My love of aviation and engineering was growing.

Support from many sources

I benefited from the generosity of my aunts and uncles.

Once my aunt and uncle took me on a trip to Washington, DC, with my first cousin, who was a few years older and already in high school. They picked me up on the farm during the summer vacation after my sixth grade. We drove up the Blue Ridge Parkway to our nation's capital and stopped at various sightseeing sites along the way, such as Luray Caverns in Virginia.

We toured all the tourist sites in Washington, including all of the museums. I was particularly interested in the exhibits featuring the most famous explorers and inventors and their experiences. Seeing the Spirit of St. Louis and realizing how amazing the feat was fueled my early interest in aviation.

When I started going to the new school in Jefferson in the eighth grade, we switched classes for the different subjects instead of staying with a single teacher for all subjects with two grades per room. Being exposed to more teachers who were specialized certainly improved the quality of my education.

My science teacher loved chemistry the same way I did. He got me even more interested in pursuing this subject in high school and perhaps later in life.

Falling in love with rockets

In the summer between my ninth and tenth grade years, I started a new engineering project. It was inspired by the October 1957 launch of the first space mission, Sputnik 1. It was all I could think about. I was riding in our family car on our way to Atlanta to visit relatives when the announcement was made. I was thrilled that we were going to open the space frontier during my lifetime. I wanted to get started right away learning how to build a rocket. I had help from a surprising source.

My folks purchased an encyclopedia for the family, and the company offered to do research studies for owners of the set. Without my parents' knowledge, I ordered a research study on rocket engines and space boosters. It was a college-level study, complete with the appropriate math equations, physics concepts, and diagrams. After receiving and studying it, I bought materials and started building a small rocket in the basement. I mixed solid propellants to fuel it.

The test firing of my propellants in my backyard was spectacular. The fuel burned bright hot with many sparks from the embedded metal shavings that were mixed into the black powder. I didn't have a nozzle yet, and without a nozzle, it couldn't get enough force to overcome the weight of the heavy metal pipe.

So it was basically a pipe bomb. You would load a pipe up, closed off on one end, with this fuel—a mixture of black powder and ground-up aluminum, because that's what they were doing with rockets to get more energetic fuels—and then light it off. It just took a match. Then lots of flames came out. This was not the world's greatest rocket fuel, but it sure made quite a startling experience in the backyard.

I was secretive about this project, fearing that my parents might not approve. I was doing these experiments in the backyard of the house. My parents were at work. Nobody else was around because they would have been horrified. So I did it when they weren't there. My mom was working as a nurse, weird hours of the day, and my dad was working as the credit manager at the hospital. They got home at dinnertime.

Eventually, I used up all of the fuel in my test firings and reluctantly gave up on completing the rocket since I didn't have access to the machine tools needed to construct a nozzle. I may have failed in my first attempt as a rocket builder, but I never lost my dream to build and fly rockets.

Advanced Chemistry

In high school, I loved chemistry and took two years of it. Mr. Carter was my favorite high school teacher. He gave us a lot of exciting experiences in our school's laboratory.

He nominated me and I was accepted for a summer program at the University of Georgia between my junior and senior years. Only thirty students from across the Southeast were selected for the six-week program. We stayed in a dorm at the university.

We built a complex laboratory device to assist our professor with a research project. After building the device, which involved intricate construction with glass tubing, we assisted him in collecting data. We also audited several courses, including Organic Chemistry, which blew my mind. I had a lot of fun.

Chapter 7: High School—Learning to be a Leader
Grades 9–12, Age 14–17

After the Christmas and New Year break from school in my ninth grade, we moved to our new home in Gainesville. It was a new brick house in a development near Gainesville High School, which would be my new school. The home had three bedrooms plus a full basement that wasn't finished except for a roughed-in bath and laundry room. Our home was across the street from waterfront lots on the newly completed Lake Lanier, which would provide easy access for swimming in the summer months.

I now had my own bedroom complete with new furniture, including a desk for studying and a couch for relaxing. My two sisters shared one of the other two bedrooms. The privacy and comfort were amazing.

Football

My transition to the new high school was relatively easy. I decided that in addition to band I would try out for the football team by participating in spring practice.

At one hundred and nineteen pounds, I was physically too small to be legitimate competition. Our team was one of the best in North Georgia and was often in the running for a state championship.

Because of my small stature and unlikely success, the coaches and managers gave me the shoddiest of equipment. My shoes were particularly bad, and I quickly suffered with painful strained Achilles tendons for the rest of the spring training. In addition, practice was held at the stadium several miles across town. Finding transportation to and from proved to be a challenge. I often walked home after practice.

I endured all of spring practice, but in the fall, I met with the head coach and said, "Coach, I've decided to go out for the marching band this fall instead of football." He just gave me a big smile.

Leadership lessons

Having given up on becoming a jock, I looked around the school for other opportunities and settled on joining the Key Club. This junior Kiwanis Club was active in school and community service activities. I jumped in with both feet and got a lot of experience in organizing and executing projects. This helped me to get to know my new classmates and gave them an opportunity to get to know me. Our Kiwanis Club sponsor owned the town's theaters. For some reason, he took an interest in me and became a mentor. Over the next couple of years, I grew out of my natural shyness and became more extroverted.

I especially liked being a project leader. I had to encourage other members to volunteer their time, plan events, and do the extensive in-person and on-the-landline phone calls to coordinate everything needed to bring the project to a successful conclusion. I also spoke to the Kiwanis Club's adult members at their luncheon meetings about our efforts and to encourage their support, which helped me build confidence in my public speaking and leadership abilities. Leading groups doing complex things would be a big part of my life. I didn't know that then; I just knew I liked it.

My favorite project involved collecting food and clothing for our local nonprofits that supported our poorest community members. My team and I set up collection posters and bins in stores, which meant that I had to convince the owners/managers of why it was important to help us. Then I worked with the local radio station and newspaper to publicize our project to encourage support and participation on a large scale. As a grand finale, we set up a Saturday collection session where people could call in their address to the radio station, and we would dispatch a Key Club member to collect their items. Then we worked with local charities to identify the needy families and their Christmas wishes.

We collected over $4000 and 2800 toys and items of clothing, which we delivered to 1600 people in 333 families in time for Christmas. The project won both state and national Key Club awards.

That project was the pinnacle of my early leadership experiences, and I thrived on it. And I just discovered it by the act of doing. It was really a kind of serendipity. Its success resulted in my being elected as Key Club president in my senior year.

The primary fundraising activity for the Key Club was running the concession stand at the home football games, which were well attended. We had to provide the labor to order, prepare, and deliver the menu items, including people to walk through the stands during the games with trays of items for sale. We did well enough to be able to fund the equipage for the high school's new language lab in my senior year.

I was happy to have opportunities to attend both a state convention of Key Clubs in Savannah, Georgia, and a national convention in Boston, which necessitated my first commercial airline trip on a Lockheed Electra, operated by Eastern Airlines. I didn't know what to expect on my first takeoff. The pilot pushed the throttles to maximum power while holding the brakes. The noise was deafening and my heart was racing. When he released the brakes, the plane accelerated quickly and pushed me back into the seat with amazing force. When he rotated for takeoff, we leaped off the ground. The feeling and sight of the land falling away was exhilarating. I wanted to do more of this.

Although I was too small to succeed as a varsity football player, I did continue to develop talents in one sport: long-distance running. My neighbor across the street was one year ahead of me in high school and joined me in practice. There was a dirt road, more than a mile long, running through the undeveloped lots in our neighborhood. We raced each other on this road and eventually joined the varsity track team, participating in both the mile run and the mile relay. While I never won any races, I enjoyed the competition. The training built endurance that would prove valuable for physical challenges to come.

I managed to "graduate" from the summer tobacco-harvesting business. In my sophomore and junior years, I found weekend work at the local Dairy Queen store. I made a whopping sixty-five cents per hour, which was the prevailing wage for that entry-level work in local ice cream parlors.

I was elected as junior class secretary. Class positions were ceremonial. We didn't do much except to organize a junior-senior prom and get a group picture of the class officers into the yearbook. We didn't campaign for the positions, either.

During the spring of our junior year, the school changed the timing of class officer selection to the spring of our junior year instead of the fall of our senior year. Although I had gotten a lot of visibility with my classmates as a result of my Key

Club leadership activities, I was still surprised that one of my classmates nominated me to be senior class president. Several other seniors were also on the ballot. Being a transplant into the high school halfway through our freshman year, and given that many of my classmates had been together since kindergarten, I was a long-shot candidate.

I was stunned when the results were posted. The once-shy kid from the farm won.

I never realized until that moment that my classmates saw something in me that elevated me to that honor. At our reunions, I thanked them for their recognition of me in such a special way.

I managed to graduate number two in academics in my class of 117, behind a smart woman. In the yearbook, I was selected by my classmates as "most dependable," along with a different young woman. The local Elks Club also awarded the two of us "Most Dependable" scholarships as a result of our many leadership activities during our school years. The Elks Club also awarded me their Youth Leadership Award.

The recognition that I received as a leader and my academic success in high school gave me a taste of what was to come. This boost of confidence helped me through some difficult days ahead.

Section 2: United States Air Force Academy (USAFA)

Chapter 8: College Dreams
Age 15–17

D uring my sophomore year of high school, I was sitting on my couch scanning the latest issue of *National Geographic*, which was one of my dad's favorite magazines. I discovered an article with a lot of photos about the new United States Air Force Academy (USAFA).

The article intrigued me: it promised an exciting curriculum and the opportunity to get into aviation, which I regarded as being a career on the leading edge of technical advancements in 1959. Just like that, it had me hooked.

I had never even thought about military academies or anything. But I thought, this is really different than just your regular old college. And I *like* it. I mean, this is adventurous. These guys, not only have they got a great school, they get to go fly airplanes and stuff. And it's free. That was a big deal for me. How was I going to pay for college? My folks did not have the money to send me to college.

After thinking about it all day, I got up my courage and rather excitedly said to my dad, "Dad, take a look at this article about the new Air Force Academy. That is where I want to go to college."

Dad laughed as if he knew this would be a tough nut to crack, and said, "Son, you will need to get a Congressional appointment to attend, and I don't know any Congressmen or Senators."

Then he proceeded to help me in my quest.

Dad

My dad, Roy Dubard Bridges, grew up in East Atlanta, Georgia, the youngest of nine children. He was drafted into the US Army Air Corps when he was twenty-five. He served most of the time during the war in California at Hamilton Field, guiding planes from the Pacific theater to safe landings there. He was released from service at the end of the war.

He demonstrated remarkable alacrity and resilience through his long lifetime, reinventing himself again and again as he transitioned from one career and skill set to the next—farmer, carpenter, credit manager, picture-frame maker and shopkeeper, guide to help planes land safely, extraordinary supporter of his children's dreams—a man deeply devoted to his family. He was adamant that both of my sisters attend college, and they did. But first, he contrived a plan for me to pave my own way into this most exclusive of colleges—the United States Air Force Academy—as improbable as it seemed.

It takes a village

Several times over the next two years, when he would learn of a visit to town by our representative, Phil M. Landrum, 9th District, Georgia, he would keep me out of school that day and order me to dress up in my one suit. He would drive me to the only hotel in town and tell me to go and visit the Congressman.

He would wait in the car.

I would go to the front desk and get the Congressman's room number. I would cold-call the Congressman and tell him that I was Roy Bridges and I wanted to attend the USAF Academy. He would invite me into his room for a visit. Over the course of several visits, he got to know me well.

Dad also arranged visits with graduates from the other established military academies who were running businesses in town, including a bank president. These helped me understand the obligations of attendance as well as the advantages: you're going to get a free education, but you're going to have to serve a certain amount of time in the military after you graduate.

I learned that the USAF Academy had a liaison officer in town, and Dad arranged for me to meet him. Lieutenant Colonel Garrard was a retired USAF lieutenant colonel and had been a pilot when he was on active duty. He was currently managing the big local ice plant that serviced the large and growing chicken processing plants in Gainesville, which billed itself as the chicken capital of the world. Garrard told me that there was one other person in town currently attending the USAF Academy and arranged for me to visit him during one of his visits home. That was encouraging. I wanted to follow in his footsteps.

Lieutenant Colonel Garrard gave me many other helpful recommendations regarding the application process for the academy. He explained that I would have to fill out the paperwork for a security clearance and would be required to pass both a medical and physical fitness examination at a USAF base.

When I was a senior in high school, my advanced math teacher proved to be inspirational. He gave interesting and exciting meaning to our studies in advanced engineering math.

He had a unique way of explaining how these methods were helping scientists and engineers to uncover secrets of our universe and build amazing machines such as spaceships and satellites to explore our planet and the universe. I resolved to study engineering at the USAF Academy and join those who were building these new machines.

Leaving nothing to chance

I became a little obsessed with my desire to attend the USAFA. I worked hard to get several prominent people who knew me to write letters of recommendation to our Congressman. I had no way of knowing what my competition was for the appointment, but I knew that he had only one slot to give.

Given the long odds of getting the academy appointment, I applied and was accepted into Georgia Tech. I worked a deal with my uncle who lived in Atlanta, Georgia, and ran an auto repair facility where generators and other automotive products were rebuilt. He agreed to employ me every other quarter so that I could earn enough money to attend. At that time Georgia Tech had a program of study that would allow such a schedule. I put down a three-hundred-dollar deposit for a dormitory room at Georgia Tech.

I became paranoid about my eyesight, which needed to be 20/20 to get into the USAF Academy. My mom was a nurse at a local textile plant and had a clinic with a vision test machine. I visited often to check my eyes.

I also increased my training regime to assure that I could pass the physical fitness test. In addition to long-distance running, I borrowed a set of barbells from a neighbor and worked out several days a week with them. I did sit-ups, push-ups, and pull-ups.

When I was finally invited to travel to a USAF base in Tennessee for a medical exam and a physical fitness test, I was ready. Before getting on the train to head home, I learned that I had passed both.

Destiny arrives by registered letter

Imagine my surprise when I got a call from the US Post Office in May of 1961 that I needed to pick up a registered letter. I drove to the post office, went to the window, and showed them my driver's license. The clerk gave me the letter. It was from the USAFA.

My fingers seemed to be burning hot as I slit it open and unfolded it inside the building. I dreaded that what I might see was that they had declined to admit me. As I read the letter, I was shocked to see that I had been accepted.

I felt light-headed and floated out of the post office on a cloud of joy and wonder that my dream had come true. I would join the Class of 1965 at the USAF Academy in Colorado in June 1961, shortly after my high school graduation.

When my folks came home from work, I showed them the letter and thanked Dad for all of his efforts to assure that I was successful in this quest with the Congressman. I thanked them both for all that they had done in my life to give me this opportunity.

My adventure would soon begin!

Chapter 9: Doolie Summer 1961
June–August 1961

In the summer of 1961, air travel was expensive. I took a train to Colorado from Gainesville direct to Chicago and changed trains for the overnight trip to Denver. In the morning, I switched trains again for the short journey to the academy in Colorado Springs. I arrived at the station in the afternoon and walked up the hill to the Antlers Hotel for the evening. I saw mountains that were over fourteen thousand feet high for the first time. They were majestic, and I was thrilled to have completed my journey.

I was floating on a cloud of joy to be on my own and on the verge of starting my new adventure. I was now living my dream.

I was determined to be on the first bus from the Antlers Hotel to the academy to begin my processing. My seatmate and I were both glued to the window as we got our first glimpses of the academy buildings and athletic complex. Everything was so green and new. We chatted excitedly about becoming cadets and the opportunities in our exhilarating future.

The dream becomes a nightmare

As the bus pulled to a stop, a member of the training cadre boarded and began yelling that we were all doomed and should just quit now. He ordered us off the bus and instructed us on how to line up in formation. I had a sinking feeling. This was going to be a tough day.

A member of the cadre got in my face and yelled, "Stand up straight. Tuck your chin in, smack. Did you hear me? Let's hear it. Yes sir. No sir. No excuse, sir."

Smack was a favorite derogatory term that many of the upperclassmen used when offended by a doolie's screwup.

The meaning of the word *doolies*, used to describe our status in the cadet wing, was becoming clear to me. The word is a corruption of the Greek word *doulos*. It means slaves, and we were.

"Already told you, chin in. Give me twenty-five pushups now. Maybe that will help your memory."

Since we were on the first bus, the cadre was in no rush to continue our in-processing. The final cadets wouldn't arrive until three hours after we did. Finally, we were ushered into a room where we were administered the oath of office. After that we were marched to the barbershop where we endured the shearing off of our hair. Then we were assigned individual cadre members to double-time us to the area where we were issued uniforms and equipment.

After being issued my gear, the upperclassman assigned to guide and torture me marched me at double-time with the heavy bag of equipment to the far end of Vandenberg Hall, the dormitory, as I was in the Twenty-fourth Squadron, the last in the wing.

He harassed me the entire way, pushing me to go faster. "Come on smack, pick up the pace. I don't have all day. This is nothing. If you think this is hard, maybe you should just give up and quit now."

I was winded, tired, thirsty, and dispirited as we arrived in the squadron area. The altitude of 7250 feet was already taking a toll.

He ordered me into a room and instructed me to put on a certain uniform, report back quickly outside the room, and stand at attention in the hallway. As I exited the room, I collided with the squadron commander.

He was incensed by my cardinal sin. "Hit the floor and give me fifty push-ups, smack. Next time watch where you are going. I don't like smacks touching me and stepping on my shoes."

It went on like that for the rest of that eternal day.

I should have taken the last bus.

Starvation

After many more painful training sessions, we were marched to Mitchell Hall, the so-called dining hall.

Not much nourishment came from that place. We were told to sit on the edge of our chairs with eyes downcast and to follow a strict protocol on how to get through a meal. Any transgression resulted in being ordered to sit and not eat.

We had descended into hell.

We were issued a small gray book, *Contrails 1961-62*, which was a collection of fourth-class (freshman year) knowledge. We were expected to memorize everything in the book and be able to recite it on command perfectly. We were quizzed on this during meals, and any mistakes were punished by not being allowed to eat.

Soon we were starving.

Abuse as authority

We were often stopped anytime that we were outside of our room—such as during trips to and from the restroom—and quizzed on fourth-class knowledge. Any mistakes meant more pushups. They delighted in trying to trip us up by asking more obscure questions. Other times we were stopped to correct our posture. Anything was fair game.

There were no freedoms and no justice. We were at the mercy of the upperclassmen. They abused us mentally and physically.

After dinner back in the squadron area, the punishments continued. Finally we were lined up in the hallway for our turn in the shower. I drew the far shower of the eight stalls. The warm water felt so good that I ignored the commands to speed it up and just relaxed for a moment.

Moments later I was surprised to see a cadre member standing in front of me. He yelled, "I told you to hurry. Get out of here now." I had just lathered up and so was covered in soap. I used a washrag in my room to remove the suds.

The punishment (physical and mental hazing) continued all summer and felt like an eternity. While life on the farm had been physically hard and at times uncomfortable because of the temperature or humidity, life now was also mentally exhausting.

Small respites

My first roommate was religious. He discovered that we could attend a small prayer service before breakfast every morning. I decided that I needed all the help I could get, including divine help, and attended regularly. The prayer service helped to keep the hell we were living in perspective. We also avoided the hazing in formation before marching to breakfast. We could double-time to the dining hall after the prayer service.

My first room was opposite the place where buses unloaded the USAF Academy Drum & Bugle Corps to play reveille live outside of the dormitory. I recognized the pattern the second time that they did it. After that I woke up to that sound at 5:30 a.m. every morning. Another day in hell was about to start.

My roommate was selected for the morning trash detail. He had to dress early, push a trash cart around to all the squadron rooms, and collect garbage. As I was shaving at the sink next to the open door of our room, I heard a low whistle as he neared our room. I positioned myself at the door, and he lateraled a football-size aluminum-foil-shaped package, which I luckily caught. I hid it in the dirty laundry bin. That night we opened it and discovered a solid ball of milk chocolate that we ate for dessert after lights out for weeks.

I was thankful for the chocolate, since none of my care packages made it past the upperclassmen.

A culture of cruelty

Everyday was one of continuous activity. We formed into our squadrons to march to and from all meals. We had daily physical fitness training on the athletic fields. Much time was spent learning to march well in formation. Some activities seemed like torture, such as running in formation with our rifles for long distances. Anybody who couldn't keep up the pace was punished by push-ups and other exercises. We had to master a physically challenging obstacle course.

Our classroom training sessions on military history and the details of our air force were welcome relief. It was hard to stay awake in the dark auditorium.

There were other cruelties designed by the upperclassmen, such as uniform inspections. While in formation on the terrazzo, we would be ordered to go to our rooms and report in a few minutes in a different uniform. This would be repeated until we had cycled through the three combinations of uniforms multiple times.

On one occasion, the last uniform combination was fatigues with combat boots and rifles. I didn't know what was coming next, so I took a shortcut to save time by leaving off my socks. To my surprise we then spent hours drilling in formation. My feet were badly blistered by the new, stiff combat boots. Short cuts were dangerous, and I didn't take any more.

Friday nights were difficult; we had to spit-shine our shoes, rifle, and rooms to prepare for a room and open ranks inspection on Saturday morning. The open ranks inspection was often followed by a parade on the parade grounds.

On Sundays we went to chapel and ran from the chapel to Mitchell Hall for breakfast instead of marching with our squadrons. We had open seating. If lucky, I would sit at a table with a humane table commandant who would dispense with the quizzes on fourth-class knowledge and let me eat in peace. If unlucky, I had a sadistically cruel table commandant who spent the entire meal torturing me and leaving me little time to eat. It was hard to spot the good ones. Just a crapshoot.

Life-threatening hazing

We switched roommates halfway through the summer to give us new challenges and remove any support that we had developed. My second roommate seemed to always be in trouble with the upperclassmen. They often nominated him for special punishment with the Zulu Squadron. After the evening meal, he would have to report in his combat gear, rifle, and poncho. The cadre ran them in formation until all were exhausted.

Once he was carried into our room and dumped on the floor after completing the punishment. He was unconscious from heat exhaustion. I took off his poncho and shirt and used a washcloth and cold water to revive him. That was a real scare for both of us. We have been close friends ever since that event.

I was furious that an upperclassman had been so cruelly sadistic. He came close to killing him. Had I not been able to revive him by cooling him down, I would have had to call the same sadist to get him medical attention. I'm glad that I didn't have to test his humanity further.

Hope for better days

Later in the summer, work began on a new picnic and recreation area in the woods above the academy. I could sign up for a Sunday work detail clearing brush and wood. The reward was that we could eat all that we could hold from the field kitchen. I was so starved for a good meal after all of the harassment during my daily dining experiences that overdoing it was a danger. I felt so full that I hurt. I kept going back Sunday after Sunday.

My hope for better days came when I had my first orientation flight in a T-33 jet trainer.

The recreation area that we were building was named in honor of our classmate who had died in a T-33 accident during his orientation ride. There were going to be real dangers in my chosen career.

Near the end of the summer, we were introduced to survival training, which involved a trip to the Rampart Range Mountains behind the academy. At our rustic campground, we built lean-tos out of parachutes. We were provided some beef that we converted to jerky in a tent built out of parachute cloth where we smoked it. We also were provided with a rabbit that we combined with wild vegetables to make a stew.

If we could catch anything, we were allowed to eat that as well, but with so many cadets hunting, there was not much to catch.

This was idyllic relative to the hell at the academy. There was one big qualification. It rained buckets every afternoon and the parachute cloth simply turned big raindrops into a fine mist. After a few days my nylon-covered wool sleeping bag became wet. Since there was little sunshine in between rainstorms, mine never dried for the rest of the week. Sleeping in a soggy and cold sleeping bag was miserable.

After several days learning survival skills in the camp, we set out with a single upperclassman guide and practiced using terrain maps and compasses to find our way back to the academy. This involved several days of strenuous hiking in the mountains. All we had to eat was the little bit of jerky that we had prepared and a single survival kit can of food. I was soon starving again.

Arriving back at the academy late one morning, I was unprepared for the feast waiting for me at the dining hall, during which I could be at ease while doing some serious chowing down. I ate more than my body could tolerate, given how small my stomach was after days with little to eat. There were a lot of people hanging over the wall that surrounded the terrazzo level of the dining hall, vomiting. I didn't get sick like many of my classmates, but man, I hurt.

Light and dark at the end of the tunnel

Near the end of the summer training on a Sunday afternoon, I decided to visit my bus seatmate from the first day. That turned out to be a really bad idea because I had to endure a gauntlet of punishment on my way. As I transited the long hallway to get to his room, I was stopped in every new squadron, asked my purpose for being there and then punished with push-ups for daring to enter their domain.

When I finally reached his room, he told me that he was going to resign and leave the academy. He said, "I'm only here to please my dad. I never wanted to be here and I hate it." I was stunned. We were almost finished with the worst. I hated the constant mental and physical harassment too, but I had never considered quitting.

I wished him well and fought my way back to my room, vowing to endure to the end.

Work hard, do my best and don't complain. Things will get better.

On August 16, it finally ended, and we were recognized as cadets and members of the USAFA Cadet Wing. Many of my classmates could not tolerate the ordeal and resigned before the end of the summer as my friend on the bus did. I felt fortunate to have made it and was determined to stick it out for all four years, no matter what.

Of the 822 who entered the academy on that first day in June 1961, over 300 would either resign or flunk out before graduation in June 1965.

I felt fortunate that I was able to tolerate the physical and mental torture of that first summer. Now if I could just do as well with academics, I knew I could get through the next four years.

I would to do whatever it took to graduate.

Chapter 10: Fourth-Class Year
1961–1962

The fall semester and beginning of academics were a welcome relief from the constant physical and mental torture of the indoctrination of Doolie Summer. Having all classes back in the squadron instead of the relatively small summer training cadre provided a more balanced view of what our future might hold.

Daily routine

From 6:00 a.m. to lights out at 10:00 p.m., life was hectic. There was never enough time to study for the demanding academic courses. I had to reprioritize constantly to try to hit the high points in preparation for the next day's classes and frequent tests.

My roommate was older and more experienced than I was because he had been in the army and had attended prep school. He had a detailed and rigid technique for his academic preparation, which consisted of a three-part method. He would first scan the textbook assignment. Then he would read it in detail and outline all of the key points in a notebook. Finally he would memorize the outline. While it was thorough, he could not complete it for all subjects every night before lights out. I tried to get him to take some shortcuts so that he could concentrate on the big events such as upcoming tests, but he just couldn't adjust.

Every day I would spring out of bed, dress, clean the room, make the bed, march in formation with the squadron to breakfast, double-time back to the room, grab books, and double-time to classes. Then it was double-time back to the room, march to lunch, double-time back to the room to collect notebooks and books, and double-time to classes. After classes were completed, we would double-time back to the room and then double-time to the gym for intramural athletics on two days a week from 3:45 to 5:45. After intramural athletics, we showered, dressed, double-timed back to the room, marched to dinner, double-timed back to the room, and studied until lights out.

On days without intramurals, the squadron would practice marching or we would have other military training events such as lectures on the honor code or ethics.

This was repeated four days a week from Monday through Thursday. Friday was about the same, except the afternoon period after classes was reserved for preparing the room, our shoes, and our rifles for the Saturday inspections. The detailed preparations for inspections continued after dinner until lights out.

Weekends and holidays

On Saturdays, after the room and open ranks inspections, we often had a parade. There was some relief on many Saturday afternoons, which were needed to catch up. In the fall many of the Saturday afternoons were spent at home football games.

Occasionally there were cultural events on Saturday evening at Arnold Hall, such as movies, plays, or concerts. On some of the Saturday afternoons the academy hostess arranged dance lessons to teach us the finer aspects of becoming an officer and a gentleman. She invited young women from nearby colleges to attend and be our partners. After we completed the lessons, she would occasionally schedule mixers on Saturday afternoons and would also invite local young women to attend. I didn't find the love of my life there, but they were fun.

On Sunday, we went to chapel and then had some time off. Again, it was badly needed to catch up on academics or sleep.

On home football weekends, we marched into the stadium and stood throughout the game. During my fourth-class year, we were bussed up and back to a stadium in Denver. When the Falcon Stadium was completed on the Academy campus the next year, we were "seated" on the east side of the stadium, facing the afternoon sun. My face was always sunburned except for a section shielded by the short, front brim of my uniform "wheel hat." My fair skin and red hair continued to be a real pain.

There were very few other opportunities to leave the academy grounds. Upperclassmen had more opportunities for time away from the academy; however, it was very limited for third- and second-classmen. First-classmen (seniors) could have personal cars and had a more liberal time-off policy for weekends. Third- and fourth-classmen (sophomores and freshmen, respectively) had to wear uniforms when allowed off the academy grounds.

Contact with my family was limited to an occasional evening collect phone call from the squadron phone room, which had a number of phone booths for this purpose. I was surprised that my folks and sisters had such thick southern accents. Apparently mine was already a little less thick than when I left home, since I had not noticed theirs before leaving.

I could still summon my thick southern accent when it served me well. For example, I could get our dining table to sit at ease if I could get the table commandant to laugh at something that I said. Some of them were actually not sadistic and enjoyed some humor. One sure way that I discovered with one of my favorite table commandants was to phrase my request to pass the ice cream when it was served for dessert. In a thick southern accent, I'd say, "Sir, please pass the 'arse' cream."

After the table commandant had a good laugh at my antics, he would tell us to sit at ease for the rest of the meal.

I also sent my family letters frequently. I mentioned some of the horrors. Eva Mae and Nancy said that Mom and Dad wondered if they had made a mistake by encouraging me to attend the academy.

During the spring I joined the Ski Club and went on several Sunday ski trips to nearby areas. The equipment was much different than modern boots, bindings, and skis. They were just boards with one end curled upward that we strapped our boots to with spring bindings. I didn't have the money for lessons and had never skied before, but the opportunity for some freedom was worth the risk. Since I couldn't turn well to control my speed and was unable to stop without falling on my side, I am surprised that I survived the first few trips without injury. I gradually got better over the years but was far from competent.

During our first year we were not allowed to travel home during the Christmas and New Year holiday break. We had to remain behind. That did bring some welcome relief from the relatively constant harassment from the upper classes as they continued to haze us physically and mentally for the slightest infraction or failure to have memorized perfectly our fourth-class knowledge from *Contrails*. My folks traveled to Colorado during this first break. I really enjoyed my short visit with them.

They got to eat a meal in Mitchell Hall, and Eva Mae went to a mixer dance with the cadets.

First year comes to an end

Academics had been tough. While I did pretty well on the midterms, grades were strongly influenced by term finals. They all were given in a single week before Christmas, another hell week. I hoped that I had done well.

When grade reports were issued for the first semester after the Christmas break, I received a perfect 4.0 grade point average for my academic courses and a B for my physical education class (wrestling, boxing, swimming, and gymnastics) for a total grade point average of 3.94. Grandmother Roberson would have been proud. That gave me confidence that my time management and study habits were paying dividends. I continued to practice them with small tweaks throughout the rest of my time at the academy. I made both the Dean's List and the Commandant's List, which meant that I was on the Superintendent's List.

My roommate flunked out.

I was the only cadet in our squadron whose weight could possibly qualify for the lowest intramural boxing weight class, which was 137 pounds at weigh-in before the weekly matches. I didn't want to box, but during the spring semester, I was ordered to do it to keep the squadron from having to forfeit that weight class each week. My normal weight was 143 pounds, which meant that I had to lose a minimum of six pounds every week to qualify. That was difficult. I normally dieted from Saturday until the weigh-in on Thursday afternoon. I would then eat a lot on Thursday night and Friday before starting the diet again. I won more bouts than I lost, but they all took a toll. I was usually so dehydrated and energy-deprived that I wasn't at my best, but I gave it all that I had.

At the end of our first year, we had to endure hell week.

This was the last week before we were to be recognized and see the end of the constant hazing that we had experienced since our arrival. Hell week was shorter, but even more intense than Doolie Summer, with mental and physical hazing on steroids. We endured long runs with rifles, which were exhausting. During meals we sat at attention and recited our Doolie knowledge. There was little eating.

Finally it was over.

The reward for surviving first year

After graduation activities during June week, we departed on our field trip to air force, army, navy, and marine locations across the continental United States. That was a real treat.

We sailed on navy ships based in San Diego. I wasn't lucky and was assigned to a destroyer escort, which was the smallest of the navy's capital ships. Overcoming seasickness during the first day as we churned through constant large ocean swells was a chore, but the navy fed us well. I enjoyed the freedom of being able to eat as much as I wanted, including plenty of ice cream. For me, having a relatively full stomach seemed to ease my nausea from the constantly pitching and rolling ship.

The air force and army entertained us with firepower demonstrations, which were impressive. At Fort Benning, Georgia, the army treated us to a massive nighttime firepower show with dozens of tanks and howitzers firing hundreds of rounds. The sounds of the guns and the flashes of light from the barrels were something to see and hear. I was happy that I wasn't an army soldier having to face that kind of threat. We were also given the opportunity to fire all of the army's small arms as well as machine guns and recoilless rifles.

The air force bussed us to the bombing range, and we watched as dozens of fighters fired rockets and dropped bombs on nearby targets. Again, I would rather be flying than stuck on the ground trying to dodge such overwhelming firepower.

I had an opportunity to fly in the back seat of an F-100 fighter at George Air Force Base (AFB), California. The F-100 was a real supersonic fighter. I felt the rumble of the afterburner during takeoff and supersonic flight. I was inducted into the Mach 1 Club, and my instructor pilot showed off the maneuverability by performing some impressive aerobatics, loops, and rolls. The one-hour flight was way too short.

I couldn't wait to get my own F-100.

We commuted between the different bases on C-124 cargo aircraft and were housed in dormitories. We enjoyed social activities at our stops. Barbeques and formal and informal dances with blind dates from the local area were fun. I didn't win the "ghoul pool" on these blind dates, but again I didn't meet the love of my life.

Overall, the trip was well planned and carried out. After the trip, we were allowed to go home for a few days of vacation before classes started again.

What a relief to have that first year behind me!

Chapter 11: Upperclass Years
1962–1965

My upperclass years were a stark contrast to that awful Doolie year. Academic, physical fitness, and leadership standards were high, but there was now freedom to explore other opportunities offered at the academy.

The academy's academic program was challenging all four years. All cadets were required to complete 143½ semester hours, which is a heavy load compared to the 120–130 hours at the average liberal arts college. Adding military training and physical education courses brought the total to 186½ hours.

Academic excellence

Although all cadets had to take the same courses to be awarded a degree in Engineering Science, the curriculum was balanced to include courses from the departments of Basic Sciences, Humanities, and Social Sciences in addition to Engineering Sciences. While I naturally loved the Basic Sciences (chemistry, physics, and mathematics) and Engineering Sciences (aeronautical, electrical, mechanical, and astronautical engineering), I learned to enjoy the Humanities and Social Sciences.

They provided both some relief from the intensity of the science and engineering courses and opened my eyes to the richness of studies in these other fields. From learning Russian to exploring the world of renowned philosophers, I found these subjects to be challenging in a different way and surprisingly refreshing. Russian was tough for me, as I do not have a natural talent for languages, but I scraped by with a B average.

Chemistry was a snap for me, and I excelled, especially in the lab exercises. My engineering courses were extremely difficult. I dug in and mastered them. Since my grades were good enough, I was allowed to take double overloads (two additional courses per semester above the basic requirements). This resulted in my being able to take some graduate-level courses that qualified me for the astronautics masters degree scholarship program after graduation.

That was my top-level goal.

My first experience with astronautics was not successful. I realized that I was behind in mastering the basic concepts and dropped the course before the first graded review. I was depressed by my failure but determined not to give up.

The next semester I tried again and applied myself more diligently from the get-go. I got an A for the course and was ready for more.

Leadership training and scuba diving

Our military training was broad. In addition to classroom training, where we became familiar with all things air force, we practiced leadership by taking positions of leadership in our squadrons, groups, and wing command. My leadership experience in high school helped me excel in these opportunities. I was appointed as my squadron's First Sergeant during my second-class (junior) year. Later, I was appointed as the Wing

Sergeant Major during the first summer training period during my first-class year.

I earned the nickname "Sarge," which was an honorable one.

During my third-class year, I joined the Academy Scuba Club and became certified. I continued with the club for the rest of my time at the academy and eventually became an instructor. One of the yearly highlights was a spring break scuba trip to the west coast. We usually were hosted by the navy at the naval base in San Diego or Port Hueneme near Oxnard, California.

My first dive was with the Navy Seals off the coast of San Diego from a flat-bottomed landing craft modified to support dive operations. The first dive had to be accomplished with an instructor. Many became seasick from weathering the high swells that we encountered en route to the dive site and while waiting on our turn to dive. My instructor became seasick, which delayed and prolonged the agony of nausea. I was finally assigned a new instructor and completed the dive. It felt so good to be under the water rather than being pitched around on the boat.

We also dove from a beach in La Jolla, California, on a trip to an undersea canyon. On other trips we dove on wrecks near Catalina Island and a full underwater tour of the Channel Islands off the coast near Santa Barbara. Nearer the academy, we made a lake dive at a high-altitude lake, which was partially covered in ice. When we surfaced near an ice fisherman in our all-black wet suits, he became so frightened that he ran away.

Europe: touring

The military training also included summer field trips. My favorite was our overseas field trip after our third-class year. I selected the Northern European Field Trip, which had an itinerary including the United Kingdom, Germany, and Norway. We visited many U.S. military installations as well as a lot of tourist sites.

In the UK, we visited their academy at Cranwell. After a formal dinner in our mess dress uniforms, we played silly games, which was their tradition. One of them was a jousting match with one cadet riding on the shoulders of another and trying to knock off others with a broomstick while defending with a trash can lid shield. There was much damage to our uniforms and some injuries but nothing serious. We also visited London and observed a parade in honor of a visiting head of state.

We flew into Berlin and crossed over into East Germany at Checkpoint Charlie for a short walking tour. I tried speaking to some Russians in their language, which I had studied that year. I guess my attempt was poor as they just ignored me. We cruised on the Rhine River.

In Norway, we were treated to a cruise on a three-mast sailing ship that their military used for training new sailors.

Third Lieutenant

After several weeks of touring, we transitioned to our first military assignment.

The assignment was called "third lieutenant"—an intern phase before second and first lieutenant ranks. Everybody had assembled in one of the academy's auditoriums to select our assignments before the field trip started. Those highest in order of merit selected theirs first, which meant that I got one of the earlier choices. We weren't given advance notice of available locations, so I just had to go on a gut feeling and selected Majorca. At the time, I didn't know the details of its location, but it sounded like an adventure.

Majorca is an island in the Mediterranean Sea and a part of Spain. It hosted a mountaintop radar station that was operated jointly by an American and Spanish military crew. My USAF officer sponsor had an apartment in the main town of Palma, and I stayed with him on weekends. We took a train to the main base, where I was assigned a room in the officers' quarters during the week.

Typically, everyone got an aviation experience during the third lieutenant tour, but not all of them were in fighters. I was lucky and got another supersonic fighter thrill ride in an F-102 interceptor. Midway through the three-week tour, I was picked up by a T-33 and flown over to the mainland. There I got a ride in an F-102 at Zaragoza AFB. After that thrilling ride, I flew in the T-33 back to Majorca to complete my tour.

The Spanish worker who was the caretaker of our officer's quarters took a liking to me for some reason. He invited me to visit with him and his family for one of the weekends. We traveled to his home in a nearby village on his motor scooter. I spent Friday and Saturday with him and his family and traveled back to Palma by train on Sunday. While visiting, we went to a local bullfight. Afterwards, I was treated to a home-cooked feast with the rest of the family.

After dinner he took me to the village square for an after-dinner glass of wine and visits with his friends. I spent both nights in the bedroom with his daughters, but in a separate bed, of course. I got a good taste of family life in Spain and enjoyed every minute of it.

Europe on $5 a day?

After my third lieutenant tour was completed, I traveled to Frankfort, Germany, to meet up with three of my squadron mates. We rented a VW bus and traveled around Europe for a month. We bunked in the bus on a few nights and at pensions on other nights to conserve cash. Pensions were cheap hotels, more like a bed and breakfast, with meals included in the price. We were trying to see Europe on $5.00 a day, which was supposedly a possibility at the time. We also bought gas at U.S. military installations and purchased jerry cans to carry extra fuel with us on some of the longer legs of our trip because gas on the economy (purchased locally, not on U.S. military installations) was very expensive.

We spent a few days in Paris. Then we traveled to Madrid, Spain, and saw a bullfight at the famous arena.

We drove to Barcelona and caught a ferry to Majorca. We rented a small cottage overlooking the waterfront in Palma and rented motor scooters for transportation around town.

Majorca was a popular summer vacation for young people from northern Europe. We ran into a lot of good-looking girls on vacation at the beach. We invited some of them to join us for water skiing at the air force recreation marina in town, where we checked out a ski boat for free. We all had a blast.

I had a couple of close calls during this adventure. During a Fourth of July party at the beach in Palma, I stayed in the sun too long and was severely sunburned. I tried to buy some lotion at a local drugstore. Because of my poor Spanish and a misunderstanding with the pharmacist, he assumed that I had contracted poison ivy and sold me what turned out to be calamine lotion. I used it once before figuring out that it was no good for healing sunburn. I just had to suffer through the painful weeklong healing process without the soothing lotion that I had used at home.

I also hit some gravel while turning left on a motor scooter and slid beneath a large dump truck that was waiting to turn onto the main road. My Spanish was just good enough to get the driver's attention and alert him to remain stopped until I could retrieve my scooter from under his truck. Fortunately, I was going slowly enough to avoid serious injury.

Finally, on one of our last nights in Majorca, we went to our favorite restaurant for a great steak dinner. We all became deathly ill from food poisoning and filled every available receptacle in the bathroom with vomit. The next morning, I was up earlier than others and joined the next to arise on a trip to the military dispensary to get some medication. We were so weak that we had to stop and rest every hundred yards. The medical technician asked us what we had eaten and the timeline of our illness. He concluded that the hamburgers we had all eaten at lunch at the USAF military exchange cafeteria most probably caused our illness.

I also almost ran out of cash. I called and asked my father to wire some money to me in Spain, but it did not arrive before we had to leave. Fortunately, I was able to borrow enough from my travel companions to complete the trip. It took my father months to get his money back.

After taking the ferry back to Barcelona, we retrieved our bus and continued our trip with stops in Monaco and several stops in Italy, including the towns of Pisa and Rome.

When it was time to conclude our trip, we traveled through northern Italy and Switzerland to Frankfort, Germany, where we caught our return flight to the US. We were running late and had to stop on the side of the road to change into our uniforms to save time. We just barely made it in time.

After this great experience, I dreamed of securing an assignment in Europe after graduation and completing pilot training.

First-class year: practicing leadership, righting wrongs

During the summer of our first-class year, I was on the very first detail training new Doolies. I was appointed Wing Sergeant

Major and was responsible for training the cadre on our new guidelines for acceptable discipline activities.

Foremost in my mind was eliminating things like the Zulu Squad that almost killed my roommate during my Doolie summer. A few push-ups as a disciplinary tool was okay, but running people until they collapsed from heat exhaustion would not be tolerated.

I knew that some upperclassmen could become sadistic if not checked by their peers and reminded that there were limits to assure the safety of the cadets. I rotated around the wing to observe behaviors and corrected situations on the spot when limits were being exceeded. Overall, we were successful in implementing a set of tough physical discipline activities without any of the excesses of previous years.

Jump training

In late July, I turned over my detail activities to those in the second increment and traveled to Ft. Benning, Georgia, to complete the US Army's Paratrooper Training Program and earn my jump wings. Since I was one of the most senior cadets, and since my name began with a *B*, I was appointed as the cadet in charge of our small group of about a dozen cadets.

Initially, the army integrated us into an enlisted dormitory; however, that turned out to be a bad idea. The enlisted troops were confined to their barracks in the evening. Cadets were allowed to go to the Officers' Club for drinks and dinner. Naturally some friction became evident.

I went to the army officer in charge and explained the issue. Initially, he rebuffed my suggestion to move into a separate dormitory. He said, "You guys are just too spoiled. Grow up and get with the program." I stood my ground and insisted that it was bad for the morale of his army troops. He eventually got it. We were moved into a separate dormitory that housed only cadets. This turned out to be a better solution for all concerned.

The training was tough physically. Combined with the August heat and humidity, the conditions were miserable. To avoid heat exhaustion, the army instructors marched us through outdoor showers every hour or so. We were soggy by the end of the day from the combined effects of a lot of sweat and showers. Fortunately, we cadets were able to drop off our boots and soggy clothes for professional cleaning and polishing on our way to dinner and pick up a clean and polished set for the next day. Not having to clean and shine in the evening left us some time to relax before sleeping and dressing for another day.

Roy at the USAF Academy on the Wing Staff
in his first class, senior year

After completing the rigorous preliminary training, we boarded C-119 Flying Boxcars for our first of five jumps. I was somewhat unlucky on my first jump: I was closest to the door and ended up standing in the door as we approached the drop zone at 1200 feet. That wasn't a comfortable position for someone with a fear of falling. When I was tapped on my buttocks by the jumpmaster, I was so tense that I sprang vigorously out of the door. After a terrifying few seconds of free fall, the chute opened with a jerk. From that point on, I enjoyed the sensation of falling to Earth while gently swaying under the canopy.

My first three jumps were uneventful; I wasn't injured during the landings.

My fourth jump was with full combat gear, including a rifle strapped to my leg. This made me so heavy that I could barely walk. I shuffled to the door and tumbled out when it was time for me to jump. Poor timing and a weak jump resulted in my landing on top of the parachute of the person who had jumped out of the door on the opposite side of the plane. I was fortunate to be able to scramble off before my chute collapsed. I said some nasty things to him as I fell off of the top of his chute. Despite a relatively hard landing, I walked away uninjured.

Our fifth and final jump was without the combat gear and a pleasant way to finish jump training. I was happy to leave Georgia for Colorado and vowed to do all in my power to avoid jumping out of any other airplanes. I have always greatly admired and respected the army's paratroopers for all that they endure to keep our country safe. Jumping out of an airplane with full combat gear into hostile territory is about the most hazardous activity that I can imagine. Real courage is required to do this professionally.

Back to the Academy

First-class cadets could own a car. My parents ordered my first car so that it would be ready to pick up during my short leave after jump training. I was able to obtain a low-interest loan from a bank in Kansas that used these to attract a lot of new military customers. I am still using that bank, so it turned out to be a good strategy for their business. They also deferred my first payment until after graduation.

I drove my sporty new MGB back to Colorado. After the years of lost freedom at the Academy, driving over the hills and valleys to Colorado felt so great. I couldn't wait to get through my last year and regain my full freedom.

During the fall semester, I was on the wing staff as the Wing Activities Officer. The four wing staffers marched behind the Wing Commander during our parades and other formation activities. We ate our meals on the staff tower and had rooms in a special section of the dormitory but otherwise didn't enjoy any other additional amenities or privileges.

I was responsible for planning and organizing several wing activities during the semester, such as our big evening party at the Broadmoor Hotel. I set up the food, beverages, and entertainment. Everything worked out well, and the cadets who attended reported having an enjoyable evening.

Scandal

One morning in January, after forming up to march to breakfast, I was stunned to see that military police were arresting a large number of cadets and handcuffing them. I learned that an investigation had implicated 101 cadets in a cheating scandal. One cadet stole the answers to tests and several others sold them. Many of those implicated were athletes. All were discharged from the academy as required by our honor code.

I participated in a focus group to try to understand the root cause. We evaluated all of the available metrics and the results of a survey that we constructed and administered to all cadets. While 101 of 1750 upperclassmen (5.8%) were implicated, 29 of 80 upperclassmen (36%) on the varsity football team were implicated. The survey showed that the Air Officers Commanding (AOC) assigned to each squadron were not as respected or admired by the cadets as were those officers serving as academic instructors. The AOC had offices in the squadron areas and were more focused on documenting minor infractions by cadets and assigning demerits as opposed to reinforcing the values that the academy was trying to instill in us.

We determined that many cadets regarded cadet life as a game between cadets and the institution. The football team became a peer group that commanded more loyalty than the cadet wing and the academy. We advocated that the cadets be more in charge of enforcing discipline as opposed to the AOC. Cadet leaders on the football team also needed to take on the task of making sure that their teammates put more of an emphasis on cadet wing values as opposed to just winning games.

Questionable choices

Later that month, we were invited to march in the inauguration of President Johnson. I had a bad sinus infection but decided to go anyway. I failed to realize what flying would do to me in that condition. I developed a raging middle ear infection. After a miserable night of pain, I went to the emergency room and spent the day in the hospital instead of marching in the parade. I went back to the academy by sleeper car train after recovering a few days later.

I was so pleased with the new freedoms of a car and more time on the weekends for visits to town and dates that I got a little carried away with my fun time. As a result, I ran into my most serious academic trouble during the spring semester.

I didn't do well on the first graded test in my advanced astronautics course, which was a graduate level course that I would have to complete successfully to be eligible for the scholarship program in astronautics at Purdue University after graduation. I wanted to win that scholarship. I needed a B average or better to qualify, and currently I had an F. I was put on academic probation, which restricted my off-duty weekend privileges.

I knuckled down and got an A on my independent research project for that course. I studied well and effectively for the final test. I was amazed that I found the problems to be exactly what I had studied; consequently, I finished the test in record time and scored a perfect 100%. The instructor awarded me an A grade for the course. That was a close call.

I served as a member of the Cadet Professional Ethics Committee. As one of a group of twenty-four elected representatives, I became familiar with the moral and the ethical problems I would face as an officer and gained a deeper understanding of those by teaching ethics to other cadets.

Competing for Rhodes scholarship

My philosophy professor was also the officer in charge of encouraging some of the seniors to compete for a Rhodes scholarship. He was impressed with an essay that I wrote for his course as well as my overall grade point average and leadership achievements. He urged me to apply, which I did reluctantly to please him.

A couple of thoughts that I included in my Rhodes scholarship application still resonate with me today. I started the application with the following paragraphs:

> "Life can be viewed as merely a haphazard course of events beginning with birth and ending with death, but this picture of life surely does not apply to meaningful human existence. As a thinking being, I have the responsibility to influence the development of my own essence and to control my environment, but any man who wishes to engage in more than the mere struggle for survival must develop the best he has in him....
>
> "Though I feel that this goal is a responsibility of life, it is more like an exciting and challenging adventure than a burden. Daily adding to my knowledge of myself and the world about me and seeking to find ways of applying these new things to make the world a better place in which to live makes life a joyous affair."

I was invited to an interview in Atlanta, Georgia. A team of college professors, presidents, and former Rhodes scholars interviewed us. Their questions were tough. I did the best that I could but was not selected.

I was depressed immediately after leaving the interview and admit to buying a six-pack of beer on the way back to my hotel to self-medicate.

But I actually wanted the Purdue scholarship more because that would open the door to the life of adventure in aviation and space that were my goals.

I do have a high degree of respect and admiration for those who were selected for the prestigious Rhodes scholarship program. The cadet wing commander during my time on the wing staff succeeded in winning a Rhodes scholarship. He had an impressive résumé as the top cadet in leadership, a high grade-point average, and was a member of the varsity football team. He and I have been friends over the years, and he is a great American. He served the minimum number of years in the air force and then retired to become a successful and wealthy businessman. He gave back a lot of his wealth to the academy for a new athletic facility.

Graduation

The fall semester wing staff was selected to lead the wing through June week of graduation activities. That was an honor and a good way to finish our four years at the academy.

I graduated on June 9, 1965, as a Distinguished Graduate with an Order of Merit of 9 out of 517 graduates. I was on the Dean's List, the Commandant's List, and Superintendent's List (top 12%) for every semester. I was elected as the secretary of our class, which would allow me to participate in organizing reunions and other activities of alumni.

Although everything that I experienced at the academy would be important as I moved on to my ultimate goals in life, I was happy to see the academy in the rear view mirror of my MGB, on the way to begin my master's degree studies at Purdue University. The feeling of freedom and accomplishment were sweet as I drove across the country. I'd had enough of the constraints that the academy imposed.

Later in life, when reflecting on my academy experiences, I realized how important all that I had learned there was to my future successes. Over the years, my classmates from my squadron at the USAFA met often at academy-sponsored reunions. We have remained close friends ever since.

Section 3: Advanced Training

Chapter 12: Purdue University
June 1965–January 1966

After arriving in West Lafayette, Indiana, I rented a furnished apartment with one of my fellow USAFA Class of 1965 graduates, John Blaha, who was attending Purdue as a scholarship winner like me. We found a nice place at the relatively new Williamsburg on the Wabash apartment complex, which was within a short drive or long walk to Purdue University. Classes started on June 21, 1965, which was barely long enough to complete our move, stock the pantry, and set up housekeeping.

Grad school eye-openers

My roommate and I were so happy to be free of the restrictions we had endured at USAFA that we made some bad assumptions and initial choices of how to spend our time. For example, we joined a sailing club at a nearby lake. We learned to sail on their fleet of small sailboats and had fun cruising the lake and setting up races with other members. Not long after beginning our summer term of classes, we got a wake-up call that would put severe, voluntary restrictions on how we spent our free time between classes.

We had three intensive graduate courses in the first summer term: Hypersonic Aeronautics, Applied Stochastic Math, and Information Transmission—an Electrical Engineering (EE) course. The wake-up call was my grade on the first EE examination. I made a 21%. Fortunately, others did even worse.

Our professor was unhappy with our performance. He decided to give us a chance to redeem ourselves. He set up ten pop quizzes to be given on days of his choice and not announced in advance. He would replace our first examination grade with the sum of our performance on these quizzes. I used to drip sweat from my fingertips after arriving in class each day until it became clear that we would not have a pop quiz that day. Clearly, I needed to spend more time studying and preparing for all my subjects.

My sailing club activities were over as I settled into the grind of graduate school. My renewed efforts at applying myself better paid dividends. I received one A and two Bs on the grade report.

After completing the first summer term, we had a single intensive course for a short second term. Since I had transferred two graduate courses from my last semester at USAFA, I needed five more to complete my degree in the fall semester. I had courses in Orbital Mechanics, Theoretical Methods (advanced engineering math), Viscous Flow Theory, Propulsion Gas Dynamics, and Space Propulsion System Design.

These were all difficult courses. I never got closer to having an ulcer than I did near the end of the fall semester as I prepared for final exams. I got some advice from my mother, a nurse, on healthy foods to counter my stomach issues, and barely survived the finals. I needed a B average. I received four As and one B for the fall semester, which was more than good enough. I would get my diploma for a Master of Science Degree in Astronautics in January.

One of my summer professors was also my academic advisor. He was extremely personable and genuinely interested in my plans for my career after graduating from Purdue. We stayed in touch over the years. He was instrumental in inviting me back to Purdue to receive some awards as my career progressed. Purdue had a major, positive influence on my career and successes that I had in several high technology positions.

A serendipitous dinner party

I did not have time for any social activities during that fall term except attendance at home football games. One other exception was a Thanksgiving Day dinner party at a neighbor's apartment in our apartment complex. He had graduated a year earlier than I did from USAFA but had failed to maintain a B average; consequently he had to stay for an extra year to get his Purdue degree.

One great thing happened at that party. I met a young woman, Benita Allbaugh, who was also living at our apartment complex. We had an enchanting conversation. I recalled seeing her walking to work a few times over the Wabash River Bridge that was adjacent to our apartment complex. In addition to her engaging personality, I admired her shapely legs. Given my upcoming exams, I had to put my desire to get to know her on hold.

After the exams were over and a few days before our graduation ball, I called my neighbor who had hosted the Thanksgiving party and asked for Benita's phone number so that I could ask her to be my date for the ball. He gave me the number but also called to warn her. She told him that she wasn't going to date a redneck Southerner. Somehow he convinced her to give me a chance.

We had a great time at the ball and at a friend's apartment afterwards, where we spent a lot of time conversing about our interests and dreams for work and goals. I asked her how busy she was for the next week, which was my last week in West Lafayette, and she implied that she had time for me. She and I dated every evening of that week and had a lot of fun. I promised to stay in touch, and we exchanged letters frequently as I moved on to my new assignment for pilot training in Arizona.

I packed up my MGB and drove through a snowstorm to my parents' home in Gainesville, Georgia, for some welcome Rest & Relaxation (R&R). I didn't need to report to Undergraduate Pilot Training at Williams AFB, Arizona, until March, so I had a couple of months of R&R. It was restorative. I also had Benita on my mind and traded letters with her about my R&R plans and adventures and her activities in Indiana.

During a portion of my R&R, I met up with one of my Purdue and USAFA classmates at a USAF base near Charleston, South Carolina. We caught a flight to Puerto Rico. After a week of vacation, we repeated the journey back to South Carolina.

I also visited other friends and relatives along the East Coast before returning to my parents' home to pack for my trip to Arizona. One stop was a visit with my favorite aunt, my mom's youngest sister, in Hartford, CT. In response to her questions about my life at Purdue, I shared something personal that I had not shared with anyone else.

I told her, "I have met the woman I would like to marry."

Chapter 13: Undergraduate Pilot Training (UPT)—T-41
March–May 1966

I began Undergraduate Pilot Training (UPT) in March 1966 at Williams Air Force Base (AFB), which is located just southeast of Phoenix, Arizona, near the small town of Chandler. I initially resided in the Bachelor Officers' Quarters (BOQ) on base with the same roommate I had at Purdue. I was appointed second in command of our flight and reported to a German air force major who was also a student and, by virtue of his rank, our class flight commander. He wasn't familiar with USAF customs and traditions and asked me to take care of day-to-day details.

Our class was split into two flights and each was assigned to a different flying training squadron for the duration of UPT. The two flights rarely did anything together other than to attend some parties and graduation ceremonies.

Our initial tasks were to begin academics and T-41 training. The T-41 is the military designation for the Cessna 172, which is a single-piston engine, high-wing aircraft with fixed tricycle landing gear. The T-41 pilot training was conducted at a small airfield located approximately 40 miles south of the main base near the town of Casa Grande. We were bused to and from Williams AFB. My first Instructor Pilot (IP) was a young civilian.

Most of the other instructors were also civilians, but USAF officers were assigned to oversee the operation.

I was looking forward to learning to fly. I had no prior experience flying a plane other than a few orientation rides while at USAFA. My young instructor seemed to think that I should already be skilled in flying.

After demonstrating a maneuver to me, he expected me to repeat it with instant perfection rather than coaching me on how to do it better and better over time. He yelled at me and berated me on the poor quality of my attempts. His yelling and constant criticism continued during the debriefings, which were humiliating, as my fellow students overheard just how poorly I was performing in his eyes.

Chair flying

I grew despondent and began to sense that I was headed to a failure in this first crucial step toward my goal of becoming a great airman. The feedback was the same for my first nine flights. I was graded *fair* on each of them, which was one step better than *unsatisfactory*. Despite the string of *fair*s, I began to practice my flights in my BOQ room every evening.

I named this *chair flying*. I would sit in a chair and put my hands on an imaginary control yoke and throttle. I mentally practiced where to look and how to perform the maneuvers over and over again. I stayed with the technique even though I wasn't getting the sense from my instructor that I was improving. I added tweaks to my mental preparation based on each new flight. This practice helped me learn to think ahead of the aircraft, which was crucial during dynamic maneuvers such as flying the patterns and landing. I also learned the landing procedure called the flameout landing, an essential skill to master if for any reason you lost engine power and had to land the plane like a glider. I was not giving up.

After my ninth *fair*, I was identified as someone not likely to succeed. The T-41 was a cheap way to screen out poor performers before beginning the more expensive training in jets. I was scheduled for a check ride on my tenth mission. If I did poorly on the check ride, I would be dismissed from UPT. The instructor for that flight was an older USAF major who was the senior officer in charge of the T-41 training. He gave me a briefing on what he wanted to see me accomplish during the flight. After the briefing, he rarely opened his mouth and let me perform the maneuvers on my own. After we landed, he said little in my debriefing, but he awarded me an *Excellent*. I felt a huge weight drop from my shoulders. *I'm on my way now. I'm not looking back.*

Under the tutelage of a new civilian instructor pilot, I successfully completed my first solo flight. I endured the initiation ritual after my solo flight, which was being dumped in a large cattle water tank by my classmates. Fortunately, I had prepared for that by bringing dry clothes to change into for the bus ride to the BOQ.

I was thrilled to have completed that first big step and to be able to practice flying by myself. My flying skills and confidence continued to increase, and I completed the rest of the T-41 syllabus without any problems. I never got another *fair* grade, only *good* or *excellent*. After passing the written exam and filing an application, I received my Federal Aviation Association (FAA) pilot's license, which was good for single-engine land aircraft in visual flight-rule weather conditions.

I attributed my eventual success to my chair flying, which I continued throughout T-41 training and later during T-37 and T-38 training, where being ahead of the aircraft was even more important, given the higher speeds and more dynamic maneuvers in the jets. I was not a natural talent at flying, but I improved every day and never got another poor grade. Looking back on it, my first IP actually did me a favor. The chair flying evolved out of desperation.

Our class celebrated the end of T-41 training with a loud, raucous, and joyous party at the Officer's Club. We consumed a lot of beer.

Chapter 14: Undergraduate Pilot Training (UPT)—T-37/T-38
May 1966–March 1967

T37 training was conducted at Williams AFB, all with military IPs. Each IP had three to four students, and we took turns flying. The T-37 was a twin-engine jet with retractable landing gear and side-by-side seating. It was capable of more advanced aerobatic maneuvering and more complex emergency procedures such as a single-engine-out landing, spin recoveries, and unusual-attitude recoveries. We also practiced flameout landings as we had in the T-41. The really fun parts were the opportunity for cross-country flights to nearby bases, and formation flying.

My IP was professional and great at teaching and coaching me, and I advanced rapidly in my flying skills. I continued to practice and mentally prepare for each flight by chair flying in the evenings in my room. I did not have any trouble progressing to my solo check-out flight.

Safe landings

After completing eight flights, I started another one with my IP. We practiced a couple of touch-and-go landings. When he deemed that I was ready, he asked me to do a full-stop landing. We taxied back to the departure end of the runway. I shut down the engine on his side of the aircraft, and he exited and walked across the runway to the mobile control facility where he would watch and grade my landings. I restarted the engine and requested permission for takeoff. My task was to complete two touch-and-go landings and then a full-stop landing.

After I successfully completed my solo flight, I was allowed to fly solo missions to practice maneuvers. They were wonderful. I had a sense of freedom like I had never known before.

In addition to training during flight, our instructors drilled us on the procedures for safe and emergency operations in our main briefing room. We were often called upon to recite in front of the entire group. There was a lot of professional and peer pressure to recite all emergency procedures perfectly on demand.

One day, not long after my first solo flight, I was walking back to the parachute shop to stow my gear after completing a mission. I heard an emergency situation playing out, involving one of my classmates on a solo mission. The radio calls to and from mobile control were broadcast on loudspeakers on the flight line. He was in the traffic pattern, setting up for a landing. As he turned to line up with the runway on initial, he called, "I have a low oil pressure on one of my engines." Mobile control responded just as he started his 60-degree bank turn to downwind, "Shut the engine down." As he rolled out on downwind, he said, "I accidently shut both engines down." I stopped and stared up at his aircraft as he started his turn to final approach with his gear and flaps down. I knew this could not end well.

He asked for permission to land. Mobile control said, "Turn away from the runway. You are not cleared to land. You will not have enough energy to make it to the touchdown zone."

To make a successful engines-out landing from his position, he needed to be a lot higher in altitude.

He rolled out perpendicular to the runway and shortly afterwards crashed. Later I learned that he was able to land in an adjacent pasture. He stopped just before running into a large irrigation ditch and was not injured.

He never returned to our group to continue his training. After being checked out by the flight surgeon and being released, he and his wife had a heart-to-heart conversation. He resigned from pilot training. The incident had been too traumatic.

We were happy that he had not been injured but were sad that he was gone. It was a sobering moment for us: we all faced some risk in this occupation. Emergencies could happen suddenly. Some could end tragically. It was traumatizing for me as well. But I was committed.

Flying in the dark, and other skills

Once we had mastered Visual Flight Rules maneuvers, we transitioned to Instrument Flight Rules training, which meant that I would fly with a device fixed to my helmet that prevented me from seeing out of the cockpit. This is referred to as flying under the hood. I had to use my instruments for orientation from takeoff to landing.

Under the hood, it was possible to develop a disorienting phenomenon called vertigo. Sometimes I would feel like I was turning, even when my instruments showed that I was straight and level. To resist the urge to turn, which my brain insisted was the correct thing to do, was incredibly stressful.

As I got more practice, it became easier to overcome vertigo. I learned a variety of instrument-landing approaches, which had to be done precisely. After becoming proficient, I began night flying, which was another challenging environment.

Sometimes the horizon was visible, but one had to be careful to keep up an instrument crosscheck to be on the safe side.

The most fun was learning formation flying, which was one of the final chapters in our T-37 syllabus. Learning to join with another aircraft and then fly a few feet off of his wingtip required judgment and manual skills to make small corrections with my control stick and throttle to maintain the position.

In addition to flying, we had other training such as academic, ejection seat, and altitude chamber training as well as some military training. This latter training was more designed for Reserve Officer Training Corps (ROTC) graduates than those of us from USAFA. Frankly, I found the academics easy compared to what I had experienced at USAFA and Purdue University. Aeronautics was especially easy compared to my previous advanced courses.

New options, privileges, and fun

On Friday and/or Saturday nights, we often gathered in the Officers' Club or its swimming pool for socializing. As we became more competent in our chosen profession, we had time to enjoy other fun things in life. After a few months of living in the BOQ, we were given another option for housing. We could choose to live off base if we liked. My roommate and I teamed with several other classmates and rented all of the rooms at a "dude ranch" just outside of Chandler.

We had access to the main ranch house for larger social activities and the connected cottages. My roommate and I drew the former caretaker's cottage, which was a separate one-bedroom cottage with an eat-in kitchen. We could use the large swimming pool for recreation during the long, hot summer. A small staff provided maintenance and upkeep. This was a definite improvement over the adequate but rather austere BOQ, and we enjoyed it immensely for the rest of UPT.

We began our T-38 training approximately halfway through our one-year UPT. The T-38 is still in use today for UPT. It is a sexy twin-engine supersonic jet with tandem seating. Flying it required me to use more precision and thinking ahead of the aircraft because of its higher speed for landing approaches. We again practiced both Visual Flight Rules and Instrument Flight Rules flying as well as cross-country trips that involved more legs. I planned and flew one to San Francisco with my IP and had fun visiting famous restaurants and nightclubs.

Overall, I enjoyed the T-38, and all that we got to experience at UPT. We especially concentrated on formation flying, which all fighter pilots would need to have mastered. In the course of my long career, formations would serve to save lives, take others, and commemorate yet others in ways I would wish had never come to pass.

Chapter 15: Falling in Love
Summer, 1966–March 1967

I had continued to communicate with Benita, whom I had met at Purdue. I was pleasantly surprised when she let me know about her plans to return to her parents' home in Tucson and seek a job there. She and a woman from Germany who worked at Purdue were going to make an extensive sightseeing journey across the country in Benita's car.

When they arrived in Arizona, I invited Benita and her companion to join me for a weekend outing at our dude ranch. I arranged a date with my German superior officer for Benita's German friend. The two Germans didn't hit it off too well.

But Benita and I were happy to see each other again. After completing the trip with her German friend, Benita returned to Tucson and found a job there. I was thrilled that she was living nearby and resolved to visit as often as she would have me. I generally had Saturdays and Sundays free for visits, with an occasional Friday evening as well. The trip to Tucson took about one and a half hours in my MGB each way. In addition, there were social opportunities at the base or our dude ranch where I could bring a date. Benita was willing to get together frequently.

Given my lack of funds on my meager salary, her parents were hospitable and allowed me to camp out in one of their bedrooms during my weekend visits. I appreciated their hospitality and acceptance of my designs on their only daughter.

Benita and I engaged in a wide variety of activities during my visits. She was an expert on the must-see spots around the general area of Tucson and its beautiful outdoor spaces in the nearby mountains and desert. We picnicked often during good weather. We went camping a few times with another couple on Mt. Lemon to escape the desert heat. She took me to her favorite spots, such as the Sonora Desert Museum and the San Xavier Mission. We even went on a double date across the border in Mexico for dinner at one of her favorite restaurants.

Of course, we did some of the usual things on our dates, such as a Saturday night movie. Our favorite was *Doctor Zhivago,* based on the novel by Boris Pasternak, which was awarded a Nobel Prize. The Soviet authorities forced him to turn it down and banned the book. The love story resonated with the two of us.

The question

I was in love and was pretty sure that she was, too. I wanted to propose marriage but was conflicted on the timing, with a trip to Vietnam likely a few months into my future.

As graduation approached, the list of possible assignments was posted, and we applied for our top choices. My top choice was the F-100, but they were limited in number. Fortunately, my class ranking of number 4 was good enough for me to land the last available F-100 slot. I was also designated as an Outstanding Graduate. That was quite a change in status from my humble beginning in the T-41. My passion, persistence, and deliberate chair flying practices trumped my lack of natural talent.

Time was running out at UPT, and I still wrestled mentally about whether to propose marriage, knowing that I would be headed to Vietnam for a year within months after finishing my advanced training in the F-100. The F-100 was used as a main-stay for close air support and was used by fighter wings at four bases in Vietnam. A lot of replacement pilots were needed; at the time, pilots were only required to fly one tour in the war for a year.

Would asking her to marry me be too selfish, given the odds of dying over there?

Although we had been dating steadily for only about nine months, we were both deeply in love. Without getting into the gory details, she managed to signal her exasperation with my inability to communicate any commitment to our future to-gether. I finally got the hint, purchased a ring, and proposed.

The answer

I am forever grateful that she accepted. My late proposal meant that she had little time to plan for our wedding, but she pulled the details together in time for an Easter Sunday wedding in Tucson at her Methodist church on March 26, 1967, which was two days after my UPT graduation. My roommate from UPT and Purdue served as my best man, and several other class-mates attended our wedding. My parents drove to Arizona for my graduation and our wedding. Many of Benita's friends and relatives attended as well. The wedding in the church sanctu-ary was magnificent. The reception in a nearby church building was also a lot of fun.

The hotel where I had initially reserved a room for our one-night honeymoon somehow lost my reservation. I had to scram-ble to find a replacement at the last minute. I was lucky to find a new motel with separate cottages complete with fireplaces.

After the reception was over, we got my car—which had been well decorated by my friends—defrocked and washed. We then stopped at Benita's parents' home and "borrowed" some firewood. We turned the air conditioner down and enjoyed a romantic first night together in front of that fireplace.

Fireplaces continued to fill a need later in life as a place to share our deepest feelings for each other and our family. We both found solace in the quiet comfort of the flickering flames as we found ways to soothe hurt feelings or work through worries about some incident, illness, or coming event. We enjoyed sharing our happiest thoughts there, too. Our love for each other and fireside chats continues even today.

We had originally planned a honeymoon trip to Carmel, California. Just before graduation, the air force moved up my reporting date for F-100 advanced training at Cannon AFB, New Mexico, and we had to cancel that trip. The new timing required us to hit the road for Clovis, New Mexico, on the day after our wedding. We spent one night on the road in Ruidoso, New Mexico, before arriving in Clovis.

We quickly located an apartment and moved what little we could haul in my MGB into our furnished, one-bedroom apartment. The moving company that I had contracted through the air force delivered the rest of our goods a few days later.

One other Williams AFB UPT graduate from my class moved into the same apartment complex. Steve Amdor had been one of our dude ranch residents and had married Vallerie while we were in UPT. We had friends nearby right away.

I was a happy man, a jet pilot, and married to the love of my life.

Roy and Benita with their parents at their
wedding in March 1967

Section 4: USAF Operations and Staff

Chapter 16: Cold-Weather Survival School
March–April 1967

Within a few days after arriving at Clovis, New Mexico, and signing in at Cannon AFB, I had to depart for Fairchild AFB near Spokane, Washington, for cold-weather survival training. It was still cold in early April there, especially in the mountains. After some classroom training, we started several days of training outdoors to practice necessary escape and evasion skills.

Escape training

The exercise started at night with us crawling through a simulated battlefield on cold, muddy dirt and trying to avoid being captured. That was kind of a joke as the instructors basically herded us toward a pickup point after several miles of crawling by ringing the perimeter and shooting off their guns and flares over our heads.

After we were "captured," we were isolated into small rooms about the size of a telephone booth. Loud, foreign-sounding music blared away constantly. The guards came by often and kicked the doors to make sure that we weren't sleeping.

At some point, which seemed like an eternity, the guards opened my door and took me to a torture device to stimulate claustrophobia. I was placed into a small space inside of the machine, which immobilized me in an uncomfortable position and shut off all light and sound. While this was uncomfortable, I was used to cramped spaces and had never been bothered by claustrophobia. After another eternity of this torture, I was removed and placed into an outdoor prison camp with the other prisoners.

We milled around inside the barbed wire, which was ringed with tall guard towers and illuminated with bright spotlights. It was chilly. There were a few bunkers with pot-bellied stoves for warmth, but there was not room for everybody at once. We had to take turns warming up.

One of my fellow *prisoners* issued me an escape chit. The instructors had assigned him this task prior to us beginning the exercise. Getting a chit meant that I had to try to escape. I plotted with a few others to arrange to get on one of the work details of prisoners who were allowed to go outside the wire to cut wood for the stoves. Of course, the details were guarded.

After the detail exited the gate and arrived at the woodpile, we began the task of chopping as much wood as we could carry. As we worked, I kept an eye on the guard. When he was momentarily distracted by something and turned away from us, I slipped quickly into a nearby drainage ditch and remained motionless until the detail went back inside the camp without me. Our guard did not notice that I was missing. Then I crawled in the ditch until I was several hundred yards from the camp. Since it was dark, I could then crouch to minimize my exposure and walk around the camp until I came to a road on the other side.

A short distance up the road was a small building that contained the match to my chit in a box. I went inside and picked it up. Then I walked a short distance down the road toward the camp entrance and again hid in a drainage ditch. When the next large work detail formation marched by on the way back to the camp, I paused until they passed me and then jumped up and joined the rear rank of the formation. The guards didn't notice.

At the guard gate, I approached the guard in the guardhouse and showed him my matching escape chits. He quickly grabbed and pocketed them. I thought that he was trying to cheat me out of credit for my successful escape and raised my voice in protest. "Why are you hiding my chits? I want credit for my successful escape." He quickly pinned me against the building wall and whispered, "Shut up. We have to put you back into the prisoner population so that you can complete your training. You must keep your escape a secret. You will get credit."

He then escorted me to a room inside the building and debriefed me more thoroughly on the rules of the road going forward. I was also given a cup of coffee. I remember adding a ton of sugar to it because I was so tired and hungry. Wow, that was a real pick-me-upper. After a short time, I was placed back into the general prison population. It was a long, cold night in there.

Survival training

In the morning we boarded buses, which took us into the nearby mountains. There we were each issued a parachute and a survival kit similar to ones that would be in our aircraft ejection seats and attached to hooks on the harness of our parachutes so that it would go with us when we ejected.

We were instructed to build a lean-to tent with the parachute for the night. Having learned from my earlier survival school experience at the USAFA, I wanted my sleeping bag to remain dry; therefore, I carefully made a deep bed of pine boughs on the floor inside of my tent. I also trenched around the outer edge of the tent to divert water in the event of rain. After sleeping in it overnight, I arose in the morning to discover several inches of wet snow on my tent. Thanks to my careful preparation, my sleeping bag was still dry. My earlier lessons paid off.

After camping for several days and learning more survival techniques, we practiced escape and evasion while hiking to a simulated partisan camp for lunch, which consisted of soup boiled in a trashcan. We then hiked to our pickup point for extraction. Along the way, simulated enemy soldiers tried to capture us and shot at us with blanks if they spotted us. Basically, that meant we had to stay off the logging roads and remain in more difficult terrain where we could hide in the underbrush. The trees in this rain forest were massive. If we encountered one that had fallen across our path, we had to detour for several hundred feet to get around it. It was too thick to climb over.

While hiding from some enemy soldiers with my fellow prisoner and hiking partner, who was an enlisted airman, I smelled chocolate. I whispered to him, "What are you eating?" He offered me a whole chocolate bar. I gladly accepted it and marveled that he had been able to smuggle in food. We had been ordered not to do that. I didn't rat him out.

When we arrived back at our lodging, I was overjoyed to get a hot shower and some clean clothes. The course was over for most, but those of us headed to Vietnam had to stay for an extra week of training on how to devise and send messages in code inside of Red Cross letters to our loved ones in the event that we became prisoners of war—and then explain to them how to decode those letters, should the necessity arise.

Simple life as newlyweds

Benita met me at the airport when I returned. She laughed at my new mustache, which I had grown while at survival training. That was embarrassing, so I shaved it off the next morning. She'd had an interesting time while I was away. She drove Vallerie Amdor to the hospital and helped her at home after the birth of her son, since Steve was at survival school with me when the child was born. Vallerie and Benita have remained friends.

Given our limited income, my wife and I struggled financially. I had to pay my car loan each month as well as a loan that I had taken out to buy engagement and wedding rings. We had little left for other expenses. Our big outing for the week was a trip to the local A&W Root Beer drive-in on the night that they had root beer floats on sale for half price, five cents each. We ate a lot of spaghetti and meatballs and other inexpensive menu items. Benita was adept at managing our limited grocery budget to make sure that we wouldn't go hungry during the last few days before payday.

We had received an unusual wedding gift, a beautiful Siamese cat, Saki. Saki would walk on a leash during our late-afternoon outings. The only problem was that he only wanted to go in one direction: away from the apartment. As soon as we turned around, Saki would balk and refuse to move. We had to carry him home in our arms.

Benita played bridge with the other wives. On Friday nights, we would gather with my classmates and their wives at the Officer's Club. We enjoyed our simple life as newlyweds. I dreaded leaving her to go to war, but I also had to do my duty to the country. I just hoped that I would return.

Benita, however, had reassurance from God that I would be all right. By mutual agreement, we never discussed the possibility that I might not come home.

Chapter 17: Flying the "Hun"
April–December 1967

On one of my first days on the flight line at Cannon AFB, I had an opportunity to climb into the cockpit of an F-100 for orientation. I also drove out to the end of the runway and observed a four-ship formation takeoff, which was a great demonstration of the raw power of the engines as the pilots selected afterburner for takeoff. The deep-throated roar rattled the bones in my chest. Learning to fly the F-100 Super Sabre, or more affectionately, "Hun," was going to be a great adventure.

F-100 academics and flying were fun. They revealed that the "Hun" was a versatile and capable fighter. I felt privileged to learn all about it.

In ground school we learned all aspects of the aircraft and the munitions that it was qualified to expend, including nuclear bombs. After a couple of flights with an instructor in the F-100F two-seat model, I was cleared to fly solo in the F-100D single-seat model, and most of my remaining flights were in it. We learned how to strafe with the four 20 mm nose-mounted cannons, bomb accurately with both simulated conventional and nuclear bombs, and fire rockets accurately. We learned both low-dive angle and steep-dive angle deliveries for bombs. We practiced aerial refueling using the probe-and-drogue method.

We flew to the range in four-ship formations. We practiced aerial gunnery by shooting at targets towed by another F-100.

For the nuclear drops, we learned to navigate at low level to the target on the range and then release the bomb while in a steep climb to allow us time to safely exit the target area before the bomb exploded. F-100s were on nuclear alert in Germany, as we were still fighting the Cold War as well as the conventional war in Vietnam. Some of us might have a future assignment to Germany and were required to be competent in nuclear deliveries. I looked forward to an assignment there after Vietnam, although my vision of nuclear bombs and alerts was to deter war and never have to drop one.

By far the most fun was practicing bombing on the tactical gunnery range, which gave us a more realistic sense of how we would employ the F-100 in Vietnam for close air support than the tightly formatted gunnery range where we had learned the basics. At that bombing range, a range control officer monitored our runs to assure that we released our ordnance at a safe altitude. If we violated one, we would be fouled off the range.

We were required to be certified by an instructor pilot before returning for solo flights. We flew in tightly controlled patterns on the range and always rolled in on the same heading. At the tactical range, we would roll in on the best heading to maximize our ability to hit the target.

Self-improvement

I did have some issues along the way. One was my difficulty in getting up on time for early missions. At USAFA my roommates learned to keep yelling at me until I got out of bed. Apparently, I could say some nasty things when someone tried to wake me up. My wife didn't appreciate that, so one morning when I was particularly abusive with my comments, she let me sleep, and I was late to a flight briefing. I got into some hot water over that incident with my instructor pilot. It turns out that I needed this tough-love lesson to cure me of my bad habit.

I eventually learned that I liked getting up early to mentally prepare for my flights. I never made that mistake again at Cannon AFB or later in my career.

I also flunked one flight practicing at the gunnery range. I made two errors. The first one happened on the rejoin after takeoff. I was the number three in the formation. As I led the rejoin, the instructor in the number four aircraft on my wing thought that I had passed too closely behind the leader as we slid into formation from below and behind. I thought it was absolutely perfect, but that didn't count. On the same flight, I was fouled off the range for being too late to pull out of a strafing run. I never made those mistakes again, either. It was my only unsatisfactory flight during F-100 training.

Finals and graduation

My final mission was a simulated close air support mission that included an aerial refueling and attacks on targets on the tactical gunnery range. It was a check ride with an instructor pilot in the back seat. He praised how I had conducted the mission.

The final issue during F-100 training occurred after I was back on the ground. I landed late in the day and was met at the aircraft by a fellow student who handed me a bottle of champagne. The pre-graduation party was already well underway. I was tired and hungry and left the party early to go home. Apparently one of my fellow students became drunk and went into the parachute room and pulled the ripcord on a couple of chutes. All in our class were called and ordered to report in Class A blues early the next day to stand at attention while the technicians repacked the chutes. Our graduation ceremony followed. And then it was over.

After the year of UPT and eight months of F-100 training, we were all now fully qualified fighter pilots.

Bittersweet goodbyes

We received our next assignments well before graduation. Most of us were headed to one of several F-100 bases in South Vietnam. My classmate neighbor Steve Amdor and I were both assigned to Phu Cat Air Base. We had a couple of weeks of vacation, which gave us time to clear our apartments and move our wives to where they planned to stay during our one year in Vietnam. Benita decided to move back into her parents' home in Tucson for the year. After arranging for the move of our household goods, we had time to visit with my folks in Georgia and then her parents in Tucson.

Before the Christmas holidays, we rejoined with our Cannon AFB neighbors, Steve and Vallerie Amdor, in Phoenix, and carpooled together to Travis AFB, California, to catch our flight to Clark AFB, Philippines, which is where we would complete a jungle survival course before taking the second leg of our flight to South Vietnam.

On the way to Travis we made a stop in Lake Tahoe, Nevada. This was my first visit to Lake Tahoe, which was one of Benita's favorite spots on the planet. She had lived and worked in a nearby Nevada community for a short time after high school. The view from our hotel room was stunning.

After departing Lake Tahoe we traveled to San Francisco and stayed in a navy residence lodge to save money while visiting Fisherman's Wharf for great seafood and seeing the other tourist spots around town. After a couple of days, we departed for our final stop at Travis AFB. We learned that our departure would be delayed one day, which gave us time for a farewell dinner with our buddies from Cannon AFB who were also scheduled on that flight and their wives. It was a bitter-sweet party, knowing that we wouldn't see our wives for many months, if ever.

Chapter 18: Vietnam War—Jungle Survival School
Late December, 1967

And then I spent Christmas in the jungle.

Jungle survival school in the Philippines was somewhat less miserable than my cold-weather survival experience. We learned how to survive for a few days in the jungle in the event that we had to eject from our aircraft. The focus was how to enhance our chances of staying alive and making contact with rescue forces for extraction.

We learned to make hammocks out of our parachutes but actually bunked in manufactured hammocks equipped with mosquito netting for safety. We gathered and cooked food growing in the wild after learning what was safe to eat.

We also had a mini escape-and-evasion exercise, which involved hiking into the jungle and trying to hide from a group of indigenous people who had been engaged to act as the enemy and find us. If they did, they would collect a chit from us, which they could trade for goods such as a bag of rice.

The exercise began in the afternoon and lasted all night. Steve Amdor and I hiked for a while and were on the lookout for a good spot to disappear for the night. We happened upon a dense thicket of brush on a hillside. We burrowed into this by crawling on our hands and knees. We suspected that the "enemy" knew of the general area, as they observed the initial direction of our hike using lookouts. We were well hidden and thought that we might have a chance of escaping discovery.

After dark, the initial search party was visible as they neared our hiding place because they were using bright flashlights. They searched around our thicket but then moved on out of our general area. We relaxed a little and opened some tins of survival rations for dinner.

But then we made a mistake. After finishing dinner, we allowed the cans to roll down the hill, deeper into the thicket. When the "enemy" came by a second time, they spent a considerable amount of time near our thicket. Unfortunately for us, they frightened some rats that had apparently found our empty dinner tins. When the rats ran away, they clinked the tins together and the "enemy" had us. One of them crawled into our hiding place and collected our chit. It's a wonder that we didn't come to harm from a snake or other local creature, but we made it through the rest of the night in our hideout.

After ending the exercise and our survival school course the next day, it was great to get a hot shower and some clean clothes. Afterwards I went to the base barbershop. I got the works, including a massage. I had never been so pampered.

Chapter 19: Vietnam—416th Tactical Fighter Squadron (TFS)

January 1–July 14, 1968; November 10–December 1968

On New Year's Day 1968, Steve and I were in the passenger departure lounge at Clark AB at 4:00 a.m. waiting on our flight to Da Nang. The flight was uneventful. After landing, we were able to find a C-7 Caribou, a small cargo aircraft that would transport us the rest of the way to Phu Cat AB.

On a stop at another airfield along the way, we were surprised and delighted: our crew knew that there was homemade ice cream to be had at that airfield. They wanted some. After devouring it on the ramp by our aircraft, we all boarded again and continued to Phu Cat AB.

The BOQ at my new base for the first month was an unpainted plywood building with open, screened windows in the hallways for ventilation. The rooms had window air conditioners, but they were noisy. Even in January, it was still warm enough for us to trek to our communal shower and bathroom in shorts and t-shirts. New house trailers were being installed but weren't ready for occupancy yet.

My new unit was the 416th Tactical Fighter Squadron. The pilots and staff welcomed us warmly. It was a close-knit group with a lot of experienced pilots who quickly got us integrated into daily operations. Initially, we were at a relatively low operations tempo; however, as we reached the end of January, the infamous Tet Offensive kicked into high gear. Our unit was ordered to night duty, and we flew many missions, providing close air support to units under attack.

Tet Offensive

It was dangerous duty, as visibility was often compromised by fog or smoke. The forward air controllers dropped parachute flares to enable us to see the terrain and spot the target. We had to spot targets based on ground features or sometimes with directions relative to fire logs dropped on the ground by the forward air controllers. Targets as well as the surrounding terrain were often hard to discern in the dark.

So it was extremely tense and draining flying at night, often in compromised visibility. I had to operate at peak proficiency and alertness to put my bombs on the right target to deter the enemy, not hurt any of our troops, and avoid crashing into the ground in the process. They were stressful flights.

Fortunately, before starting this phase, we had moved to new trailers, which came complete with a bathroom, shower, and two bedrooms. I roomed with Steve Amdor and drew the top bunk. They had quiet and effective air conditioning, which helped us sleep better during the warm days. Nevertheless, I often felt sleep-deprived.

Returning from night missions at breakfast time and eating a dinner of reconstituted powdered eggs at the mess hall was a daily, disappointing routine.

You felt like you deserved a steak dinner. You got powdered eggs.

Roy beside one of the F-100s that he flew at Phu Cat Air Base South
Vietnam in 1968 with the 416th Tactical Fighter Squadron and
Misty on 226 combat missions

R&R in Bangkok

In March, after Tet wound down, several of us were given the
opportunity to fly to Bangkok, Thailand, on the base's C- 47 for
a few days of R&R. After arrival and checking into the hotel, I
went to bed in the late afternoon and slept almost around the
clock. What a relief.

Much better rested, I hired a local "taxi driver and tour
guide," and he showed me the local tourist sites, including a
Thai kickboxing match, which was one of his favorite activities.
These few days away were enjoyable and refreshing. I bought
some jewelry for my wife as an anniversary gift. I also put together a slide show and audiotape to share my Thailand adventure with her.

After returning from R&R, I resumed taking my turn on
the flying schedule. We returned to day operations, except
for taking our turn on night alert duty at the alert shack for

several days at a time. Depending on the schedule of my flights, I jogged around the base before or after to stay physically fit. There wasn't much else to do other than hang around the ready room at the squadron and play darts with my squadron mates or visit the Officer's Club for drinks and dinner.

A miracle and an unintentional porpoise

Some of our most exciting missions were undertaken to help our troops caught in desperate situations. One of those early in my tour was almost my last mission.

We were called to assist our troops in contact with enemy forces. Given where our troops were dug in, we had to attack headed into steeply rising terrain. Following delivery of my low-altitude-released bomb, I had to make a sharp and relatively high g recovery. Unfortunately, one of my gravity-activated leading-edge slats did not extend, which caused my aircraft to bank sharply to the left. The only way to recover was to relax to one g momentarily and then begin the pullout again, hoping that the slat would extend on the second try.

Fortunately for me, it did; I completed the pullout with only feet to spare above the rocky terrain.

I was awed by this miracle. Five hundred miles an hour, and you're clearing the hillside by inches...right then and there, I thanked God for saving me.

Another exciting mission started with my wingman and me being scrambled—a call on the phone in the alert shack telling you to move with haste and abandon because people are dying and they need you right now—from our day alert facility. On these missions, we pre-cocked our aircraft and gear so that we could be airborne within 15 minutes from the scramble call, which included a stop in the arming area at the end of the runway so that the ground crew could arm our bombs and guns. So we were literally running out the door. We pushed the engine start button as we were sliding into our seats and parachute harnesses.

After takeoff we were instructed to rendezvous with a KC-135 tanker in South Vietnam and then to rendezvous with a Misty fast Forward Air Controller (FAC) near the Mu Ghia Pass in North Vietnam. It was unusual for us to fly up into North Vietnam. I had not refueled since Cannon AFB and was so hyped up by this unexpected and dangerous mission that I got into a Pilot Induced Oscillation (PIO) approaching the refueling basket.

A PIO is an unintentional porpoise—imagine the movement of a porpoise swimming through the water—that can build to dangerous and rapid cycles if not checked by releasing pressure on the control stick. It happened because I overcontrolled in trying to place my refueling boom into the small basket, which was only three feet in diameter.

I backed off a little, took a deep breath, and relaxed enough to resume my approach. This time I hooked up and completed the refueling successfully.

We rendezvoused with Misty, a top-secret unit attached to our wing. They briefed us on the target, which was a railroad siding and storage area, including a number of railcars being used by the enemy for storage. They put a smoke rocket on the first railcar target. I rolled in and put a bomb directly on the target, which destroyed the railcar.

After dropping the rest of our bombs, we strafed the remaining railcars with our 20 mm cannons. On my first strafing pass, I was so hyped up that I failed to remember to arm the guns with a switch on the front console. When I realized my error, I leaned forward to arm them, which again started a small PIO. This actually increased the effectiveness of my pass as my guns raked back and forth across the line of railcars. The railcars were filled with ammunition and blew up as I pulled off the target.

Misty was impressed with our accuracy and put us in for a decoration. I received a Distinguished Flying Cross (DFC) for that mission, which was the first of two in two days. I was submitted for another the next day for a mission near Khe Sanh, South Vietnam, during which we destroyed a North Vietnamese army truck park and storage area.

Danger comes in many shapes and forms

The weather could also be an enemy. We were subjected to monsoonal rain and thunderstorms, which often reduced visibility to marginal levels. On one mission, I was flying with another F-100D near Khe Sanh for close air support. The weather closed in quickly and prevented a rejoin as we departed the target area. We confirmed that we had altitude separation and proceeded home as single ships.

On the way home, I was struck by lightning. I was flying through cumulonimbus clouds, which are quite turbulent, really focused on flying my instruments—trying to stay straight and level, hold my altitude—not expecting anything bad to happen. When the lightning bolt hit, it was literally a bolt out of the blue.

I was blinded by the flash. My hearing was interrupted by the deafening crack. Everything was suddenly silent. I thought I had lost my engine. Disoriented, I was trying to check gauges with my vision disturbed by the blinding light and thinking, well, this is really bad.

I hadn't lost my engine after all, and I made it home, although I was shaken by the incident. To add insult, a forklift pulled out in front of me as I was taxiing to my parking spot, and I didn't have room to stop before hitting it, which caused minor damage to the aircraft. The forklift had come flying out of a bunker as I turned a corner in the maze of bunkers that protected our aircraft while parked. It was a big surprise to both of us.

There were dangers and perceived dangers on the ground at Phu Cat as well. One day, while serving on duty in the alert shack, I thought I heard a knock on the door. I walked over and opened it. To my surprise, it wasn't somebody knocking on the door.

It was a mortar shell. It had landed nearby in the shack's front yard.

While our aircraft parking areas and our dormitory trailers were protected with revetments to avoid extensive damage from mortar attacks, the alert shack was not. I shut the door and dived under the pool table in the middle of our ready room. Unfortunately, I knocked heads with one of the other pilots on alert who had dived under from the opposite side. We narrowly escaped injuring each other.

One of my perceived dangers was serving at our mobile control facilities at night. These small mobile facilities were placed near the end of the runways so that we could check landing aircraft to make sure they had their landing gear down. We would make a radio call and fire a flare gun if we saw that the gear was not down. The location meant that we were far from the nearest building or security personnel.

To reach the mobile control for my night shift, I drove solo in a truck to the small facility located near both ends of the runway. While our airbase defensive forces, consisting of a South Korean army unit, did a great job of protecting us, I still imagined being attacked by a stealthy hostile force in the visible, vulnerable facility. The mobile control facilities had a colored light on the roof and were easy to spot. They provided little protection, with glass panels on all sides to give us 360-degree visibility. Many nights we could see gunships flying overhead and firing tracers to keep hostile forces at bay. I often kept my pistol aimed at the door during late-night duty, as it was both lonely and scary.

One other perceived threat was getting a haircut by the South Vietnamese barber. I was often by myself in the barbershop. While I never heard of anyone being hurt by a barber on an American air base, I was never comfortable getting my neck and sideburns shaved with his straight razor. It wouldn't take much effort for him to slit my throat. When I heard the barber stroke his razor on his leather strap to sharpen it, I would tense up with fear. I always said a little prayer at that time—and afterwards, when I walked out without injury.

Chapter 20: Vietnam—Misty
July 15–November 9, 1968

On July 15, 1968, I volunteered for and was assigned to Commando Sabre Operation, a top-secret unit assigned to the wing. The office and ready room were located behind a door marked *Top Secret* in an attachment to the wing headquarters building that was accessed by an outside staircase to the second floor. The unit was known by its radio call sign: Misty.

We flew the two-seat F-100F on fast Forward Air Controller missions in North Vietnam with pilots in both seats. With rare exceptions, we flew our missions in the area designated as Route Package 1 (RP1), which was the area directly north of the Demilitarized Zone (DMZ). There were a total of six RPs. RP1 was assigned to the air force. RP2 was assigned to the navy. Mu Ghia pass was on the northwest border of RP1, between the two areas. While we occasionally worked in RP2 at the request of the Airborne Command, Control, and Communications airplane (ABCCC—a flying command post) to check out some suspicious target such as a Surface-to-Air Missile, we didn't routinely work in that area so as not to interfere with navy operations.

We were equipped with "Willie Pete"—2.75-inch white phosphorous smoke rockets—which we used to mark targets for fighters to attack with explosive ordnance. Primary targets were truck parks and supply storage areas, which were part of the extensive transportation network used by the North Vietnamese army to haul supplies to the South. The primary road network was known as the Ho Chi Minh Trail. We were also on special alert to identify and destroy any Surface-to-Air transporters or sites.

Whenever anyone bailed out in the area, we participated in the Rescue Combat Air Patrol primarily to knock out Anti-Aircraft Artillery (AAA) sites to permit the Sandy A1E Skyraider fighters and Jolly Green Giant rescue helicopters to fly in for the pickup safely.

For more detailed insights into the Misty mission and results, I highly recommend that you read an excellent book: *Bury Us Upside Down: The Misty Pilots and the Secret Battle for the Ho Chi Minh Trail* by authors Rick Newman and Don Sheppard. Affectionately, we renamed this book *Bury Us Upside Down so the World Can Kiss Our Ass,* based on a verse from a fighter pilot song.

Misty missions

My Misty mission durations were much longer than those I had experienced as a close air support mission pilot. Misty missions varied from two and a half to eight hours each, with aerial refueling completed as many times as necessary. Misty had its own refueling tanker in a track off the coast of North Vietnam to maximize flight time over the target area. Most missions were at least four hours. After completing a set of ten check-out missions, five each in the back seat and five in the front seat, we alternated flying in the front and back seats on missions.

The back-seat pilot handled the radio calls to and from ABCCC. When targets were spotted, the back-seat pilot would mark them on a detailed map of the area. He kept notes on the results of attacks that we directed to have an accurate Battle Damage Assessment (BDA) report for the mission debriefing with our intelligence officer. Misty was key to collecting real-time intelligence that was distributed to Seventh Air Force. Given this focus, the back-seat pilot was crucial in recording enough detail to make the intelligence usable by others. Details included the map positions and other critical items such as the defenses surrounding it. The back-seat pilot also carried a handheld camera, which was used to obtain photos of targets for debriefing.

Occasionally, targets spotted by other aircraft in the area or sent to the ABCCC by headquarters were transmitted to Misty in code, which the back-seat pilot would decode using a decoding device that we carried. He would then locate the target on the map. We would fly to the target and investigate it. If conditions were suitable, we would call for fighter aircraft to strike it.

Jinking and refueling

Since we generally flew at relatively low altitudes to enable us to spot targets better, we had to "jink" in three dimensions constantly. Jinking means not flying in a straight line, ever, to make the plane harder to hit. We kept our airspeed at 450 knots and our altitude at or above 4500 feet as protective measures against the heavily defended area, which hosted many AAA sites.

Initially, this became a challenge for me to avoid airsickness, since I often had my head down, working the map on back-seat missions. After my first check-out ride in the area in the back seat, I felt unstable after landing, when exiting the aircraft. I had to hold on to the ladder until my head quit spinning. My first five checkout rides in the back seat lasted from five to seven hours each. These were tough missions, but I gradually learned to accommodate the constant high-g-force turns while head-down without any complications during or post-mission. I naturally preferred my flights in the front seat so I didn't have the head-down duties, but trading spots every other mission was fair play.

Both the front- and back-seat pilots participated in refueling. These involved sticking our ten-foot-long wing-mounted boom into a three-foot-diameter basket behind the tanker and stabilizing there for enough time to fill up the tanks. Refueling was also a good time to guzzle some water and relieve ourselves in bottles designed for that purpose and mounted on the front panel.

Roy and Vietnam roommate Steve Amdor
with their Misty F-100F aircraft

Misty's effectiveness

The front-seat pilot handled the flying duties and kept a lookout for other traffic in the area. Both front- and back-seat pilots became expert at spotting the well-camouflaged and almost invisible targets. It took a few missions and some coaching on how to spot the targets, but with some practice they magically stood out with little effort from our eyes and brains. Fighter pilots who typically flew at higher altitudes had little chance of spotting these targets or assessing BDA accurately, which is where Misty added so much value to the effectiveness of our air warfare campaign in North Vietnam.

Our reports of enemy activity and assessments of bombing results were compiled by our assigned intelligence officers and sent to Seventh Air Force. Misty as an organization often made suggestions to Seventh Air Force on ways to improve the effectiveness of the air warfare campaign. Sometimes these were well received, but not always. It seemed that some pilots and outfits just wanted to get counters toward their 100 missions over the North so that they could go home. Accuracy was not always more important than safety. High-altitude releases on targets were not as effective as we would have liked. We were committed, though, and stayed at it. As a result, Misty developed a reputation as an effective player in the war to interdict the massive quantities of supplies flowing down the Ho Chi Minh trail.

My most memorable Misty mission

Although many of my Misty missions were memorable, the most memorable one was on July 26, 1968. I was in the back seat for that mission, and Steve Amdor was in the front seat. We were engaged in a rescue attempt for a pilot who had bailed out the day before and spent the night hiding in a riverbank.

After making radio contact with him and identifying his position, we identified the dozens of gun sites around him and on the flight path for the rescue helicopters. We then proceeded to put in flights of fighters on these sites.

We desperately wanted to get him home. And we were in a very, very tough situation. Those helicopters were not going to be able to get in unless we knocked all those gun sites out. We felt duty-bound to rescue him, but we had to be careful—careful not to run out of rockets, not to run out of fuel, not to get hit—and efficient. Get these gun sites knocked off as soon as possible so the rescue helicopter could come in and pick him up. It was an intense mission.

So we persisted. We flew for eight hours and refueled five times. Eventually, only one gun was left active; we had pummeled it but not gotten a direct hit yet. The gunner hooked his gun up to his truck and motored out of the area. Just gave up.

And after eight hours in the air, we succeeded. After putting in dozens of fighter strikes, we silenced the guns, they came and picked him up, and we all went home and had a beer.

Steve and I were awarded medals for this mission. It was my third Distinguished Flying Cross.

Close calls

I had several close calls with Misty. On one mission, the airborne command post informed us of heavy AAA activity near the DMZ, which was prohibiting slow-flying forward air controllers from operating in the area. I was in the front seat. After surveying the AAA gun sites in the area, we identified the most likely culprit, which was a 57 mm site surrounded by 37 mm and smaller-caliber gun sites.

After arranging for a flight of fighters and rendezvousing with them, I marked the main 57 mm target with a smoke rocket. The lead fighter attacked but missed the target. I gave the number two fighter directions off of the lead's bomb explosions, but he insisted that he did not have a good fix on the target. In my passion to knock out this site, I violated one of our standard operating procedures, which was to never mark the same target, especially a gun site, twice.

As I rolled in to mark the target again, all hell broke loose. Basketball-sized 57 mm shells streamed up and headed straight for us. After marking the target and pulling out, I was hit by small-caliber AAA in the wing and began to stream fuel from the hole. I headed to the ocean and began a climb to 30,000 feet to try and get enough altitude to make it back to Phu Cat before running out of fuel. I set up on a long straight in to the runway and managed to land successfully before the fuel tank was exhausted. The Wing Commander wasn't too happy with the damage to the aircraft, but I didn't get into trouble.

I nearly died in a midair collision with another Misty over North Vietnam. Normally, we flew each Misty mission solo in the area. As one Misty was exiting, the replacement Misty would be given a briefing by the departing Misty. For some reason on this mission, there was a mix-up in communications.

I was in the back seat, and we were taking a last look at a potential target before departing. As we were turning left, I looked over the right side of the canopy rail and saw another F-100F with its belly up to us in a turn that put him on a collision course. I immediately put my hand on the stick and pushed hard. As I did, we heard—and felt—the shock wave of the other aircraft as it passed within inches of us.

I don't know if my hand on the stick at the last minute had any effect or whether we were just destined to pass close by and not hit each other. The fact that I even looked out in the other direction was weird. My front-seat pilot never saw it. Why did I do that? Looking back on it, the fact that I even saw this guy before he made that unearthly sound was phenomenal. Maybe even miraculous.

Fortunately, we were soon on our way home. While flying back to Phu Cat, I was too stunned to talk. I silently reflected on just how close we came to dying that day.

On another mission, we were spotting targets for the battleship *New Jersey*. We were at 10,000 feet and had momentarily stopped jinking when a 37 mm shell passed so close to our canopy that we heard a sharp shock wave. Normally we had a mutual pact with gunners: we won't shoot at you if you don't shoot at us. You mess with us, we're gonna kill you.

Those gunners got a good dose of 16-inch shells from the *New Jersey* as a result. Take that, and no more cheap shots.

Once at the end of a Misty mission, we returned to find that Phu Cat was socked in. While in the holding pattern waiting for our turn to try an instrument approach, we heard aircraft after aircraft calling missed approach and diverting to another base with better weather. We had hit a tanker earlier and had enough fuel to try an approach. When our turn came, I completed the instrument approach to minimums. I could see the approach lights but the visibility was so low I couldn't actually see the concrete runway itself. The guy in the back seat said, "Watch your air speed." That was when we touched down. I'd completed a perfect landing and rollout, but it was hairy.

Assessing our effectiveness

There were two other special missions that I flew with Misty that were interesting. The first was an experimental night flight. I flew several of these missions over North Vietnam. These turned into more of an intelligence-gathering exercise about the effectiveness of our efforts to disrupt and destroy truck traffic moving supplies to the South. To illustrate it, I was flying in the back seat on one of these missions and using a starlight scope to observe activity on the ground. The scope was several feet long, which made it somewhat unwieldy in the confines of the cockpit; however, I was able to see some interesting activity. We were not employing fighters but were observing the results of flights of fighters attempting to interdict the many truck convoys moving through the area.

The activity on the ground that I observed was surreal. When the fighters began dropping bombs in the area, the long string of trucks in the convoy stopped on the road. The drivers got out, lit cigarettes, and took a smoke break standing beside their trucks. They showed no sign of concern or fear such as diving into a ditch or running into the trees. They apparently realized, based on experience, that their hooded truck headlights were impossible to see from the altitude where the fighters rolled into their dives for their bomb drops.

As the flight of fighters completed their drops and headed for home base, they would summarize their BDA in a radio call to the ABCCC. We also observed any damage and formulated our own BDA but kept it quiet to share with our intelligence officers after returning to base. The comparisons were always widely different. The fighters often reported a lot of damage to trucks and mysterious secondary explosions. We saw little to no damage to anything.

In the meantime, the drivers got back into their trucks, and the convoy motored on south without any damage. If it hadn't been so serious, it would have been laughable.

These missions were when I actually knew—despite our best efforts—that we weren't making any difference.

And the really frustrating thing was that we'd send this intel to the Seventh Air Force and, as far as we knew, nothing changed. Clearly, the USAF did not have the right technology to stop the truck traffic on the way to South Vietnam. A lot of supplies were getting through. This did not bode well for winning the war.

One other interesting special mission of my Misty tour was spotting for the battleship *New Jersey*. I had the opportunity to assist them in attacking several high-threat targets by adjusting their targeting to try to achieve hits with their 16-inch guns. The projectiles weighed about two thousand pounds and could travel over twenty miles.

The shells were deadly when hitting hardened targets such as another battleship or a concrete-reinforced surface target such as a gun emplacement in a bunker on a hillside to defend the beach against an invasion. Those types of targets were plentiful during the war in the Pacific against Japan during WWII. There were none in North Vietnam in RP1.

There were plenty of gun sites employing AAA in RP1, and they were not protected with hardened bunkers. They were simply emplaced on the soft ground typical of the coastal plain of North Vietnam. Many were surrounded by earth bunkers a few feet high to protect the gunners from near misses. A direct hit from the *New Jersey* was required to damage them.

The shells from the *New Jersey* did not have fuses that would blow up the shells on initial contact with the ground, which would have proved more effective for a near miss by creating a bigger surface blast. Their shells penetrated deep into the soft ground before exploding, which muffled the surface blast.

We looked for good targets for them such as the occasional ferry, railroad train, or high-threat gun site. It was somewhat less tense to employ them since we were at high altitude for spotting; therefore, we were at much lower risk from AAA.

Battleship cruise

Misty was invited to send a few pilots to the navy shipyard at Subic Bay, Philippines, to cruise with the battleship *New Jersey* back to Vietnam after one of their resupply runs to the shipyard. I was one of the pilots selected to make the trip, and it surpassed all expectations. I bunked in one of the rooms occupied by Admiral Halsey's staff in World War II when he used it as his flagship of the US Third Fleet. It had been overhauled and re-commissioned in April 1968. It employed nine 16-inch, twenty 5-inch, eighty 40 mm, and forty-nine 20 mm guns.

Early one morning after starting our cruise, I was rudely awakened when a 5-inch gun located just on the other side of my stateroom's outer wall fired as part of a gunnery practice. In my rapid awakening from a deep sleep, I momentarily thought it was another mortar attack at Phu Cat and hit the deck. I was happy to find myself on a battleship instead.

The Captain treated us royally on our cruise, including a dinner with him and a comprehensive tour of the ship. Overall, we had a great adventure. A helicopter picked us up from the ship as we arrived off the coast of South Vietnam and transported us back to Phu Cat.

R&R

Our social life at Phu Cat after flying was pleasant. We often gathered in the ready room of the 416th TFS for a beer and a game of darts or just conversation. Misty did not have a ready room, so the preferred location for socializing was the Officer's Club. There were frequent going-away dinners where we would cook out and fix some good food that we obtained from the army supply depot in the nearby city of Qui Nhon. We had an ample storeroom of supplies and alcoholic beverages for these periodic dinners and after-flying socializing. Eventually, we purchased "party suits" for our going-away feasts from Hong Kong on one of our mini R&R trips. In addition to my Bangkok R&R mentioned earlier, I was able to go to Hong Kong twice during the year for three or four days each.

Back in my trailer room, I made frequent audiotapes to send to my wife. I would listen to ones that I had received from her. These seemed more satisfying than letters, although we did some of both. We were much in love and longed to be together again. The extensive written and verbal communications to and from Vietnam played a big role in making our marriage even stronger over the years by helping us communicate better despite the stress of the situation in front of us at the time. It helped me even more, since I had not had much experience communicating with women as I matured, given my few dates in high school and at USAFA.

The most special event of the year was my one permitted R&R to Hawaii, where I met my wife for a wonderful week. It was the honeymoon we'd never had. My flight from Da Nang was delayed by one day, but the rest of the trip was great, although there was one other incident that was a close call of a different type.

My other trailer roommate, besides Steve Amdor, was a flight surgeon. He occupied the other end of the trailer and had a single bed because of his irregular work schedule. He gave me an R&R medical kit to help me adjust from my recent night flying and the time zone changes. He told me to take two of the red pills after we had refueled in Guam. That was about midnight. He said that they would assure that I got a good night of sleep before arriving in Hawaii the next day. My first indication that something was wrong was the feeling of someone shaking me violently while holding my shirt to wake me up after landing in Hawaii. Everyone else had already exited the plane when the stewardess found me still sound asleep. I was refreshed for sure.

Benita and I spent a couple of days sightseeing around Honolulu and then flew to the big island of Hawaii on our way to the Kona Village Resort. We had to board a small propeller aircraft at the airport to complete our journey. Kona Village was located behind some large lava fields on the Kona Coast, so it was quite remote. We had a nice thatched-roof hut right on the beach. There were hammocks suspended between palm trees on the side facing the beach. Everything was included on the "American Plan." It was an idyllic setting and a suitable replacement for the honeymoon that we'd had to cancel after our wedding because the air force changed my reporting date to Cannon AFB.

One day we asked for a picnic lunch and took that by a chauffeured boat to a small, uninhabited island nearby. We snorkeled on the reef there and enjoyed our picnic lunch and an afternoon of catching up with each other as well as planning for a true homecoming in December at the end of my tour. As evening approached, our chauffeured boat picked us up for the short trip back to the resort. I hated to see this second honeymoon come to an end.

Only five months to go.

Back to work

One thing that I noticed after my R&Rs was how strange it seemed getting back into my F-100. I could sense a lack of proficiency because I had lost touch with some of the more subtle sounds and feels of the aircraft. I regained my comfort level after a flight or two but found it remarkable what flying almost every day and sometimes two or three times a day does for your overall proficiency. I liked feeling "one" with my aircraft as if it were an extension of my senses.

I flew a total of 666 hours in the F-100 in less than two years, and most of that was flown in the year in Vietnam.

Misty flew its last mission in North Vietnam in late October; President Johnson announced an end to the bombing campaign on October 31, 1968. I had flown a mission with Misty the day before, quite a dangerous one. I directed fighters in placing sensor pods at selected spots to monitor activity remotely along the Ho Chi Minh trail. To assure correct placement, the fighter had to fly at low altitude and in a straight line during the deliveries. This resulted in an increased risk of being shot down by AAA fire.

I was not told that there would be a bombing campaign cessation the next day. That upset me. I had exposed some brave men to a lot of danger. Fortunately, no one was shot down. To my knowledge, these sensor pods never produced any useful intelligence. Misty had provided plenty of evidence that the enemy could move the supplies needed down the trail despite our best efforts at interdiction with fighters. Now they would be unimpeded by anything.

At the time that I volunteered, Misty pilots were limited to four months with the unit because of the high risks involved. Some earlier Misty pilots were allowed to stay for 100 missions to provide continuity and orient new Misty pilots in the fine arts of the mission.

I flew my November Misty missions primarily over Laos. My last mission was on November 9. During my four months, I recorded 297 hours and 50 minutes on 67 missions over North

Vietnam with 203 area penetrations, and 188 hours and 55 minutes over North Vietnam territory. I flew five missions over Laos for 15 hours and 10 minutes in November, which increased my total missions with Misty to 72, for a total of 313 combat hours. Note that many fighter pilots flying missions into North Vietnam were allowed to go home after completing 100. I made the equivalent of 203 missions in my four months with Misty and had to stay for a full year. It wasn't really fair, but that was the deal.

I returned to flying operations with the 416th TFS for my last few flights of my tour before departing Vietnam in mid-December 1968. I completed a total of 226 combat missions during the year.

I have enormous respect for the pilots with whom I flew and served in Misty as well as those in the 416th TFS. Given the number of close calls that I survived, I felt lucky to be going home without injury. Over the three years of the unit's existence from June 15, 1967, until May 12, 1970, 157 pilots served in Misty. Thirty-seven were shot down while in the unit, for a loss rate of twenty-four percent. Three were captured and interned as prisoners of war. Seven were killed in action. After leaving Misty, eight were shot down while completing their tours flying combat with their original units.

I came close to death several times during my year in Vietnam. My faith helped me to face the prospect of death on an almost daily basis without fear. I summed that up as a motto: You can't live fully until you have faced death. Benita was confident that I would return from the war unscathed, which is why she had been so irritated by my initial reluctance to marry before returning from the war.

Roy returning from his last Misty mission

Roy enjoys a celebratory glass of champagne after his last
Misty mission

Next assignment

When my next assignment was sent to me by message from the Military Personnel Center, I was most displeased. My desire was to go to Europe and continue flying the F-100 to gain more supersonic fighter time that would help me get into Test Pilot School. Instead I was ordered to report to Vance AFB to become a T-37 Instructor Pilot (IP). I appealed my assignment through my chain of command but was informed that the USAF desperately needed IPs for Undergraduate Pilot Training (UPT) to handle the heavy workload of turning out new pilots in a time of war.

I was so irritated that I manufactured a banner and hung it on the outside of my trailer. It read, "The Air Force sucks."

I was encouraged by my superiors to remove it rather quickly.

I did so, but it took me some time to come to terms with it. I wanted the extra flight time in the F-100 to help me qualify for test pilot school as soon as possible and was concerned that the T-37 time would not be considered as relevant for the purposes of competing for a slot.

I filled out my application for test pilot school before leaving Vietnam so that I could obtain letters of reference from my chain of command at Phu Cat. My application was put on hold by the school until I had achieved the minimum number of hours of first pilot time. I was still a little short of the required 1500 hours.

Finally the day came for me to leave Vietnam and return to the states. Benita met me at the Phoenix airport after the long journey home. We spent the night at a nearby hotel before driving to Tucson the next morning. Saying that I was happy to be home is a gross understatement.

After a short reunion with my wife's parents, we traveled to Enid, Oklahoma, and rented a house near Vance AFB, which was my next assignment. After getting settled, we traveled to Georgia for a visit with my parents. I came down with the Hong Kong flu while there and spent a couple of days in bed. It turns out that Benita was just recovering from a case of it when we met at the Phoenix airport, so I have to assume that I caught it from her.

We did kiss a lot that first night home.

Reflections

I have reflected often on my combat tour in the years since returning home. Shortly before departing for Vietnam, one of my relatives asked me why I was going. The war was unpopular.

The question seemed sort of ridiculous. I was in the air force as a fighter pilot, and the nation was at war. Like it or not, it was my patriotic duty to do my best that I could to help us win it. I did, and I feel good about my contributions.

On the other hand, a lot of people died needlessly in Vietnam, including many innocent civilians.

Did they die for a good reason? The answer is complicated. Political leaders of the era were terrified of something called the domino theory of Communist expansion in Southeast Asia and felt that we had to stop it there. In hindsight it is clear that we took on a nationalistic civil war created by French colonial imperialism.

The Vietnamese people wanted a reunited nation. Yes, the North Vietnamese were governed by a Communist system, which was unfortunate. The war and sanctions imposed afterwards devastated the country for decades.

Bottom line is that our politicians and military leaders made bad decisions about getting us into the war and had little understanding of the ultimate cost of our failed effort to stop the reunification.

Some of my colleagues went back to Vietnam for a second tour in fighters. I thought about it on several occasions but finally decided not to. Because of all that I had seen and done at Misty, I was convinced that no matter how much I could give to the war effort, it would not be enough to win.

It was a lost cause.

I wanted to make a positive contribution to society by helping to develop better fighter jets and space craft as a test pilot and, hopefully, eventually as an astronaut.

In the years after leaving Vietnam I would often awake after dreaming to realize that I had been flying the roads and trails of North Vietnam looking for targets.

Some of my Misty colleagues went back to North Vietnam and walked the ground that we flew over so many times. I have never had the urge to do that.

There are just too many ghosts there for me.

Chapter 21: T-37 Instructor Pilot—Vance AFB, Oklahoma
January 1969–June 1970

After our arrival at Vance AFB, we initially had to arrange for a short-term rental in downtown Enid, Oklahoma. After my initial checkout in the T-37, I would go on Temporary Duty to Perrin AFB in Sherman, Texas, for several months to complete Instructor Pilot Training. For our short stay in Enid, we rented one half of a furnished, ancient duplex on Maple Street for a month. The walls were thin, and our neighbors treated us to regular Friday night drunken brawls. We were happy that our stay there would be over in a couple of weeks.

During my first few weeks after checking in, I completed several initial check-out missions in the T-37 with instructor pilots. These were easy compared to the difficult flying in the F-100 in Vietnam.

Soon we were on our way to Sherman. There we initially rented a furnished two-bedroom apartment with a promise by the landlord to let us transfer to a cheaper one-bedroom as soon as one became available in about a month. This apartment was luxurious compared to Maple Street but too expensive for our budget. I had been promoted to Captain while I was in Vietnam, and since Benita worked—and lived at her parents' home—we had saved some money during the year. Our resources were much better on a month-to-month basis than before, but we needed to buy furniture to equip our base house at Vance AFB once I completed Instructor Pilot Training.

Life, landlady, and cookies: all good

Although we were spared the Friday night drunken brawls, we were treated to our neighbors' pillow talk when we were in bed. The landlord reneged on his promise, so we searched and found a cheap garage apartment in nearby downtown Denison, Texas. It was owned by an elderly widow and was located behind her home and over her standalone garage. She had installed a bell in our apartment, which she would ring when she had freshly baked goodies to share with us.

Life was good.

After my academics and flying duties were done for the day, we would enjoy a good home-cooked meal and play some cards or a board game such as Scrabble. We loved being with each other again, and we had much to share after a year of communicating by audiotapes and letters.

I found that I enjoyed learning how to teach someone to fly, which, I learned, was quite different than perfecting that art in myself. My instructors were great, and I made good progress.

While I was in class one day, someone ran into the back end of my MGB in the parking lot. That was a shame since my wife had had it repainted and expertly detailed as a homecoming gift to me when I returned from Vietnam. I took it to a local dealer to have it repaired. While negotiating the repair, I noticed that a nearly new 1968 Ford Thunderbird, light green with a dark green matte vinyl roof, was for sale. I asked for a ride in it with the salesman. After Benita and I discussed it, we decided to trade in the MGB for it. We needed a larger car for traveling and to accommodate the child that we hoped to have someday soon. The MGB was too small for a car seat for a baby.

After I successfully completed Instructor Pilot Training, we drove in our new T-Bird back to Vance AFB and were issued a house in the base housing area. It was a small two-bedroom home with a carport shared with our neighbor next door.

Witnessing the moon landing

We moved in just before the first moon landing, which was on July 20, 1969. There was no way I was going to miss it, but the timing was tight. We didn't own a TV, so I rented a small black-and-white TV for the historic occasion. Since we were about 80 miles from the nearest TV station in Oklahoma City, I had to purchase some wire and insulators so that I could rig an antenna among the trees in my backyard.

There was literally no furniture in our house. I was sitting on the bare, tiled floor in what was to be our living room, with this TV, the only one I could get. It was a small screen, but I could actually see what was going on up there. And it was cool.

As Neil Armstrong stepped out onto the moon, I was sitting there on the floor in our still-empty living room, facing the TV with my Pentax camera, taking 35-millimeter slides of my TV screen.

And I stayed tuned in. When the astronauts went back in and went to bed, I went to bed, too. I tuned in every time that I could, except when I was working. Since there were to be more moon landings in the coming months, I said, "I'm going to get me a color TV. We're going to watch the rest of these in style." Benita and I agreed to purchase a color TV so that we could watch them in all of their glory.

To save money, we purchased a Heathkit color TV kit and put it together over the Christmas holiday in 1969. Surprisingly, although I was the engineer in the family, Benita assumed that role and instructed me, the solder technician, which part to place next and where. We also installed a proper directional antenna on a tall pole attached to the house to improve reception. We finished the set in time to watch part of the Rose Bowl football game on New Year's Day.

Teaching other people to fly

My flying unit was great. I was in D Flight and enjoyed excellent leadership and a group of professional and sociable fellow instructor pilots. I was appointed to be the Standardization/ Evaluation Officer for the flight, which involved instructing the students in emergency procedures and testing their knowledge while under the stress of reciting their responses in front of their peers in the audience.

Some of the students thought of me as a hard-ass because of that role. However, my demeanor in the cockpit and during pre-flight and post-flight briefings was quite the opposite. Given my experience with an IP who yelled at me during my own T-41 training, I simply wanted my students to graduate with enough proficiency to advance to the next level and remain safe. None of my students had mishaps while under my supervision or later in UPT.

I did have to wash out one student because he just could not master instrument flying and would be a hazard to himself and others if allowed to continue. This was heartbreaking for all concerned, including his fellow students who tried to talk me out of it. I explained that my conscience would not let me do it, given the potential instrument conditions that he would face during his flying career.

Most of my students were motivated and talented, although some were quicker than others to master the art of flying.

I did have another difficult challenge. I had inherited a student from Saudi Arabia who had washed out of the previous
class but was being given an extra chance. The USAF was training a number of foreign students from many friendly countries
at the time. Part of his problem was the language difficulty, and
the other was his complete lack of experience in operating a
vehicle of any type, including a car. For example, he was having
difficulty planning and executing cross-country flights, which
involved planning a detailed navigation card showing way-
points, navigation aids, time, distance, and fuel used. To help
him advance, I got approval for a multiple-leg, overnight cross-
country and had him prepare many flight plans. He made progress, and I thought that he might have overcome his difficulties.

But when we were returning to Vance AFB and the FAA
controller asked him for his ETA (Estimated Time of Arrival) to
the fix for his instrument approach, he turned to ask me what
ETA was. I was incredulous; I momentarily lost my temper and
yelled at him.

He looked me in the eye and said, "I should kill you for in-
sulting me and would if we were in my home country."

I realized my error; I should not have yelled at him. That
was against my way of teaching people. I took a deep breath
and gently coached him on the way to respond. I helped him
complete T-37 training satisfactorily. He was quite a challenge,
but I never had any problem with him after that.

Given the USAF's need for an increased number of new
pilots to fill the ranks during the Vietnam War, we had a heavy
workload to complete the training on time. We were on a twelve-
hour-per-day schedule, which would allow us to fly four flights
per day. Some of these were night flights, in the evening or before dawn, depending upon the overall total for the day. Twelve
hours allowed us to spread the flights throughout a longer day.

From our home we were treated to the sound of aircraft flying at all hours, from early morning until late evening.

Family life

Social life after work was generally pleasant for my wife and me. She and I often hosted or attended dinners with friends from the base. Benita played bridge with a group of wives and participated in other Wives' Club activities, and we attended regularly scheduled squadron social activities. We also had time for an occasional short vacation, but one of them nearly got me into hot water.

We scheduled a vacation, a road trip with a small house trailer to Tennessee, where we met my parents for some sightseeing. I returned to find that I was in trouble with my squadron commander: I had missed the annual Squadron Toga Party! After I explained the details of why we had planned the leave on that date, he let me off the hook. Apparently, others had avoided the party for some reason, and he felt slighted.

In the fall of 1969, my wife surprised me one day with wonderful news. She announced that she was pregnant with our first child, with a due date in the spring of 1970. On a cold day in March of 1970, my Squadron Operations Officer met my student and me at our aircraft after landing as we pulled into our parking area.

"You need to go home now. Your wife needs you. You can debrief your student later." I hustled home to find that Benita was in labor and needed to get to the hospital downtown immediately. I double parked at the hospital entrance and got her up to the delivery ward. I went back to the entrance and parked my car, but by the time I returned, she had already completed the delivery. I saw my beautiful wife being rolled out of the delivery room with a gorgeous, red-haired baby girl. I thought,

"She is so beautiful that she will be Miss America of 1988," and I said as much to my wife after I got to her room. We named our daughter Tanya Marie.

My wife and our new baby did not suffer any complications and were soon ready to be discharged. When they returned home, however, we did experience some unexpected difficulties. We had endured a heavy snowstorm while they were in the hospital and now the roof was leaking badly as the snow began to melt. It was a flat-roofed home, which made the situation worse, as it would take several days before the snow melted and the roof could be repaired.

We protected our furniture as best we could with plastic sheeting and buckets. We were assigned temporary accommodations in a repurposed old hospital building until the roof could be repaired. The fallout from the repair job was almost worse than the leaks. The constant pounding of the roof to remove the old roofing material produced immense quantities of dust and dirt, which fell in all areas of our home. After all was done, we had to launder or dry clean all of our clothes and have the couch and chairs vacuumed and cleaned. What a mess!

Air Force Aerospace Research Pilot School

Not long after our daughter was born in March, I was notified that my application for the Air Force Aerospace Research Pilot School (ARPS) had been approved, and that I should report to Edwards AFB, California, in July 1970 to begin school with the Class of 70B. What a pleasant surprise. This had come much sooner than I expected.

After all the prep work I'd done, filing my application before I ever left Vietnam, and getting all these first-pilot flying hours as an instructor—and suddenly I was already in? I expected to be at Vance for years. Now, I was not only getting a new, beautiful baby, but I was getting my new, beautiful assignment to do exactly what I'd always wanted to do.

My assignment to Vance AFB had allowed me to fly often relative to others who were assigned to Europe to fly the F-100, which had been my first choice when leaving Vietnam. As a result, I was able to achieve the required amount of first-pilot hours to qualify for ARPS in record time. At twenty-seven, I would be the youngest pilot to ever attend ARPS. (I didn't hold the record for long; a student in the next class was a few months younger when he arrived at ARPS than I had been.) Nevertheless, getting into test pilot school so soon proved that my displeasure with my T-37 assignment—succinctly expressed by the "Air Force sucks" sign that made a short appearance on my trailer in Vietnam—was wrong-headed. It was, in fact, exactly the right thing to do, given my aspiration to attend ARPS as early in my career as possible.

I would be happy transitioning out of the T-37 and leaving Oklahoma behind.

In the wintertime, it seems there is nothing between the North Pole and Oklahoma but a few barbed wire fences. Doing a preflight inspection before daylight on a cold winter morning was agony. When the cold was extreme, I would instruct the student to get strapped in and complete his pre-start checklist. I would do a thorough but much faster preflight inspection and strap in. We would start immediately so that we could close the canopy and begin to warm up.

Summers were equally miserable, with the heat, humidity, and wind. Strapped into a T-37 while taxiing for takeoff seemed to take an eternity. We could not close the canopy since there was no air conditioning on the ground with the engines in idle, which meant having the piercing scream of the T-37 engine intake close to my right ear. That sound is what earned the T-37 the nickname "Screaming Mimi." Those experiences explain my lack of high-frequency hearing and tinnitus today. Our helmets provided inadequate hearing protection and, given the unpressurized nature of the T-37, we couldn't wear earplugs under our helmets.

The one great thing about the weather conditions was the ability to teach student pilots how to fly well when it was windy. I had not gotten much experience dealing with windy conditions when I was in UPT at Williams AFB, so I had to acquire this expertise once at Vance. During our daily pre-flight briefing, with the entire flight as the audience, we made the students explain the adjustments needed to counter the day's forecast to keep the landing pattern correctly aligned to assure safe conditions. I once had to land at Vance in such a strong crosswind that I had to use full rudder to stay aligned with the runway in a wing low touchdown. Frequent thunderstorms and occasional tornados could pop up quickly and require us to land immediately.

And that's not all tornados could do.

When our daughter was two months old, we finally felt comfortable enough to hire a babysitter so that we could make the trip to Oklahoma City for a nice dinner and evening out, and one evening we did just that. While we were away, a tornado hit the area between Oklahoma City and Enid. We saw some destruction along the highway on our way home and worried about what we would find when we arrived. This was in the era before mobile phones, so we were kept in suspense until arriving at home. We were spared a disaster, but we were happy to be leaving Oklahoma for our next assignment.

On our cross-country driving trip to California, I talked to Benita about what becoming a test pilot meant to me. She understood.

When I returned from Vietnam, she had picked me up at the airport in Phoenix. The two days we were driving to our new assignment in Enid, Oklahoma, were a time of catching up, and that's when Benita chose to tell me that while I was away she had paid for pilot training and had successfully soloed. She didn't continue to get her pilot's license, but her experience showed me that she shared my interest in aviation. I wished that she had shared this with me earlier, while I was in Vietnam, but she hadn't wanted to worry me.

Together, we looked forward to the next adventure.

Chapter 22: Aerospace Research Pilot School (ARPS)
July 1970–August 1971

We arranged a military household move from Vance AFB to Edwards AFB as summer began in 1970. On the way, we met my wife's parents in Lake Havasu, Arizona, for an overnight visit. They had purchased a lot in that resort and retirement community.

It was extremely hot while we were there. To cool off, we took a swim in the motel pool. I had fun helping our three-month-old daughter enjoy her first swim. Benita was upset with me for being a little too athletic with her on her first swim, though.

As we continued our drive and approached Edwards AFB from the east, we traveled through towns such as Barstow and Boron, California. I had built up an exciting mental picture of what Edwards would be like and had shared it with Benita in the months leading up to our trip.

Alas, the reality was far from what I had pictured. It wasn't quite the "magnificent desolation," words that Buzz Aldrin used to describe the lunar landscape. Instead, it was a bleak, flat desert without any visual relief except for the occasional weird Joshua tree or the promise of the distant Sierra Nevada mountains on the western horizon.

As we turned off the main highway and entered the north gate, the landscape didn't improve. The highlight, as we topped the hill leading to the Visiting Officers' Quarters (VOQ), was a great view of the extensive flat lakebed that had hosted so many aerodynamic accomplishments over the years. There was a similar scene in the movie *The Right Stuff*, which I saw years later (it came out in 1983), where one of the Mercury astronauts traveled to Edwards AFB for the first time with his wife. Of course, I wasn't going to Edwards for the view or the environment. I wanted to be a test pilot, and this was the place to achieve that goal. But, man, at first glance? That place was *uggg-lyyy*.

Settling in

It was hot when we arrived at the VOQ in the afternoon to inquire about a room for a few nights until I could sign in and arrange for housing. Alas, there was no room available at the inn until at least 4:00 p.m. I told the gentleman at the front desk that he would need to host my wife and rather upset child in the lobby while I ran errands around the base in the afternoon heat. At 4:00 p.m., when I returned, there were still no rooms. We headed for the nearest town—Lancaster, about 30 miles to the south—to rent a motel room until the VOQ could accommodate us the next day.

After a few days in the VOQ, we transitioned to our temporary dwelling in Desert Villa, which was a Spartan, ancient military motel for residents awaiting availability of their permanent base house. I was the most junior ranking officer of my ARPS class, so I was last in line for a house. The quarters at Desert Villa consisted of a combination family room, bedroom, and minimal kitchen all in one room, with a separate bathroom. Cooling was by swamp cooler (a unit that uses moisture to cool the air), which was okay in the dry desert. Our army cots had thin mattresses and olive drab wool blankets.

We met some of our new classmates and their families while there. On the weekend, we picnicked in the nearby Tehachapi Mountain Park with one couple, Paul and Gloria Nafziger. We spread an old wool army blanket for our daughter to play and lounge on. The view from the mountain was breathtaking, our picnic dinner was delicious, and most of all, we enjoyed getting to know each other. We became best friends for life and had many other visits during our Edwards tour and later in life.

During the week, I began to get set up for flying at ARPS and got my first check-out ride in the T-33 with an IP, after which I was cleared for solo flights. "Your flying is solid," he complimented me in our debriefing. My interpretation was that he perceived that I was totally in command as an aviator on my first flight as pilot of the T-33. It was an unexpected but reassuring start!

After several weeks, we were allowed to move into our base house, which was a small three-bedroom home with a detached garage. It was to be our home for the next five years, and after we finished furnishing and adapting it for our family, it was comfortable and enjoyable. We made friends with our many neighbors. Even today, we are still in touch with a number of them.

Homework

I set up a Spartan desk, which I had purchased from Sears, in one of the small bedrooms, and buckled down to review engineering subjects during the few days before classes started. I had purchased some special textbooks—engineering math and aeronautics—to help me cover a lot of ground, along with practice problems. Engineering math and other technical subjects had not been my focus since leaving Purdue University, and I knew I was rusty. Fortunately, I quickly regained my proficiency and confidence. That would prove to be helpful as we began the ARPS curriculum in earnest, with flying every morning and academics every afternoon. Looking back, I think of ARPS as earning a PhD in flying and a master's degree in related engineering subjects in one year. It was to be another exercise in time management, which would require extreme focus and frequent reprioritization to do well.

After classes started, I studied at my desk every night after dinner with my wife and daughter and my one luxury, which was to watch an episode of the new TV show, *Star Trek*. I also spent time with my daughter, especially as she got older. She liked for me to read her a story. When she had enough leg strength to graduate to a walker, she used to paddle around the house on our tile floors, and she would frequently visit me at my desk in my study room. She took delight in emptying my lower desk drawer and throwing the paperwork on the floor. I had much fun watching her innocent mischief.

Classroom in the air

Many of my flights were early in the morning to take advantage of the cooler temperatures and smoother air, which helped us achieve the desired accuracy of our data-gathering flight exercises. Walking back to the school building from the flight line at an early hour, it was easy to say that we had done a day's worth of work well before noon.

We began to learn all aspects of how to determine the specifics of aircraft performance and flying qualities and be able to reduce the data from our onboard flight test instrumentation and prepare detailed test reports on the results, which were graded. In addition, we had periodic graded check rides with

IPs where we were evaluated on our ability to efficiently plan and execute test flights safely, and to achieve accurate test results.

This required preplanning so that we could do specific tests in specific areas of the airspace at Edwards with a minimum expenditure of fuel. My earlier transition to being an early riser paid dividends. I was often awake at 4:00 a.m., mentally preparing for an early briefing and flight over a cup of coffee and a light breakfast at home before leaving for the school. My wife and daughter would be sleeping soundly, so my activities were not a burden to them.

One particular flight provides a good example of how difficult and rigorous the flying curriculum was. Our first flight in the F-104 required us to demonstrate how well we could prepare for the first flight of a new aircraft or to perform a qualitative assessment of a previously unknown aircraft, such as a captured enemy aircraft.

We had to take the flight manual and teach ourselves how to operate the aircraft without any instruction or assistance from the IPs. We had to plan the flight to gather all pertinent data so that we could debrief our IP and write a comprehensive report on the most important aspects of the aircraft's performance and flying qualities.

Faster than sound

In the F-104, this required us to go supersonic to gather data at its higher speeds, which used a lot of fuel and had to be performed in the supersonic corridor. This was a specific area for speeds faster than the speed of sound, to avoid subjecting population centers to potentially damaging sonic booms. We had to be precise on each test point since we would not have enough fuel to repeat maneuvers. I managed to pull off an excellent flight on my first F-104 mission, which established my reputation with the ARPS IPs as a quick learner and on my way to being a competent and proficient test pilot of high-performance fighter aircraft.

After that first graded F-104 dual flight with an IP, I was cleared to fly solo to learn more about flying this high-performance fighter. Since we didn't have enough fuel on our first flight to reach the F-104's maximum speed of more than Mach 2, I had a separate solo mission to reach a test point at Mach 2 in the supersonic corridor.

As I was accelerating in full afterburner toward Mach 2, I suffered a violent event passing Mach 1.7. In addition to a loud "bang" noise, I was thrown into the instrument panel with such force that I was surprised that I had not cracked my helmet. I quickly pulled the throttle out of afterburner and did an emergency return and landing at Edwards. After landing and writing up the incident in the maintenance log so that the engine could be inspected and repaired, I headed back to the operations counter at the school.

The Operations Officer asked me how I had enjoyed my first Mach 2 flight. I had to explain what had happened. He asked, "Did you remember to deploy the engine bypass flaps at the appropriate speed as required by the checklist?"

I thought about it for a moment and then replied honestly, "I don't remember doing that."

He laughed and said that I had caused the engine to compressor-stall as a result. The only disciplinary action he ordered for my mistake was that I return to the flight line and immediately repeat the flight in a different F-104, which I did, and successfully reached my Mach 2 test point.

I admired the way that the Operations Officer taught me not only a valuable lesson in how to fly the F-104 but how he didn't overreact to my error. In that demanding environment, one needs to understand that even professional test pilots are human and will potentially make an error. The lesson is to set up an environment where supervisors can assure that the most critical errors don't become a statistic from a fatal accident. Downstream, I would be a supervisor of those flying hazardous test missions and would need to help my test pilots avoid making fatal human errors. It was a good lesson to learn!

Roy in front of the F-104 jet that he flew at the Aerospace Research Pilot School (ARPS) and while serving with the 6512th Test Squadron at Edwards AFB

AIRCRAFT

While many of our basic performance and flying-quality missions were performed in the T-33, T-38, and F-104, ARPS provided many other opportunities to develop our ability to fly other aircraft safely and efficiently and write detailed reports on their characteristics. We flew dual missions with IPs in the vintage B-57 bomber. We were able to experience the hazardous single-engine-out flying characteristics in that twin-engine aircraft with its non-centerline thrust engines. I had an opportunity to fly the B-52 bomber with an instructor pilot. With its eight engines, it was a handful of throttles.

We flew a few flights with IPs in the variable-stability B-26 bomber of WWII fame. These were insightful, as we were able to explore different handling qualities using the high-technology flight-control computer to vary the characteristics of the aircraft.

The school also owned and operated a specially modified F-106 fighter with variable-stability capability so that we could see a wide variety of flying-quality characteristics in a high-performance fighter. The F-106 flights were flown with a specially trained ARPS IP.

Helicopters, gliders, and flying with birds

We had a dozen or so missions learning to fly the UH-1 helicopter. That was a unique and great experience for me since I had no previous experience with rotary-wing aircraft.

Another real treat was flying gliders at a contract glider facility in nearby Tehachapi. That location was ideal for gliders. It was located in a pass in the Sierra Nevada mountain range, which provided ideal lift conditions on a daily basis. After a checkout, we were allowed to fly the glider solo. On an early solo flight, I got above a partially clouded deck and was blown further downwind than I anticipated. When I broke out of the clouds and saw the landmarks, I instantly realized my error. Using my training, I managed to get back to the field and land with just feet to spare.

I was cautious on future flights to never get into a precarious position like that again.

Occasionally, I flew formation with soaring birds. They knew where the best lift was. When they noticed me, they quickly moved aside.

As a fighter-track test-pilot student, I was allowed to select a fighter that I had never flown before and do a qualitative assessment of it. I selected the single-seat A-7 and flew it for two flights without the assistance of an IP in that aircraft, which put the previous training of preparing for my first F-104 flight into practice.

Zoom ballets

Without a doubt, the highlight of the school's special experiences was the zoom flight in the F-104. First we had to learn how to land the F-104 engine out. The approach was modeled on the pattern used by the rocket-powered X-15 for its landings. We began a 270-degree turn over the landing runway at 25,000 feet and used the altitude to provide the energy as we made a descent to a landing on the runway within a few hundred feet of the target touchdown spot. After being qualified by an IP, we practiced these maneuvers often on our solo missions to become proficient. They were difficult to master.

I thought of them as an aerial ballet and delighted in taking off in afterburner, accelerating to 400 knots, and pulling up into a climbing turn to 25,000 feet, where I put the throttle to idle to simulate the engine failure and began the approach. A graceful, shallow banked turn to arrive on final approach at just the right altitude and speed to nail the touchdown completed the ballet. Exhilarating!

Zooming in the F-104

Once we had mastered the landing, we were fitted with full-pressure suits and flew with an IP on graded flights to extremely high altitudes. We accelerated the F-104 in the supersonic corridor to a speed near Mach 2 and then pulled up into a 30-degree climb on our first flight and then to 45 degrees on the second mission. We zoomed over the top on a ballistic profile. The speed at the pullup determined how high we would go, and the profile was designed to assure we were low enough to assure adequate aerodynamic controls in the thin air. The engine had to be shut down before it reached too high of a temperature in the thin air. Once we were in a descent and at a lower altitude, we restarted the engine; however, we flew as if the engine would not start. We left the engine at idle and completed the flight to touchdown using the X-15 landing pattern.

The aerodynamics were tricky. The still-spinning engine acted as a gyroscope, which resulted in a yaw—the nose of the aircraft moving to the right when you push it down—as we pushed over to control the angle of attack to avoid going out of control in a stall, and potentially into a spin. These were graded flights and had to be done well the first time to be competitive in our class order of merit.

Zooming in the NF-104: my near-space adventure

ARPS students who were fighter pilots were given an additional zoom adventure. The school possessed two heavily modified NF-104 aircraft. These aircraft were equipped with a rocket engine in the vertical tail. The cockpit was pressurized with nitrogen to keep the pressure suit from needing to be pressurized, which gave the pilot much better comfort and mobility. That made it a lot easier to move the control stick more accurately than when in a stiff pressure suit.

The aircraft also had gas-operated attitude-control jets, which provided roll, pitch, and yaw control when the atmosphere was too thin for adequate aerodynamic control with elevators, rudders, and ailerons. This allowed us to design profiles that would achieve much higher altitudes.

We each got to fly two flights in the modified NF-104. My profile required me to accelerate to Mach 2.4 and then make a pull of 4 g's to a 30-degree on the first flight and on the second flight to a 45-degree angle. I invited Benita to be in the control room during my two flights to witness the thrill of this near-space adventure; I wanted her to share seeing my dream come true.

I was required to shut down the engine at a preselected altitude of 65,000 feet to prevent the engine exceeding its maximum allowable temperature. I used the rocket engine briefly to accelerate more quickly through the transonic region to preserve fuel, as that was a critical parameter for the flight, and then shut it down until Mach 2. I reengaged the rocket at Mach 2 and let it run until the rocket fuel was depleted at an altitude of over 80,000 feet.

I had some unplanned excitement on my second flight designed for the 45-degree zoom. As I completed the takeoff in full afterburner and turned out of traffic, I deselected afterburner for the climb to 40,000 feet to begin my acceleration. Unfortunately, the afterburner did not fully extinguish initially. I caught the problem after a brief time and successfully deselected it on the second attempt, but I had burned extra fuel as a result. Because of my slightly lower fuel level, I was ordered to light my rocket sooner and let it run longer in the transonic region to accelerate more quickly and regain some of my fuel margin. That meant that I would not achieve as high an altitude as theoretically possible; however, I achieved 102,400 feet—nearly 20 miles—and that was fine with me.

The sky was black, and I could see the California coastline from San Diego to Monterey Bay. What a thrill! In awe of the grandeur, for a moment I was reliving my earliest memory—alone and tiny in a vast space, staring up at that high ceiling. Only this time, the ceiling was infinite, and I was literally staring down at the Earth from miles above it.

The rocket-powered NF-104 that Roy flew to an altitude of
102,400 feet during a flight while attending ARPS

When I restarted the engine during the descent, the engine compressor-stalled as I advanced the throttle to check the engine operation after the restart. I left it in idle for the remainder of the flight, as I didn't plan on needing it to complete the X-15 landing pattern. I did one final check on the engine as I neared final approach by advancing the throttle. It operated normally, but my pattern was perfect and I didn't need it, so I returned it to idle. Not as planned, but not a problem.

Benita viewed the flight from the control room, caught up in the excitement of this special event for me. Her love and knowledge of aviation meant she could enjoy it without overly worrying about it. We had fun discussing it over dinner that night.

That flight was certainly the highlight of my flying career, up to that moment. And it would be, until I flew the space shuttle.

Classes on the ground and in the air

ARPS also possessed a spaceflight simulator. We learned to perform feats such as rendezvous and docking with another spacecraft. Those amazing experiences whetted my appetite for a real space flight.

ARPS academic classes convened in the afternoon each day and were rated as graduate level. They provided the science and engineering basis for our flying curriculum. Doing well with these courses was also critical to achieve a high order of merit. As I mentioned briefly earlier, the combination of flying, academics, and preparing and delivering our many technical reports based on our flights resulted in a complex and difficult exercise in time management to achieve excellent grades in all areas. My engineering courses at the Air Force Academy and my graduate degree in engineering from Purdue University helped me significantly; I found much of the engineering content of the courses to be more of a review and learning new applications rather than brand-new subjects to master. This let me devote more time to planning my flights, especially the graded ones, instead of preparing for academic tests.

We went on field trips to become acquainted with the test activities at the bases that needed test pilots to complete their missions. These were fun and educational.

We visited Eglin AFB, Florida, where munitions were developed and qualified so that they could be carried and expended safely from bombers and fighters.

We visited Wright Patterson AFB, Ohio, which specialized in multi-engine aircraft testing. They had specially modified and instrumented test aircraft to test new aircraft aerial refueling capabilities and anti-icing systems. They also flew a modified refueling aircraft that the pilot could put through a maneuver that allowed people in the cargo bay to experience zero g for 30 seconds or so. The cargo bay was padded, and we had fun floating and doing somersaults in the air—things you can't do in one g without hurting yourself. This adventure only made me hungrier for a real space flight. What fun!

We visited Tyndall AFB, Florida, where upgrades and modifications to interceptor aircraft were tested, and Kirtland AFB, New Mexico, where nuclear weapons were tested for safe captive carry and release by fighter and bomber aircraft. Test aircraft carried and dropped new models of nuclear weapons with instrumentation as the payload instead of the nuclear materials. This assured that they could operate safely at all airspeeds, altitudes, and profiles during captive carry and delivery, as well as survive accidents. We also were treated to an overnight cruise on an aircraft carrier to see how the navy operated in that extreme environment. And we visited several aircraft manufacturing plants in California to hear about new technologies in development that we would see being deployed soon.

Of course, we also got a detailed tour of the ongoing and planned new aircraft development programs that were being tested at Edwards AFB currently or in the near future. We were briefed and got a detailed tour of the A-12, which was developed as an operational aircraft into the SR-71, the fastest jet-powered aircraft, capable of a top speed of 2193 mph.

Graduation approaches

Edwards was the most exciting to me, as that was where the first flights and early development tests of new aircraft occurred. I resolved that if I could graduate with a high enough order of merit that I would select Edwards AFB as my first choice of assignments.

As we approached our graduation date, the school published the anticipated order of merit based on all grades to date. Most of the graded events were behind us at that point. I was pleased to see that I was at the top of the list so far and was determined to finish strong. First place would give me first choice of assignments.

The prospect of graduation was not without its regrets. My good friend and across-the-street neighbor Bill Haugen, who had been a multi-engine cargo aircraft pilot before arriving at ARPS, was unable to demonstrate his proficiency in zoom profiles to his IP and washed out of our class at ARPS. He did fine on other aspects of flying, but zooms eluded him. I personally regarded that as a tragic ending and perhaps an unnecessary one, given that he would never have to fly such a maneuver as a graduate from ARPS because he would continue to fly multi-engine bomber and cargo aircraft in the future.

But the bar for success was set high at ARPS, regardless of our backgrounds or potential future activities as test pilots. He recovered from the setback and went on to be successful in his USAF aviation career, but not as a test pilot. We remain the best of friends with Bill and his great family to this day.

There was a tragic event at the school a few months before we graduated. I was flying one day when I noticed a column of black smoke arising from the desert. I was told that a B-57 had crashed. I flew low over the site and observed the complete destruction of the aircraft. When rescue and medical forces arrived by helicopter, I returned to Edwards AFB and landed.

The news was terrible. The crew consisted of two ARPS IPs. One of them was my next-door neighbor, and he was killed. The other IP had managed to eject but was at low altitude and suffered multiple injuries upon landing. He died a couple of days later.

We adored our neighbor, and this tragedy was difficult for Benita and me. She made a trip to visit her parents in Tucson for a week to have a change of scenery. I was appointed as the summary courts officer for the other pilot to assist with the funeral arrangements as well as arrangements for his family to move to an off-base location of their choice. I grew close to his wife and family during this time.

Sadly, this was the second aircraft crash that had impacted our class. We had lost a classmate in a T-38 accident, along with his ARPS IP, when we first began our ARPS training. The student was a French air force exchange pilot. The timing meant that we had not gotten to know them well, but it certainly brought home to all of us that we were engaged in activities that could cost us our lives.

As a result of these losses, the school was short of IPs. To fill the gap until new IPs arrived, I was "graduated" early and assigned as an F-104 IP to assist our junior class with their F-104 checkouts. I was also assigned to complete the ground and flight tests of an F-104 spin chute for the school. This chute would be used to enhance the safety of flights at high angles of attack in the F-104, which had a tendency to go into a flat spin from which recovery was problematic. The famous test pilot Chuck Yeager had nearly been killed during an F-104 zoom flight when he lost control, went into a flat spin, and had to eject.

Prior to graduation, when our assignments were being decided, I interviewed with the Commander of the Fighter

Division of Test Operations at Edwards AFB for the one available slot for a new fighter test pilot. He wasn't too impressed, given my junior rank and relatively low operational experience compared to some of the more senior pilots in my class.

He said, "I have my eye on someone else in your class for that slot."

Respectfully, I replied, "Sir, by tradition, the number-one graduate has first choice of assignments, and my choice is Edwards. You'll just have to get used to me. I won't let you down."

He just smiled.

Honors

Finally, graduation day arrived. I was presented the top graduate award for the best overall record in flying and academics. It was named the Liethen-Tittle Award in honor of test pilot Majors Frank Liethen and David Tittle, who died in flight-test aircraft accidents. Apollo 11 astronaut Mike Collins spoke at our graduation ceremony and presented me the award, which was an immense honor.

Before reporting to Test Operations, I had to remain as an IP at ARPS until several new IPs arrived. One day I was at my desk preparing a test card for my spin chute tests when the new ARPS Commandant came into my office, sat down on the edge of my desk, and asked me to brief him on my activities.

I knew I was in that position only temporarily until I could transition to Test Operations at Edwards. I wasn't one of the senior test pilots, I was really a junior guy, with an office in an out-of-the-way place. I hadn't expected to have any real connection to the new commandant. So it was a total surprise when he showed up in my office, sat down on the corner of my desk, and wanted to know what the hell was I doing?

My heart stopped, but I managed to pull myself together and satisfy him about my test project.

The new commandant was Colonel Buzz Aldrin, the Lunar Module Pilot for Apollo 11, the second human being to step on the moon.

Chapter 23: Test Operations
September 1971–December 1971

After I was released from ARPS, I reported to Test Operations, which was officially the 6512th Test Squadron, for duty. Tradition required that the newest member of the fighter division would be assigned as the officer in charge of the Operations Department. It was the central nerve center for scheduling the flights of the squadron and working with maintenance to plan future schedules.

We posted the daily schedule on the grease board for all to see. Pilots signed out and in for their flights on forms maintained by me and two enlisted technicians who assisted me with the considerable workload of this operation. We also maintained the Pilot Information File that all pilots had to read and certify before each flight as well as other documents required by our Standardization and Evaluation Office. This documentation was reviewed in detail when we had our annual inspection from headquarters, and it was important that we had all of our *i*'s dotted and *t*'s crossed.

In that position, I met with the Chief of Aircraft Maintenance, a colonel, weekly to negotiate the number of aircraft sorties that we could have per day and try to get as many as possible. We needed all that we could get to meet the demands of test project schedules, which were used to provide all the base's test missions with supporting aircraft for safety chase and photo chase as well as some smaller in-house test projects that were run from Test Operations. This was a duty requiring a lot of coordination and attention to detail.

CHASE SUPPORT

Safety chase and photo chase support for test projects require a support plane to fly in formation with the test plane. If the day's project requires only safety chase, a pilot in a single-seat jet plane flies in formation with the test plane to keep a lookout for the test pilot, to warn of any imminent dangers, because the pilot is absorbed with flying the plane, watching the instruments, putting it through its paces—lots of head-down activities. The safety chase pilot reports anything unusual happening. Is another plane about to run into them? Is the plane catching fire? He's there to keep eyeballs on the other guy and be as unobtrusive as possible.

A photo chase requires a two-seater support plane. A professional photographer would be in the back seat, taking still photos and video so the engineers on the ground could have detailed evidence of how a bomb, for instance, reacted after being released from the plane, or how the plane behaved in a stall or spin they were testing. In photo chase, the front-seat pilot also serves as the safety chase.

To add to the complexity, pilots could volunteer for upcoming missions based upon their seniority in the squadron. The more senior test pilots had first choice and would pencil in their names on the next week's schedule sheet. If I could not recruit pilots for all the slots, I would have to fill in my name and fly the missions.

I also provided slides to be briefed at the daily "stand-up" briefing. This was a brief presentation to the Center and Wing Commanders and their support staffs of the results of the day's flying activities, with a focus on things that had gone wrong and a look ahead at the next day's planned flights—really focused on the here and now. Any significant anomalies such as ground or air aborts or emergencies would be briefed in detail.

Clearly, the position required a lot of gentle persuasion and diplomacy to keep things moving and people happy with me. As the junior officer in the squadron, I had no real clout.

At that time, I was checked out in the T-33 and F-104 and flew my support missions in those aircraft. One type of mission was difficult to fill on the schedule. We had to ferry the flight test instrumentation tapes produced on F-111 test flights to the contractor's plant in Ft. Worth, Texas, each time the F-111 completed a test flight. I flew many of these milk run deliveries to Carswell AFB. Weather was often a complication, requiring a lot of preplanning and variations in the routing.

I also did a lot of the more routine safety chase and photo chase missions; consequently, I became expert at those tasks, which were the bread and butter of flight test support. After serving for what seemed an eternity on the operations desk, I received a welcome invitation to join the new A-X Test Team.

Chapter 24: A-X/YA-10 Test Team
January 1972–July 1975

The A-X Test Team was formed to plan and participate in the recently announced A-X Fly-off to select competitively the USAF's next close air support aircraft. Under new Department of Defense (DOD) procurement rules, competition between two or more prototypes was deemed a best practice. In this case, the competition would be between the YA-9 developed by Northrop and the YA-10 developed by Fairchild Republic.

Our small team was composed of two senior test pilots from Edwards AFB, plus me, to do the developmental testing, and two pilots from the Tactical Air Command to perform operational testing. We were assigned flight test engineers from Edwards and maintenance personnel from Tactical Air Command to evaluate the aircraft and determine the one that was easiest to maintain.

The contractor testing and routine postflight and preflight maintenance would be performed in separate hangars and offices by the contractor test teams. This separation allowed our team a great deal of independence to assure fairness in our evaluation and avoid any chance of inadvertently passing along any of our results before decisions were made by program officials.

I threw myself into this endeavor with great passion. I wanted to help the USAF have a better aircraft for this important close air support mission than what I had flown and observed in Vietnam. As the junior member of the test team from Edwards, I drew a lot of the miscellaneous jobs, such as learning how to be a supply officer to equip our office complex adjacent to our aircraft hangar with furniture and equipment that we would need. I even went so far as to construct the top of a large conference table overlaid on some small tables that I lashed together with wire. After joining the sheets of plywood, I rounded the corners with a jigsaw and glued on some nice molding to smooth out the edges. After staining and varnishing it, it looked professional, and it served us well throughout the fly-off.

I also took on the role of operations officer by coordinating and scheduling our test and support aircraft and assuring that we filled out the forms and kept our operational records current as I had done at Test Operations. I even constructed an operations counter and grease board to mount our daily and weekly schedules. Eventually, an enlisted airman was assigned to me as an assistant. He manned the operations counter and helped me maintain all essential records.

Fly-off prep

In preparation for the fly-off, we arranged to borrow four A-37 aircraft to use for a bombing competition between our test and operational pilots to develop the criteria we would use to evaluate the YA-9 and YA-10 prototypes, as well as to become proficient in the patterns that we planned to use. We would also use the A-37s for safety and photo chase missions for YA-9 and YA-10 developmental test flights, since their performance characteristics were a good match for the prototypes and much better than anything else that we currently had at Edwards AFB. We made a trip to the Air National Guard base in Indiana to check out in the aircraft and ferry them back to Edwards.

The bombing competition involved a set of three dive angles of 25, 45, and 60 degrees. We would roll-in from a different cardinal heading on every pass and a different dive angle on every fifth pass to simulate a first-pass look for each of the 24 practice bombs that we would employ, which would be scored by the range officer. We also performed scored strafing runs on large cloth targets. Since no one was shooting at us, the bombing competition was more fun than work, and the weather was always good. I did well enough during the A-37 competition to be selected as one of the pilots to participate in that competition during the fly-off.

I was also assigned to perform aircraft systems testing on both aircraft. Our boss would participate selectively in the various test flights and our other Edwards AFB test pilot would perform most of the performance and flying-qualities tests on both prototypes.

Another part of our preparation was to travel to the Fairchild Republic plant in Long Island and the Northrop plant in California to attend ground school and observe the final construction of the prototypes. This preparation was energizing, and our excitement built to a crescendo as the prototypes arrived and were prepared for their first flights.

Near-disaster

Finally, the prototypes arrived at Edwards and completed their initial test flights, which were flown by company test pilots. After the contractor test flights to assure that the aircraft were safe for us, a date was picked to begin the formal competition, and we put into practice our planning and preparation. Since both prototypes were single-seat fighters, our initial checkout flights were flown solo, with the company test pilot as the IP in an A-37 safety chase. After a number of training sorties, we were almost ready to start the gunnery competition when disaster struck me.

I was flying a practice gunnery competition mission as number two in a flight of two YA-10s led by one of the Tactical Air Command pilots. Since we returned to land with hot guns, we had to stop on the runway, make a U-turn, and proceed to the arming area at the approach end of the runway to have the guns disarmed.

Unexpectedly, I had to use the YA-10s brakes to avoid over-running the lead aircraft. On previous flights, the aircraft had slowed on its own before reaching the center field taxiway at the center of the long runway; therefore, light braking at a slow speed was sufficient. My situation was different: I needed moderate braking to slow down more quickly and had to apply the brakes at a higher ground speed.

Everything seemed to be going fine initially, but the aircraft suddenly turned abruptly to the left. We used differential braking for directional control. As I eased up on the left brake and increased pressure slightly on the right brake, the aircraft abruptly turned almost 180 degrees and went off the runway backwards. My speed was low as it left the runway, but unfortunately there was a shallow ditch adjacent to the runway. As the tire hit the ditch going slightly sideways and backwards, the right landing gear folded.

I got out of the cockpit so frustrated by this sudden and tragic turn of events that I threw my helmet on the ground and cracked it.

I wasn't injured, so after the mandatory visit to the flight surgeon for a check and blood tests, I was allowed to go home. My boss came by my house the next day and told me to take a few days off while an accident board was convened to determine the cause of the accident. He was empathetic and supportive.

I gave my testimony to the accident board. After they had reviewed the instrumentation strip charts and other data and evidence, they ruled that it was a pilot error accident.

They blamed me.

I was sent back to Test Operations. In essence, I was fired from the test team.

On further investigation

I was shaking my head in absolute frustration, thinking, *These people don't know what they're doing, and my career is destroyed.* I knew something was wrong with this airplane. And I resolved to go find out exactly what happened on that flight.

I did my own investigation, using the same data. I went into the instrumentation tapes and figured it out. I knew what I saw and felt in the airplane. Looking at the tapes, I could see that, at one particular microsecond, something caused this airplane to suddenly, violently turn. I explained that in a detailed accident report rebuttal that I wrote and submitted up my chain of command for consideration.

The Commander of the Air Force Flight Test Center, Brigadier General Robert M. White of X-15 fame, agreed with my rebuttal and found fault with the braking system on the aircraft and the failure of the company to do a good systems test on the brakes before clearing the aircraft for the competition.

Roy returning from a YA-10 test mission at Edwards AFB while
serving with the A-X/A-10 Combined Test Force

In my description of key events in the rebuttal, I contended
that it took only a fraction of an inch of brake travel—movement
of the brake—to lock up both wheels when I initially applied the
brakes. The initial yaw resulted from the right tire blowing. The
abrupt and sudden 180-degree turn to the left was caused by my
slight release of pressure on the left brake to correct for the yaw.

That put the inflated tire and wheel into maximum braking while there was no braking capability on the right tire, since that tire was now rotating freely on the rim. The instrumentation strip charts of the timeline proved that this event happened in a split second. The evidence provided by the damaged tires and wheels supported this chain of events. Tests performed to determine the amount of brake travel required to lock the wheel, which were done after my accident, were another important piece of evidence that I had predicted.

As a result of my inadvertent maximum braking test, all ended well because it convinced the contractor and the program office to outfit the YA-10 prototype and production A-10 with an excellent anti-skid braking system, which was a well-known technology already in use on other aircraft. Fortunately, the damaged YA-10 was easily repaired and restored to service, and my reputation was cleared.

I was rehired by the test team and resumed my normal duties.

That was a close call that could have ended my test pilot career. I could have been done for right then—I would never have been on another test program and certainly would never have been an astronaut. But I survived because I had the training to do what the professional accident board missed—and because I refused to give up. Ironically, my supportive boss was partially blamed for the mishap for not supervising the contractor test team more closely and insisting on a braking test before we began flying the aircraft. He wasn't disciplined for it. Fortunately, he didn't hold the turn of events against me.

I completed the A-X Fly-off as a member of the team, including being on the bombing and strafing competition team and performing systems test flights on both prototypes. Although the YA-10 was declared the winner, we did find issues, which resulted in the need for mandatory safety modifications. These were installed on the prototypes and tested after the competition was over.

Adventures in testing

One of the more serious issues was that, when at high angles of attack, such as in a wing stall, the engines compressor-stalled and reached a temperature limit, requiring shutdown and restart. Fortunately, the YA-10 had an auxiliary power unit (APU), which helped with restarts. Otherwise a steep dive was required to get the high-bypass-ratio engines to rotate fast enough for an air start. That was impossible if both engines failed at relatively low altitudes. The contractor decided to modify the leading edge of the wing near the fuselage with hydraulically activated leading-edge slats, which would extend at high angles of attack to smooth the airflow in front of the tail-mounted engines. After installation and testing, this modification effectively resolved the issue.

Another surprise happened on an early test flight of the new 30 mm cannon. The gun was behind schedule, so a 20 mm cannon was used for the fly-off. The 30 mm gun was much larger and was a great feature for effective close air support. When the company test pilot fired the gun at high speed in one of the early tests, the gun gases stagnated in the bow wave in front of the nose of the aircraft and caught fire, which caused the engines to compressor-stall and have to be shut down to avoid an over-temperature condition.

The company quickly tried several innovative hardware fixes, such as a deflector fitted in the nose of the aircraft just in front of the end of the barrel. As the bullets exited the barrel, they traveled through a small-diameter hole in the deflector, which caused the gun gases to be ejected downward. Unfortunately, given the rotation of the barrel at high rates of fire, there was enough freedom of movement that occasionally, a bullet would not go through the hole and would damage the deflector. Eventually, the program decided to produce ammunition using a different chemical composition to avoid ignition. That would take time. In the meantime, so that we could test other aspects of the gun, we determined the airspeed above which the problem would be encountered and performed our tests below that speed. We were also careful to always have the APU running when we did tests of the gun, just in case.

Manual reversion system

Another interesting test involved the manual reversion system, which allowed the pilot to control and even land the aircraft without hydraulic power. Many aircraft had been lost in Vietnam when hit with AAA fire that damaged the hydraulic system, causing a loss of control and the need to eject quickly. Often that meant an ejection over enemy territory rather than a glide to the nearby ocean before ejecting. Many pilots became prisoners of war as a result of that vulnerability.

My boss flew the first USAF systems test flight of a manual reversion landing. He then asked me to do one and let him know what I thought of the system. He didn't give me any details of his experience. When I tried it, I discovered that the aircraft was flyable but just barely so. A lot of muscle was required to move the control stick to turn the aircraft or control pitch. Pitch control was especially difficult when power changes were made, resulting in a high workload when attempting a landing. Basically, I found that I had to get the aircraft well trimmed at the proper landing speed and glide path and avoid any power changes until touchdown.

I told my boss that the system would need to be modified in the production aircraft to be acceptable. Privately, I thought that he should have given me more insight into just how marginal this system was before I tried it. The system was eventually fixed and saved lives during combat in the Middle East wars.

High-angle-of-attack, stall, and spin program

Another highlight of my experiences with the YA-10 was being selected as the project pilot for the high-angle-of-attack, stall, and spin program. These were hazardous missions, as the response of the aircraft could be different—especially for spin recoveries—than what the engineers had learned from relatively benign conditions that models flew in spin tunnel ground tests. I had fun preparing for the tests. I was able to travel to the navy's main test facility at Patuxent River Naval Air Station, Maryland, to fly two different kinds of aircraft to become acquainted with a variety of spin characteristics and recovery procedures. I was already quite experienced in spinning the T-37 in UPT and ARPS.

I enjoyed the challenge of performing these hazardous missions. I put the YA-10 through every conceivable high-angle-of-attack maneuver as well as abruptly yawing and/or rolling the aircraft to induce a departure from controlled flight. Then I experimented with optimum recovery procedures.

My final highlight was being selected to be the first USAF test pilot to fly the new pre-production A-10A and report on its attributes. There were a few problems that would need tweaking, but overall it was well behaved and much improved over the prototype YA-10.

Adventures in family

Our first tour at Edwards was also quite significant for our family. Benita became pregnant with our second child in 1973. We had a scare when her labor began early. After treatment to stop the labor, she was able to continue the pregnancy to full term, but we were nervous for those final two months. For this delivery, I participated in training classes to assist my wife, which would also allow me to be in the delivery room during the birth. On the night of the delivery, my wife again made it clear to me that we needed to hustle quickly to the hospital. Fortunately, the base hospital was only a couple of miles from our house. I double-parked at the emergency room entry. After getting her to the delivery area, I raced down to park the car somewhere legal. I barely made it back to the delivery room in time. My wife didn't really need anything from me, but it was an awesome experience for me to be there for my son's birth.

Benita successfully delivered our son, Brian Neal, in May 1974. He was literally an answer to prayer, given the earlier close call of a potential premature birth. Also, we really wanted a son so that we would have at least one child of each sex.

Our daughter, Tanya, who was four years old by this time, started Montessori school in Lancaster, 30 miles away, which meant that Benita had to drive her to and from school each day. During the gas crisis, she would stay in town in order to avoid two round trips a day. Eventually, she was able to carpool with another family on base to ease the burden.

We worked hard to transform our bare desert backyard into a place suitable for our kids to play outside. We fenced in the yard, installed a sprinkler system, and grew a nice lawn. We purchased a swing set and set it up under a large shade tree in the back yard. Benita also did a wonderful job of configuring and decorating our little home so that it was functional and comfortable.

A highlight of our tour was our purchase of a cabin in the Sierra Nevada Mountains with another couple from our ARPS class, who had stayed at Edwards in the bomber division. Many

Friday afternoons, we packed up for the two-hour drive so that we could wake up on Saturday and Sunday at our mountaintop retreat. That was such a delight, especially during the hot summer months. We hosted many friends and family at the cabin during our tour. My dad was most impressed when he and my mom visited.

Eventually it was time to leave Edwards, but I held out as long as possible. I had turned down an opportunity to attend the yearlong Air Command and Staff College (ACSC) at Maxwell AFB, Alabama. I was offered the opportunity to attend because I had been selected for promotion two years below the zone to major, which was quite a surprise and an honor. Early promotions are critical if one is to be on track for eventual promotion to general officer. At the time of my selection, I wasn't even thinking about that. I just wanted to stay at Edwards and be a test pilot forever.

When I turned down ACSC, I was summoned to the commanding general's office. He said, "Captain, you will ruin your future chance for promotions if you homestead at Edwards and refuse to attend professional military education, such as ACSC."

"Sir," I replied, "please allow me to stay for one more year so that I can complete the YA-10 Stall/Post-Stall/Spin Program. It is the highlight of my test pilot career. I promise to attend next year."

So I stayed, and the next year, I accepted the assignment.

Although this first tour at Edwards was my dream job come true, Benita and I attended seven funeral services for fellow test pilots while we were there. Those were difficult for all concerned. I was grateful that she could accept the risks of my chosen career.

Christmas Letters 1972–1974

1972: Last Christmas, Benita bought a potter's wheel and is now somewhat of an accomplished potter. She plans to continue developing her skill in the coming year if Roy will just sweep the tons of clay from last year off the garage floor.

Tanya is passing the "Terrible Two" stage (THANK GOODNESS) and coming into the "Inquisitive Threes." We are both thankful that she is tiring of the Spot book and that we will not have to read it for the 10,000th time, but we will have to be sharp to keep her interested in new things now that she is hungry for them. She is in some kind of trance when turned loose with some of Mom's clay.

1973: "I LOVE school even if some kids don't like me—but some kids do!" Tanya shouts almost every day as we drive home from the Montessori preschool in Lancaster. She enjoyed being flower girl in Aunt Nancy's wedding and showing everyone her pretty pink panties. We think Tanya will be ready to share her room with a real baby (sister or brother) come May.

1974: Fortunately we live only a few blocks from the hospital, because when Brian did decide to be born, he arrived just 13 minutes after we left home. He is just over six months old now, with the nub of one little tooth. He refuses to learn how to crawl. He is a great roller, though, and gets where he wants to go. He is trying desperately to walk, and if he continues to progress, he may skip crawling.

Tanya is a big helper and loves her brother, even though her first words after hearing the news of Brian's arrival were a tearful, "But I wanted a little sister." She is very creative and has learned to use tape, glue, scissors, paint, felt-tip pens, bits of cloth, discarded boxes, egg cartons, leaves, bugs, and other "junk" to develop what she calls "designs."

Chapter 25: Air Command and Staff College (ACSC)
August 1975–July 1976

B enita and I rented a home in Montgomery, Alabama, for our one year at ACSC. We had nice neighbors there. We found another good school run by a local church for our daughter for her kindergarten, and she thrived. The drive to the school was only a few blocks instead of thirty miles like it had been at Edwards. We joined a nearby United Methodist church and found the members extremely welcoming and friendly. That was especially true of our Sunday school class as well as frequent social events. We were only a few hours' drive away from my parents' home in Georgia, so we visited as often as possible on long weekends and holidays.

ACSC was a pleasant if wildly different experience than my work at Edwards AFB. We were organized into small seminars of about 15 people with a USAF officer as a teacher for some of the subjects and moderator for frequent class discussions. Over the year, we were in three separate seminars, so I made a lot of friends and there were numerous opportunities for social activities.

Several of the major courses were taught in class-sized groups in the large auditorium, followed by discussions in our small seminars. We had many interesting guest lecturers, including top leaders in the USAF as well as many other speakers in the broader national security side of the government.

My ACSC training activities were interesting and would prove useful in preparing me for my upcoming assignment as a staff officer, although I didn't yet know where that would be. The USAF, like many other large organizations, had particular ways for preparing and presenting information to senior officers and formulating and documenting decisions. There were also guidelines for how to coordinate decision papers to assure that all leaders with potential input to the decision were on board.

TECH TESTING

We had to do a research project. My project looked into the possibilities of using new technologies to make testing of new combat aircraft more realistic. I received high marks for the effort; however, I was a little ahead of time in terms of the readiness of the underlying technologies. It would take several more years before we actually fielded new hardware-in-the-loop simulators. They could test efficiently, effectively, and more rigorously the ever more complex systems being fielded on modern fighters and bombers. And they could do it 24/7—a hardware-in-the-loop simulator didn't get tired.

I would be an advocate for those in future assignments in the test community. And the USAF was just beginning to invest in large-scale and realistic exercises, such as Red Flag, a large-scale training exercise that let pilots experience conditions more like actual combat. At Nellis Air Force Base, for example, they would pit several friendly airplanes against enemy systems, both on-the-ground simulators as well as opposing airplanes, to see how well they did in actual combat situations. That proved not only very effective but extremely popular.

Red Flag was more about training than it was about testing the system. But we needed to figure out how to move that forward in the development process, so we could start looking at those things right after the very first test airplane rolled off the line.

Initially, it was too expensive for Edwards Air Force Base; they're not an operational command. So going in and outfitting their range with all this fancy equipment was not in the budget. But once those things are deployed in a place like Nellis, now they're in production, and now you can—a lot cheaper—evolve them into a test facility for a brand new airplane. Additionally, new technologies for ground testing of complex new aircraft were being developed to reduce the cost and increase the amount of test time on new avionic systems. These would be important additions to our test bases in the future.

The seminars competed in intramural sports of volleyball and softball. One of my seminars won the softball championship; however, I wasn't a particularly great player in either of those sports. They were fun in terms of getting us to practice teamwork and get some needed exercise.

I was allowed to do a couple of independent projects. One was a presentation and technical paper on the YA-10 test program for the Society of Experimental Test Pilots (SETP), a professional organization I belong to, at their convention in San Diego, California.

The second independent project was a luncheon presentation on the YA-10 to the local chapter of the Order of Daedalians, which is a fraternal organization of aviators. It was well received.

Family health issues

The only downside to our year in Montgomery was the various illnesses that my family and I suffered. I had an infected tonsil that had to be lanced to relieve the pressure and pain from the associated swelling. Afterwards I had to spend a few days in the hospital where antibiotics were administered to stop the infection. This was an extremely painful event and initially I thought that I had developed cancer of the throat. After healing from the infection, I was admitted to the hospital to have my tonsils removed. That was another painful event and rather lengthy recovery.

I also had an impacted wisdom tooth removed, which was no fun.

Our daughter had repeated ear infections and was hospitalized to have her adenoids removed and ear tubes installed to relieve the pressure on her eardrums. Our son developed some sort of intestinal infection, lost a lot of weight and was listless for a while, which was scary. He recovered on his own, but it took three months. Tanya and Brian both had some minor accidents that required stitches.

We regarded our year there to be a series of one illness after another. Benita had to deal with them, and she lost a lot of weight due to stress. Fortunately, none of the illnesses caused any permanent complications.

The upside of my two hospital stays to cure my throat infection and the dental issue was that I decided to quit smoking, which was a bad habit that I had developed during my senior year at the USAFA. I had tried to quit many times at Edwards and had cut way back on the quantity of cigarettes I smoked during each day. With the help of the painful illnesses, I was finally able to kick the habit and began jogging several miles a day to regain my aerobic capability. Jogging has served me well over the years since ACSC by keeping me in good physical condition as well as being a great stress reliever.

I also started a woodworking hobby that I continued for many years. I refurbished an antique bed for my daughter and a round oak dining table and chairs, which was a favorite feature of our kitchen for years to come. Both were salvaged from

Roy & Benita with Tanya & Brian in the spring of 1976 while Roy was attending the Air Command & Staff College in Montgomery, Alabama

a relative's garage. The round table was conducive to good conversations as the kids matured and was also perfect for family meals.

Time to move on again

As the time for assignments approached, I called the Military Personnel Center often to see what the possibilities were. One job opportunity was to go to Wright-Patterson AFB, Ohio, and join the A-10 System Program Office (SPO). The SPO Director whom I had met during my Edwards AFB tour extended a personal invitation to join his team.

The other offer was to go to the Pentagon as a Program Element Monitor (PEM) in the Office of the Deputy Chief of Staff (DCS) for Research & Development (R&D). The colonel who was in charge of that division for the development programs for the F-15 and A-10 as well as their engines and some of their armament systems invited me to join his team. I had also known him at Edwards AFB, where he ran the program doing the development testing of the C-5.

I decided that the Pentagon position would offer me a greater diversity of experiences, and I accepted the assignment to be a Deputy PEM for the new F-15 fighter. I was concerned that going to the A-10 SPO would leave me with years of A-10-only experience. While I loved that aircraft, I needed to broaden my experience base to develop into a more versatile officer.

After a house-hunting trip to the suburbs of Washington, DC, in northern Virginia, we finally settled on a new townhouse that we could barely afford, using my Veterans Administration (VA) home mortgage benefit, which required no down payment and had a reasonable interest rate in a time of growing inflation. The townhouse was part of a new subdivision of mostly single-family homes in the small town of Burke, Virginia, which was near the larger town of Springfield. Both towns were just outside the expressway that circled Washington, the I-495. Transportation by bus to the Pentagon was also readily available nearby. The school system in northern Virginia was highly rated, which was important. Our daughter would enter the first grade there. We also had friends in the area.

I graduated from ACSC as a Distinguished Graduate. Everyone in the family was finally well as we organized another military family move to our new townhouse in Virginia and my new assignment at the Pentagon.

Chapter 26: Pentagon
July 1976–July 1979

After traveling to Northern Virginia, we stayed with our friends—my roommate from Vietnam and classmate from Cannon and Williams AFBs, Steve Amdor, and his family—for a few days while closing on our new townhouse and awaiting delivery of our household goods. It was fun to catch up with them again.

We moved into our new townhouse in Burke, Virginia, in the summer of 1976. It was a small townhouse community consisting of only three units with six homes in each at the end of a short dead-end street in the middle of a single-family-home subdivision. The back of our unit faced a large open area with a small creek running through it. It was developed into a park while we lived there, but it was initially just trees and native weeds.

We quickly developed friendships with our neighbors. One family had two boys, one about our son's age (two) and one a few years older. They became playmates and would get into some innocent mischief as time went by, such as wading in the creek and climbing the trees in the open space. While we were better off on my major's salary, we found that living expenses were high in northern Virginia, and we practiced frugal living to avoid going into debt.

Program Element Monitor

I began my job in the Pentagon as one of two Deputy PEMs for the new F-15 air superiority fighter, working for a senior lieutenant colonel. The three of us shared an office. The other two brought me up to speed relatively quickly, and I was assigned projects. The Division Chief, a colonel, worked for a two-star general who reported to the DCS for R&D, Lieutenant General Slay.

General Slay had a personality as intimidating as his name and often lashed out at the many PEMs working there.

I would often man our office while the other two PEMs went jogging and had lunch. This proved to be a horrible experience. General Slay would occasionally ring an alarm in our office and the offices of the other PEMs. We were allowed only a few minutes for the dozen of us to assemble in his large office. He would rail at us because we had not followed his desired format for preparing fact sheets or slides that he would use for his Congressional testimony on his programs. He required each program to present all of our financial and programmatic details on the front and back of one sheet of paper. He insisted on absolute uniformity in where each piece of information should be displayed for all programs.

During one of the general alarm calls, we were told to report with our program fact sheet. When I arrived, there were half a dozen people in front of me, all lined up in front of his desk. I took my place in line. After a few minutes he asked the first person to brief his fact sheet. A few minutes later, he asked for the sheet and proceeded to ball it up and throw it across the room. He then told us what had been done incorrectly and had us take seats in the room and make pen and ink corrections. That order was impossible for us to complete, as we would need to call our program offices to obtain the exact information that he wanted presented so I just pretended to work on my sheet, as did many others.

After a time, he asked us all to line up again and the first briefer was again determined to have incorrect information. He then ordered us back to our offices with instructions to have the sheets fixed and returned to him within 24 hours.

This is just one example of the many exercises that he had us perform. Others involved, for example, how to prepare viewgraph charts on our programs that he used for his Congressional testimony. I began to dread the time when I was alone in the office. I also had recurring nightmares during my first six months on the job.

I felt like I had descended into hell.

Many of our yearly activities involved preparing for the annual budget calls, which began with an initial run called the Program Objective Memorandum (POM). The POM was used to prepare the Department of Defense to meet what was expected to be the top-line budget for the following year as well as a complete five-year plan. This was followed by the actual budget submittal document that was submitted to the secretary of the air force to be included in the Pentagon's annual budget request. It would eventually be included in the president's budget request for the next year and included information for five years.

While these budget drills were the "main event," we also had to keep everyone up to speed on all issues within the program. For example, the F-15 had an engine issue involving a problem with the intake. This took a lot of engineering to fix. We would have to process issue papers all the way to the chief of staff of the air force, which had to be coordinated at the division, two-star, and three-star levels in departments on the air staff. We would hand-carry our staff packages to each office and wait for the authorized official to review the package and sign the staff summary sheet before heading for the next office, according to the protocol and hierarchy. Sometimes offices would non-concur with our recommendations, and we would have to find a compromise that would overcome the objection and meet with the approval of the SPO.

I wore out a lot of shoe leather on these activities. Fortunately, the F-15 was a high-priority program that was widely admired and desired by the USAF, so we received considerable help and support in solving issues and budget requests. That wasn't true of all programs, however.

We would occasionally be called upon to prepare briefings for Congressional staffers or members. Often this involved preparing a senior officer to deliver the briefing.

Another rather interesting activity was meeting with military officers from allied countries that were interested in obtaining F-15s for their air forces. Both Japan and Saudi Arabia were actively engaged with us during my tenure. It became evident in our exchanges just how different our cultures were.

For example, I was in a meeting with officers from Japan during a presentation of the F-15's capabilities. After the contractor briefer presenting the material left the room, I cautioned the officers about some potential overpromises of performance, since the F-15 was still in a test program and had not yet fully demonstrated the promised capabilities. I still remember the look of shock on their faces as they tried to understand how such a junior officer could take issue with my elders. Apparently, they didn't do that. They would not engage me with questions.

The commute to work

Initially, I drove my gas-friendly Chevrolet Vega to work. This helped with our budget as well as the ongoing gas crisis. The outdoor Pentagon parking lot was highly organized to favor carpools. Non-carpoolers had to park about a quarter mile from the nearest entrance. That proved to be cruel punishment on rainy and cold days. Once, I arrived back at my car on a cold and rainy night to find my car filled with water to the level of the doors. A new windshield had been installed incorrectly after a dust storm destroyed the original one at Edwards. What a miserably cold and wet ride home.

Traffic conditions heading south from the Pentagon to the I-95 exit at Springfield could add many minutes to what was a short commute without traffic congestion. Carpools could use the express lanes to get around the worst of the congestion. After settling into my new life, I made friends in the neighborhood who worked in the Pentagon, and we organized a six-person car pool. That allowed us to obtain both a four-person carpool pass and a two-person pass. If someone had a meeting starting earlier or ending later than our normal car pool departure time, he would use the two-person pass and drive to work solo.

Our car pool pass parking privileges were far superior to the non-car-pool parking because they were close to the entrance. Several members had a van that we used when all six of us were riding. We organized it to even out the amount of driving for fairness over a month's period.

Universal stress

Our Pentagon jobs were all stressful. In addition to shortening our trips to and from work, our car pool members shared funny stories of the trials and tribulations of our day. Laughter among our car poolers helped relieve our stress on the way home, which was a huge help. It was nice to know that I wasn't the only one having issues at work.

The other great stress reliever was the Pentagon Officers' Athletic Center (POAC). We would take turns during the day to go to the POAC for a jog, followed by strength exercises and a shower. Both of my F-15 office mates liked to jog. We enjoyed some great routes over the Potomac River bridges and around some of the National Mall's many monuments. This was a healthy respite that I took advantage of almost every day of the week.

Travels in Ohio

To do my job well required a great familiarity with the key departments of the SPO at Wright-Patterson AFB, Ohio. I traveled often early in my tour to get to know everyone so that I could call and get answers to the many questions that came our way. Also, there were regularly scheduled program reviews to the leadership of the USAF at the Pentagon. That gave us an opportunity to meet with the SPO Director and key staff before and after these sessions at the Pentagon. We became a well-oiled team.

Even though most of my travels to Ohio were not memorable, one was almost deadly. I had a minor respiratory illness but flew to Ohio anyway to attend an important meeting.

I attended the all-day meeting at the SPO. When I returned to my rental car to head to the airport, I found that it was covered with snow and ice. Despite my best efforts to remove the accumulation, I made a near-fatal mistake. When I started the car and activated the windshield wipers, they did not operate. I had inadvertently blown a fuse because some portions of the wipers were still frozen to the windshield. I drove to the nearest service station with my head out of the window to be able to see in the snowstorm.

After buying a new fuse and replacing it, I headed to the airport. On the way the car began to have engine stalls, probably because of ice in the fuel system. The problem caused the car to gradually lose speed after the engine stalled, and I restarted it many times.

At the bottom of the last hill that I would have to climb to reach the airport exit from the freeway, the car died and would not restart. I managed to get it onto the snow-covered shoulder of the road before it stopped. I sat there for some time trying to decide how to resolve the issue and make it to the airport in time to catch my flight. There was a lot of truck traffic and my car was splashed continuously with slush as they roared past my car. Finally, a jeep with a snowplow on the front end stopped. The driver asked me if he could help.

I said, "I will give you all of my cash, about $40.00, if you will take me the short distance to the airport."

After some hesitation, he finally had pity on me and agreed to do it. When I arrived at the airport, I dropped the keys at the rental car counter and explained the issue and where to find the car. I made my flight in time.

The minor respiratory illness that I had became worse over the course of the night. After arriving at work the next morning, I reported to the Pentagon Medical Clinic because I was ill with a fever and a severe chest cold. The doctor diagnosed pneumonia and explained that in the days before antibiotics, it might have been fatal. Thanks to modern medicine, I soon made a full recovery.

Defending the A-10

After about a year working the F-15, the senior A-10 PEM in the next office left the Pentagon for another assignment, and I was promoted to his position. Another more junior officer was my deputy. He had been on the program for some time. With my test experience with the A-10 and his knowledge of the issues being worked on in the Pentagon, we made a good team.

Not every program was loved with as much passion as the F-15. That was certainly the case for the A-10. The fighter pilots' "mafia" in the Pentagon was vocal with objections to the slow, ugly A-10, which was their opinion and not ours. Getting them to support us with a nickel of resources was always a fierce battle in what they saw as a zero-sum game. Every nickel for the A-10 was one less for their favorite fighter programs such as the F-15 and F-16.

As one example, the A-10 as originally fielded had basic avionics for flying in the weather. After it was deployed to Europe, the need for improvements became critical for safety as well as operational effectiveness. Getting the A-10's 30 mm cannon above the most likely routes that the Soviet Union would use for their many tanks in those Cold War scenarios where they were invading Europe meant that the A-10 needed an Inertial Navigation System (INS) that could be used anywhere and in any weather conditions.

Adding an INS was the highest priority improvement being advocated by the SPO. A Pentagon official who was not supportive of the A-10 suggested to me that they "maneuver to the target by following railroad tracks at low altitude below the clouds. There are many railroad tracks in Germany." How ludicrous!

After failing to get support in the Pentagon at lower levels, I got some support to brief the Air Force Council on the need during budget exercises. I got a nod of approval from the Council and added the money to the A-10 budget that we submitted. The fighter "mafia" was furious and tried to get it removed. I stood firm on that head-nod approval and managed to keep the dollars in the budget. That's how the A-10 got one of its most important early life improvements. There have been many others since then. The life of the A-10 has recently been extended to the 2030 timeframe after a wing upgrade was completed. It is an aircraft that has been loved by the troops on the ground, but barely tolerated by the USAF fighter "mafia." Amazing saga!

An old problem resurfaces

One day, we received bad news from the SPO. An A-10A test aircraft had crashed at Edwards AFB during a test mission with one of the new candidate ammunition loads for the 30 mm cannon that was designed to correct the problem that we had discovered in the YA-10 earlier. The test team had gotten comfortable doing gun tests without having the APU running. The test point that resulted in the accident was at a low altitude. After the test pilot shut down the engines to clear engine stalls and over-temperature conditions, he did not have enough altitude to restart the engines before reaching his mandatory bailout altitude. He had to eject and almost died from neck injuries that he suffered when landing and falling on a rock.

I had to show the photo chase video of the incident to just about every senior officer in the Pentagon. Fortunately, the gun program had other candidates to upgrade the ammunition and solve the problem. The Edwards AFB test team never flew another gun test without first starting the APU.

This was a compelling lesson of how the test community needed to find better ways to remember lessons learned so that they would not have to relearn them after future tragedies. I worked to implement such a system and culture in my later assignments at Edwards AFB.

Family at home and away

Unlike my rather stressful life at the Pentagon, we rated our family life as good in northern Virginia. Our daughter started public school and did well. We found a preschool for our son, run by the local Lutheran church. We joined a local United Methodist church and enjoyed regular attendance at Sunday school and worship services. During the summer we all appreciated the neighborhood swimming pool, which was affordable. Both of our kids learned to swim well.

Both my wife and I became active as assistant coaches on our kids' soccer teams. The sport was popular and well organized in northern Virginia. My wife was assistant coach on our son's team. I served as an assistant coach on our daughter's team for a season and then became head coach for the last two seasons. The reason that I found time to coach soccer was that I had finally figured out the annual routine at the Pentagon and always stayed well ahead of the workload. Like chair flying, which had taught me to always be at least one step ahead of my high-performance aircraft, it ensured that there weren't as many crises or catch-up events. My Pentagon PEM job became much more pleasant after I adopted that strategy.

We purchased a new piano and our daughter started lessons, which she continued all the way through her public school years as well as college. She would earn a double major in both biology and music in college, so playing the piano became a lifelong hobby for her. She also started ballet dance classes and liked them.

We had to invite a new partner into our California mountain cabin because both original partners were now somewhere other than Edwards AFB for the time being. We would later regret that decision, but it was unavoidable at the time, as the cabin needed regular visits for upkeep. For example, the park rangers required roof and yard maintenance to clear off tree leaf and needle debris to reduce the fire danger. The money that we received for this buy-in by our new partner allowed us to take a well-needed vacation. We had put off vacations to avoid spending money and never seemed to have enough to do anything special.

So we planned in advance and were able to reserve the "master suite" on the Southern Crescent passenger train, which ran from New York to Washington, DC, and then to New Orleans, for our vacation trip. It made stops along the way, including in my hometown of Gainesville, Georgia. We planned the trip to coincide with the Christmas holidays so that we could spend them with my parents. The "master suite" was in the last car on the train and was equipped with a couch that made into a large bed for us. There was a bunk bed for the kids as well as comfortable chairs. The seats faced a large picture window for viewing the countryside as we traveled during the afternoon and overnight to Gainesville. We had our own bathroom in the suite as well as our own porter, who served us drinks and food to order. It was a grand adventure, and we were fortunate to be able to do it, since it was one of the last private passenger lines. Soon after our trip, Amtrak replaced it, and the "master suite" car was retired.

We also had a few other great adventures that didn't require as much expense. We had friends who owned a pop-up tent camper. They invited us to go camping with them on several trips. One was a visit to the Gettysburg battlefield. I had always loved studying the history of the Civil War at USAFA and continued to read all that I could about it. We did a multi-stop, audiotape-guided tour around the battlefield, which was special because of all the spirits that seemed to inhabit the spots of the most furious battles.

Another camping trip with them was to Williamsburg, Virginia. We toured the restored colonial capital and went canoeing on the James River. Later in life we would get to spend ten years living in Williamsburg, so this was a great introduction.

Our last trip with them was to visit Luray Caverns, a magical geological wonder.

Applying to NASA

When the National Aeronautics and Space Administration (NASA) announced a competition for astronauts for the 1978 Class, I applied. I was accepted for an interview and medical check at the Johnson Space Center. I reveled in the experience and thought that I had done well. I was excited about the prospect of getting into the Astronaut Corps in time for the space shuttle's first mission.

When the call came to me at the office to announce the results, I was connected to someone in the Human Resources Office. My heart sank, as I knew by that source that the news would not be good, and it wasn't. I was greatly disappointed.

The immediate aftermath of getting that call was, "I feel like crap." I wasn't sure how to improve my chances at being selected if there was another competition. But the next day, I snapped out of it and said to myself, I'm not going to let this hold me back. I loved being a test pilot. Once I finished this silly staff tour in the Pentagon, I knew I could go back to something I really liked doing.

A good friend and classmate from my squadron at USAFA as well as my roommate at Purdue and UPT, John Blaha, had also applied; he went down to Texas with me for an interview. He was also passed over and became depressed, as I did at first. But I didn't want this disappointment to shatter the rest of my life, so I didn't dwell on it. I had always known that it was a long shot—a highly improbable dream. I resolved to get on with my life and career.

Christmas Letter 1978

We have lived in northern Virginia for two and a half years now. Brian started preschool this fall. He is not shy, but it is interesting to note the difference in his and Tanya's attitude toward performing. Brian's first trip to the front of a crowd resulted in a minor rebellion: he turned his back and sat down.

He loves to play any kind of ball, climb trees, roam deep into the woods (through all the poison ivy patches) and generally terrorize the neighborhood doing daredevil stunts on his Big Wheel bike.

Tanya played halfback and is blossoming into a skilled soccer player. She reads in the top of her class in school, and her work in other areas is good but would improve with less talking in class, so we are told (and believe). She still enjoys ballet and has recently started art lessons with a neighborhood teacher.

Chapter 27: Pentagon—Lt. General Stafford
July 1979–November 1979

Things at the Pentagon took a sudden turn for the good for me. Lieutenant General Tom Stafford, who had been the Commander of the Apollo 10 mission, became the new Deputy Chief of Staff (DCS) for R&D. I was invited to interview with him to be his traveling aide and speechwriter. I had done all that I could do for the A-10 Program, so I agreed to try out for the position.

I guess he liked me, because he offered me the job. I moved to a small private office that was part of his large office suite. In addition to his office, there were offices for his deputy, who was a two-star general, two secretaries, and two senior executive officers, as well as my office. The secretaries and the executive officers sat in the large outer office, which was the entry portal of the suite.

The job was quite a change of pace for me. I assisted with making travel plans and arrangements to the many places that he visited for USAF business as well as the many speaking engagements that he accepted. I also assisted with the preparation of background papers to help prepare him for visits, as well as speaking remarks. I traveled with him on the small military jet transports on his travels.

Along the way he treated me to a lot of stories about his adventures in the Gemini, Apollo, and Apollo-Soyuz programs. They were fascinating. It was a privilege to hear about his great space adventures. Sadly, since I had not been selected for the program, I thought that I would never have a chance to realize my lifelong dream to do what he had done.

An unexpected offer

Along the way to prepare me to assist General Stafford, I was briefed into some top-secret and "black" (top-secret and unacknowledged) programs. As a result of my interactions with personnel in these programs, I was invited to move to Las Vegas, Nevada, to participate in the development and testing of a new aircraft, which at that time was a black program. After consulting with General Stafford and my wife, I accepted. Benita and I managed to sell our townhouse rather quickly and arranged another military household move at Thanksgiving 1979 to our new home in Las Vegas.

Before departing, I took one other action that would eventually have a significant impact on my career. When NASA announced another competition for space shuttle astronauts that would become the Class of 1980, I didn't apply. I felt that I had had my one chance, and they didn't select me. I couldn't see why they would think I was better this time around. I was a couple of years older. I hadn't been flying airplanes. I was still just a Pentagon staff officer and was not getting any operational time in aircraft that would make my résumé look better. So why would I think they would like me better this time than last time, when I didn't get picked?

There were a lot of other really good people out there that they could choose. I thought I was just setting myself up for another disappointment. And I'd already kind of resolved to get on with life. Here I was, going back into this test program. And I knew I was going to really enjoy that.

A few days before the deadline for the application, I got a call from the Military Personnel Center. The officer who called said that they had noticed that I had not applied and wondered why not. After I explained my rationale, he strongly recommended that I reconsider and submit an application quickly. I discussed the issue with General Stafford, and he also recommended that I give it another shot. I erased the date on my previous application, put the new date on, and sent it in.

I was again invited for an interview and medical check at the Johnson Space Center (JSC), which surprised me. But I didn't take any wild expectations with me. My feeling was, look: I like going down to the Space Center and talking to those guys. I'm going to go out and have a couple Tex Mex dinners, shoot the bull with a lot of people, some of whom I knew, like John Blaha—go have a good time. But I'm just not going to get all uptight about this, because my odds of getting in are about the same as last time and look what happened. Just go have fun. Don't make up any stories about what a great thing this is going to be when I get to be an astronaut. It's just a week in Texas, having fun being around the space program. So I went. And again, I enjoyed the experience and thought that I had done well.

I did something during that interview process that I would not recommend to others. On the first night at JSC we attended a reception during which the schedule and agenda for our visit was outlined. They also said that we needed to write a 500-word essay on why we wanted to be an astronaut, which had not been required during my previous interview. I felt that was a little juvenile and decided not to do it.

As I was sitting in the green room waiting to appear before the interview board, a lady came out and said that they couldn't find my essay. I explained that I had not written one. She said that I had to do it. I asked to borrow her pad of paper and pen and wrote a 25-word essay on a yellow scrap of paper, which I gave to her.

The interview board never said a word about my essay.

Obviously, I was much more relaxed during this interview. I hoped that they would like me better this time. But I tried not to get my hopes up for fear of being disappointed again.

Christmas Letter 1979

Surprise! Our Christmas present was a new assignment to Las Vegas, Nevada. We moved over the Thanksgiving holiday.

There are many things we shall miss about Virginia/DC area. Like beautiful fall colors, Smithsonian, art museums, B.S.F., kids' soccer teams, our church, and many good friends and neighbors. We won't miss rain every weekend, annual ice age, traffic, and the Pentagon. (Hooray! I escaped!—Roy) Kidding aside, Roy did enjoy the challenging jobs he had at the Pentagon. But three and a half years at the Pentagon is more than enough, and Roy is happy to be returning to the field.

Chapter 28: Las Vegas, Nevada
November 1979–July 1980

We purchased our new home using what remained of my VA home loan benefit, which helped us immensely. Our three-bedroom house was on the small side, but adequate, and located on a quiet, low-traffic street in a relatively new subdivision. It was near a good public school for Tanya and Brian.

Clandestine assignment

Program security personnel briefed me into my new program and job. At the time it was an unacknowledged black program; consequently, I couldn't share any details about my work or my work locations with my wife and family. This made life much more difficult, but Benita rose to the occasion and took great care of our home and family during my frequent weeklong trips. I was usually home for the weekends.

My trips often took me to Burbank, California, where the Lockheed Martin "Skunk Works" was located. During my first visit, I got a tour of the plant and met a lot of the people working to develop and manufacture the new aircraft. I got to see a full-size wood mockup of the new aircraft. It was a weird shape, and I doubted that it would handle well. I soon found out.

I was assigned to work with company engineers to develop and test the flight control laws, which would enable the inherently unstable aircraft to have acceptable flying qualities under both normal conditions, when various sensors failed, and under a variety of wind conditions for takeoffs and landings.

A lot of my contribution was to be a test pilot for this new system in Lockheed's simulation facility, which was located separately from the plant. The work was interesting, and we made progress in developing and refining the flight control system; however, I did crash a few times during simulations when various sensors failed. We learned from the crashes and iterated until everything worked satisfactorily.

Since my trips were classified at the time, Benita never knew where I was at any time. In those days before cell phones, she had a number that she could call for emergencies. Someone would call me and let me know to contact her. I paid for everything with cash. I would draw travel advances in $100 bills and hide them in my wife's sanitary napkin box in our closet until I needed to refill my wallet. After each trip, I would file a classified expense report at work to settle the account.

In addition to my work in the simulator, I was responsible for developing plans for the upcoming developmental flight test program along with several other test pilots on our small test team. One area of concern for me was planning how to qualify weapons for safe carriage and delivery.

Normally test pilots at Eglin AFB, Florida, would do that part of new aircraft programs. Because of the secrecy, we would need to do it at our classified test location. How could we order, ship, and store munitions without revealing anything about the program? I decided to hire a senior sergeant who was an expert in those aspects of munitions.

Searching for and interviewing potential candidates for that job without revealing anything was another difficult issue. I finally found the perfect person and had orders issued for him to join our test team.

Finding this perfect person was interesting in itself. I made up an excuse to go down to Edwards Air Force Base and look at their munitions storage and how they ordered and stored munitions. While I was there, I ran into the sergeant who briefed me on how they did everything, and I really liked him. After I got back home, I arranged behind the scenes to get him reassigned to Las Vegas.

People of junior rank didn't normally protest assignments, and an assignment to Las Vegas could be interesting—it promises to be more glamorous than the middle of the Mojave Desert. He accepted, and I never let him know any of the details about what was going to happen. It was a clandestine activity from the get-go.

Our government and contractor team was small. At program reviews, the key leaders from the contractor, the USAF SPO, the Tactical Air Command, and the three test pilots and chief engineer on our development test team could all fit in a modest-sized conference room. Meetings were professional but much more of a collaborative discussion than what I was used to hearing in A-10 and F-15 program reviews, which always seemed a lot more formal, with only the most senior people presenting and asking questions. In our reviews everybody was invited to contribute ideas, and they did.

I enjoyed the opportunity to fly again in an actual aircraft, rather than just a simulator. We had access to T-38 aircraft for support to the test program as well as pilot proficiency flights. After being checked out by an IP, I volunteered for support duty and started the process of regaining my proficiency. I was rusty after four years of school and desk jobs.

Getting away from it all

In the spring of 1980, my wife and I had a date night to celebrate our wedding anniversary. After a nice dinner in a good restaurant, I suggested that we go to the top of the Landmark Hotel for an after-dinner glass of wine and to enjoy the view from that penthouse circular bar overlooking the Las Vegas strip. It was in a 31-story tower modeled after Seattle's Space Needle.

After we had finished our drinks, we decided to head home, which required us to walk through the large ground-floor casino. I had a few quarters in my pocket and asked my wife to let me demonstrate the interesting chances on the newer progressive slot machines. I had tried them once before, after a downtown work function without wives. I put in five quarters and pulled the lever. We won a few more quarters. I put those into the machine and again pulled the lever. To our surprise, we won the big jackpot. The machine made a lot of noise and many lights started flashing. Eventually, a casino employee came over and handed us $700 in bills.

On our way to the car, we dawdled for a while inside the casino to be sure that we weren't being followed, but we didn't gamble another nickel. Benita informed me that the winnings were going to be used to purchase a replacement dining room set for the one damaged in our move. She followed up on that by buying a nice walnut dining room set, which we still use in our home. We didn't gamble any other time while we were stationed in Las Vegas, so we were among the few who left town as winners.

We took a memorable long weekend trip with my parents when they came to visit us. We took them to a live comedy show at one of the large casinos. The next day we went on an overnight trip to the Grand Canyon. On the way we visited the Hoover Dam. We spent the night at a motel just outside the national park. Early the next morning we drove to one of the famous old hotels on the south rim and enjoyed breakfast, followed by some sightseeing of this magnificent, geological time machine. Then we drove along the south rim and stopped for sightseeing at many of the overlooks, and drove through the Painted Desert to the north rim, where we stopped for a picnic lunch.

During the afternoon, I noted we were getting low on gas, and there were no gas stations. When we finally came to a small country store with gas pumps, we stopped but discovered they were closed because it was Sunday afternoon. I took a chance and knocked on the door of a small home behind the store where I suspected that the owner lived. He did. He listened to my sad story and opened up for us to fill up with gas.

After avoiding that disaster, we drove through Zion National Park on our way back to Las Vegas. My parents, who really enjoy sightseeing road trips, were thrilled with what they saw in such a short time. They had never had the opportunity to see western national parks before. Benita and I, along with our two kids, had a great time as well.

One step closer

After I became more proficient in my flying again, I was given the opportunity to check out in a twin-engine turboprop aircraft that was used for support duties and transportation. As part of my checkout, I flew with an IP to Davis-Monthan AFB in Tucson, Arizona. We had some classified business discussions with personnel there. I used the overnight opportunity to visit with my wife's parents and spent the night at their home.

I got a big surprise the next morning after breakfast. George Abbey, the Director of Flight Crew Operations at the Johnson Space Center (JSC) called. He had tried to call me at home in

Las Vegas. On this occasion, my wife knew that I planned to spend the night with her parents and gave him their number.

George Abbey was a man of few words. I had met him before, when I went down for the interviews, and he was kind of legendary for being this inscrutable guy. He had a roundabout way of talking about things. "Roy," he said, "I know that you have a great job, so it's okay if you say no, but would you still be interested in coming to JSC to work in the Astronaut Office?"

I felt like I was on a rocket ship. And had already landed on cloud nine. I was literally floating in the air. I said, "Yes sir, I absolutely want to work for you. Thank you, sir."

He said that I would be getting more details on the assignment later but to plan to report in July.

The once-shy kid from the farm was one step closer to his dream.

Instant celebrity

My IP and I flew back to Nevada in the afternoon. I reported to my boss and told him the news. He said they would have to excuse me from the program and debrief me. I was to tell no one about my work if questioned. I was also told later in the day that arrangements had been made for me to work for the Commanding General at Nellis AFB. I was told to report to him at 7:00 a.m. the next morning in my dress blues.

I didn't get home that night until after midnight, but my wife and kids welcomed me with big smiles. Benita reported that numerous reporters had called her from the local newspaper and TV stations. She told them that I was out of town on business and would not be available until the next day. The papers and TV stations reported that I was the "missing astronaut."

After little sleep, I got up and put on my dress blues and reported to the general. He was friendly and made a joke about how pleased he was that I had worked for him for a long time. He set me up with his Public Affairs Officer, who escorted me on visits to the local TV stations and newspaper office for interviews. Amazingly, none of them asked me where I had been the day before or wanted to know what I did for the USAF, so I didn't have to make up any cover stories.

That evening, Benita and our kids presented me with a specially decorated cake with an icing caption that read, "Congratulations to the Missing Astronaut." We all had a big laugh and then discussed our next big adventure.

Destination: Houston

My immediate crisis was how to sell my home so that we could afford to purchase a new home in Texas. We had lived in it for less than a year. The market was pretty flat and interest rates were high. There was no way that I could afford to pay a realtor to market and sell it for me.

Since I had some free time away from work, I bought a couple of books on how to be successful as a "For Sale by Owner" realtor. I drew up some contracts and had them ready for signing. I also practiced my sales pitch. We put a "for sale" sign in the yard and bought some low-priced classified advertising in the newspaper. Initially, the only lookers were real estate agents who told me that I was crazy if I didn't let them sell it for me. I explained that I just couldn't afford their fees.

One morning I went out to get the newspaper and noticed a car stopped by my sign and a person picking up one of my brochures from the box on the sign. As the car started driving off, I ran into the street and waved my arms over my head. Fortunately, the driver saw me and turned around.

I showed the couple our home. They seemed interested, so I offered them coffee and a seat at our kitchen table. I told them that after they had talked about our home to let me know if there was interest, and we could set up another meeting to review and sign a contract. To my surprise, he said that he was ready to discuss that now.

I gave him my sales pitch and began to go over the contract. When I got to the part where I needed to pen-and-ink the sales price, I asked him if he had a price in mind. To my surprise, he said that he would pay my asking price. After I added that to the contract, he signed it. We set up a mutually acceptable closing date to give my wife time to arrange a move after the end of the school year. The only condition that the couple put on the sale was that I needed to let them assume my VA loan, which I agreed to do.

Benita and I drove my Chevrolet Vega to Clear Lake, Texas, for a house-hunting trip. It was murderously hot, and the car did not have air conditioning, but we made it without becoming ill. After a lot of looking around the various neighborhoods near JSC, we found a really nice home in a great subdivision, which was only a few miles from JSC. The owners were out of town on vacation.

As we were standing in the backyard with our realtor and discussing the merits of the house, to my shock, I noticed that my wife and the female realtor had fleas crawling up their stockings. The owners' dog was also on vacation, and the fleas were hungry. If we purchased it, one of our first projects would be to have the house fumigated before we moved in.

I had to arrange for a commercial loan since I had traded away my VA loan benefit. We arranged one successfully, but I had to accept one with an adjustable rate of interest in order to afford it. That was somewhat risky, as inflation was still out of control. We didn't really have any other choices, so we took the risk.

My wife flew back to Las Vegas to be with the kids until the end of school and to pack up and move. I stayed in Houston for some initial orientation before our official start of training. I camped out at the home of a member of the Class of 1978 astronauts. He was a bachelor and had some empty bedrooms. I slept on the floor along with one of my new classmates.

I flew back to Las Vegas to drive our other car with my wife and kids after closing on the house. We arrived in Houston and took possession of our home just in time to evacuate for a hurricane. My uncle and aunt, who lived in a non-threatened area of Houston, offered to let us bunk with them for a few days. It was a good visit, and we were grateful for their hospitality. We were lucky that time; the hurricane missed our area. We would see other storms during the time that we were there, and some of them didn't miss us.

A few years after moving to Texas, the USAF revealed that the new aircraft whose development I had supported in Las Vegas was the F-117. It was the first stealth fighter for our nation. It played a key role in upcoming conflicts, and I was honored to be able to play a small part in its development. Many others did much, much more to complete its development and testing so that it could do a fantastic job of destroying air defenses in Iraq and other places and save the lives of airmen. The technology would be refined over the years and be incorporated into the B-2 bomber and other later-generation fighters and bombers for our nation's defense.

And now my life as an astronaut was about to begin.

Book 2: Realizing the Dream

Chapter 29: NASA Johnson Space Center (JSC)—Astronaut Candidate, Class of 1980

July 1980–July 1981

The members of the Astronaut Class of 1980 joined together at JSC in July 1980. We were the second class of shuttle astronauts, so we were second-class citizens to the first class selected in 1978. Ours was the "no-name" class—we never settled on a nickname.

Our official introduction to JSC was somewhat dramatic. The JSC Center Director, Dr. Chris Kraft, the legendary father of Mission Control, gathered us in his conference room. He lectured us about how we could make missteps in our progress to flight status and beyond. He cautioned us to not think that we knew it all when it came to preparing for and successfully completing a space mission. We listened attentively and respectfully.

At the time, I felt that none of us were in a position to challenge any of our seniors on any matter, and I doubted that any of us would attempt such a thing. Apparently, some in the Astronaut Corps had done so in the past.

We were a rather diverse group of men and women. Nineteen of us were citizens of the USA and two were from the European Space Agency. Many of us were test pilots from the air force, navy, army, and marine corps. We had classmates who were medical doctors, engineers, and scientists. I was pleased that my Purdue and UPT roommate, John Blaha, was in the class with me. Everyone was happy to be there and anxious to get started with our training. We were also aware that we were at the end of a long line of astronauts who wanted to fly, sooner rather than later, and it looked like it could be years. The first flight of the space shuttle was still months away. Did I have the patience required to serve as support crew until it was my turn?

We would be Astronaut Candidates (ASCANs) for one year of training before being accepted into the Astronaut Corps. It was a probationary period, although no one was sure what success looked like or what event would mean failure. We were all quiet unless spoken to and devoted ourselves to our academics, other training classes, and events.

Classes, systems, documentation, field trips

The classes were interesting. We spent a lot of time in the classroom learning the shuttle systems. This was supplemented by the single-system trainers that allowed us to use the systems and procedures for normal operations and experience various anomalies in the systems, followed by use of the crew emergency procedures to safe the systems.

SYSTEMS

The systems included the electrical, hydraulic, life support, computer, propellant, and other systems. Since many of the systems were quad-redundant—meaning each system had three backup systems, like having a computer with three backup

---

computers—there were many potential failure and recovery modes. If you're going to launch up into space, you're not going to be close to anybody with a spare part.

The computer system was complex and governed by volumes of requirement documents, which defined how the software was constructed and operated. The systems were defined in engineering handbooks, which contained drawings of the components. We pored over them to understand them to the point of memorizing the details. I had a large bookcase of these documents in my office for reference. There were also many training manuals on the systems.

There were no word processing machines in use at JSC when we first arrived. The number of changes discovered during testing of the systems and software meant that many changes were required to these libraries. Keeping up with the necessary changes between updates was quite a chore for the engineers, astronauts in training, and support staff.

We were also given courses on the research that would be done using the space shuttle, space laboratory modules, and experiments that were in development. These were wide-ranging, from biology and life sciences to astronomy and physics.

Another area of focus was geology and related Earth observations from space. Compared to earlier capsules, the shuttle had many windows. We would have great opportunities for capturing photographs of some of the more interesting places and events on the planet. We were even treated to a geology field trip with a university professor in northern New Mexico. Seeing those landscapes through his eyes helped me begin to understand how the Earth had evolved over its billions of years of existence.

A special treat was hearing the stories of retired astronauts when they returned for medical checks as part of NASA's long-term medical studies. We met with them, heard their stories about their space missions, and had an opportunity to ask them questions.

We went on field trips to the other NASA space flight centers. They were all eye-openers. The highlight was our tour of the Kennedy Space Center (KSC) in Florida. Seeing the launch pads and other shuttle support facilities up close and personal made us all even more anxious to be selected for a flight soon.

T-38 check rides

Every astronaut pilot and mission specialist was checked out in the T-38 Talon, which is the advanced trainer used for US Air Force Undergraduate Pilot Training. The mission specialists were checked out for duty in the rear seat, where they assisted with planning and flying our missions. The test pilots occupied the front seat and handled the aircraft for all takeoffs and landings as well as any other critical maneuvers. Since I had been flying the T-38 in my previous assignment, I had no problems with the basic check ride and was cleared to fly solo or with mission specialists on dual flights.

T-38 training for instrument flying was the most rigorous that I had experienced in my career. There were many poor-weather days in Houston. NASA wanted to prevent aircraft accidents, which had killed astronauts in the Mercury, Gemini, and Apollo programs when bad weather was a contributing cause.

For the first time in my career, I failed an instrument check ride because of a procedural failure on my part. The IP had me simulate an instrument system failure just as I was approaching level-off altitude, which significantly increased the workload on the instrument approach. I got behind and barely missed an altitude level-off requirement. The IP was an astronaut who was famously the best T-38 pilot in the office and had more flying time in it than anyone else, and he said, "Well, that's a failure."

I was initially humiliated and crushed. It brought back PTSD-like memories of my string of straight "fairs" early in pilot training. No, this had to be corrected immediately.

After we landed and he gave me what amounted to a pink slip, I got rescheduled for another check ride the same day. I was insistent on that. I was kind of irritated. I don't flunk instrument check rides. I passed the recheck during the same day and never flunked another one.

Required flight hours

Our aircraft operations were based at Ellington Field, a few miles north of JSC. We were expected to fly a minimum of 15 hours per month in the T-38, and I resolved to always exceed that as well as complete the expected instrument and night training events. Many of the flights were support flights to deliver mission specialists to various places around the country to support training exercises, simulator support at the shuttle contractor's facility, and speaking engagements. We also flew proficiency flights to log the required number of night hours and instrument approaches.

I traveled all over the country on these support flights. Often we landed at Los Angeles International Airport to support activities at Rockwell, where the entry software was being tested and refined and the shuttles were being manufactured. I traveled to Washington, DC, Patrick AFB, Florida, Redstone Arsenal in Huntsville, Alabama, Edwards AFB, California, and many missions to El Paso, Texas, where the Shuttle Training Aircraft (STA) missions to White Sands for crew landing training were based. I even made trips to Toronto International Airport in Canada and many other places we wouldn't ordinarily go.

Another flying highlight was our initiation into zero-g flying onboard NASA's modified KC-135, which was more popularly named the "Vomit Comet." I had had an earlier experience on a similar aircraft operated by the air force at Wright-Patterson AFB while at ARPS. I didn't become ill on my zero-g flights, but I came close, so I avoided any additional flights on it. I felt it would be better to adjust to zero-g just once on my space shuttle mission instead of a dozen times a flight on the Vomit Comet.

Family life

My schedule reminded me of my Grandpappy Bridges's work ethic and professionalism. As a doctor, he worked around the clock when necessary, and his work was his hobby. But working these flights into my daily schedules proved challenging. I was often getting home late in the evening with either a fast-food burger or leftovers for dinner. Benita and the kids understood, and they didn't give me a lot of grief over it. But it was tough on us. We were—we are still—a close-knit family.

When we arrived in Texas, Tanya entered the fifth grade and Brian entered the first grade at Ed White Elementary School in our neighborhood in Seabrook. Tanya continued to be active in a soccer league, found a great music teacher, and continued her piano lessons. She also took a jazz ballet class at the dance school near our home. Brian became a member of a Little League baseball team and Cub Scouts.

Benita joined a walking club of women in our neighborhood and walked every morning. She took dance lessons in classical ballet and volunteered often at school to assist with art classes. We all joined the local United Methodist church, and Benita volunteered many hours at the church library. She also volunteered with the Houston Symphony, and we attended many performances as a family.

Given the warm weather, all of us enjoyed outings at our neighborhood swimming pool. We especially liked short trips to the beach in Galveston for a beach cookout and swim. We made these trips in the late afternoon to avoid too much sun, given that we were all sensitive to sunburn, with our red hair and light skin.

The Astronaut Office had a gym at JSC, and I worked out most afternoons, with a jog around the Center or on the circular jogging trail behind the gym, to stay in good physical condition. I would be tested constantly before flights by the flight surgeons. Any serious issues could become career-limiting. My wife and kids could also use the JSC Medical Clinic when they needed to see a doctor for treatment. Fortunately, none of us experienced medical issues such as we had in Montgomery.

Life was good.

Chapter 30: Astronaut Support Crew
July 1981–October 1984

As we neared the end of our yearlong course of studies as Astronaut Candidates, we were given opportunities to begin an engineering job to support the shuttle program. I was assigned as a shuttle simulator pilot in the Shuttle Avionics Integration Laboratory (SAIL), which was a hardware-in-the-loop simulation facility for final verification of shuttle flight software. We often worked twelve-hour shifts, five days a week, in order to meet the schedule as the first flight of the shuttle approached. For an aspiring shuttle pilot, this was a rich and rewarding assignment. While flying many ascents, ascent aborts, entries, and on orbit checkout runs, I became more of an expert on the crew procedures and shuttle systems and software.

As a teenager, I'd become an expert on the tractor and dreamed of operating more complex machines in the future. My teenage self would have been in awe of how my improbable dream was developing.

We uncovered many issues and described the more minor ones in crew notes to help the early crews understand the anomalies they might experience. We recorded any anomalies on the cockpit displays with a Polaroid camera to use in debriefing the engineers at the end of the runs. As resources permitted, IBM software engineers corrected these issues in subsequent software builds that were issued as block updates.

STS-1

I was on duty in SAIL on the day of the first shuttle launch, which became an abort before engine start because of a software anomaly. We were able to capture the details of the anomaly and duplicate it in SAIL. The software engineers patched the software, we verified it, and NASA was able to proceed with the first launch on April 12, 1981, without a lengthy delay.

What a great day for NASA.

After the flawless launch of Columbia, everyone in the office followed the mission closely. We gathered in a conference room to monitor the shuttle's entry and landing.

Given all of the important things that had to work flawlessly during entry, we held our breaths waiting for the shuttle to exit radio blackout. When Columbia called, we all gave a sigh of relief, but they still had to transit the rest of the entry from near Hawaii to a first landing on the lakebed at Edwards AFB.

We were more worried about some anomaly in the flight control system while transiting the hypersonic region than we were about the actual landing because the crew had had great landing training by flying the Shuttle Training Aircraft (STA). The STA was a highly modified Grumman Gulfstream II, twin-engine jet that could accurately simulate the flight of the space shuttle from 37,000 feet to a simulated landing. Nevertheless, this was still the first flight in the shuttle so we hoped all would go well.

When Columbia touched down and rolled out on the lakebed successfully, we all cheered. It was another great day for NASA and the shuttle program.

Many of us traveled to Ellington to welcome the crew home when they landed after returning from California. Later we celebrated again at a party with all in the office attending with our spouses. These celebrations became a tradition in these early days of the program.

Because of the many risks, the success of the first shuttle test mission was truly a miracle to many of us. Later in the program, engineers estimated the chances of a successful mission for the first nine missions as 1 in 10. Poor odds indeed.

A regular feature of life in the Astronaut Office was the weekly all-hands meeting, which occurred on Monday mornings and was chaired by the Chief of the Astronaut Office, Navy Captain John Young. Senior astronauts who were assigned to facilities such as SAIL or were tracking problem areas being worked by other engineers in the program office would briefly report on significant issues and progress toward resolution. Over the years many potentially serious issues were actively discussed.

After we began flying the shuttle, the returning crews would present frank and detailed briefings about their experiences during their missions.

As the new guys, members of the Class of 1980 sat in the back of the room, watching and listening silently.

STS-2

I served in SAIL for the first three missions. For STS-2, I was the senior SAIL person and briefed the crew on all that we had discovered in testing their software load, with an emphasis on the anomalies that were described as operational notes in a handbook. These had been deemed as non-critical and would be corrected in future software deliveries.

I also got to go to KSC and sit in the middle seat in the cockpit to observe the crew and software performance during the Terminal Countdown Demonstration Test in the Vehicle Assembly Building with the shuttle in its vertical launch configuration. That was a real thrill for me. There were only three of us in the cockpit: the ones who were actually going to fly the second mission for the shuttle program, and me in the support group. It was quite an honor, out of the hundred or so in the office, to get that third seat for that test. Up to that point, that's the closest I had gotten to launch, actually sitting in the cockpit of the shuttle when it was vertical. I *liked* this. *I wanted more of this.*

STS-3

For STS-3, I helped the Flight Data File (FDF) team, which made sure the crew had cue cards and checklists for normal operations and emergency procedures. As the crew practiced in the simulator using these, they often asked for changes to make the cue cards and checklists easier to understand and use. We were responsible for making sure that everything was perfect for flight. I assisted the rest of the team and engineers with making the crew-requested changes.

I had another unusual support role for STS-3. When the decision was made to land STS-3 at White Sands instead of Edwards AFB because the lakebed was flooded, I flew a T-38 aircraft to the El Paso Airport to be in position to ferry some data files back to JSC so they could be processed immediately. El Paso and White Sands were hit with a vicious windstorm that just barely permitted a successful landing on the lakebed. I watched the landing on TV in my motel room.

The crew used the shuttle's autopilot for the final approach to test it. The commander was to take manual control just before touchdown and complete the landing. The autopilot did not work well during the approach. It commanded a cycling of speed brakes, which resulted in airspeed variations that could be confusing. After touchdown, the commander raised the nose too high on rollout, which almost resulted in a catastrophe. They almost crashed the shuttle. Fortunately, he was able to stop the pitch up at the last moment and complete the rollout successfully. But that's when I became pretty tense—when I watched them land and he almost put the shuttle on its back, I sat up and took notice. My jaw dropped as it played out on TV. It was a close call.

The windy conditions coated the shuttle with gypsum dust, which required extensive cleaning before the next flight.

Later that evening the gear we were to transport arrived at the El Paso airport. We had learned that the weather in Houston was forecast to be marginal for a T-38 landing, so we commandeered a Southwest Airlines aircraft scheduled to depart for Houston Hobby Airport and convinced the crew to let one of us accompany the gear as an add-on to their cockpit crew and to load the gear into their cargo bay. I helped to load it and flew my T-38 back to Houston later when the weather cleared.

STS-4

For the fourth mission, I was assigned as the backup entry Capsule Communicator (CAPCOM)—astronauts in Mission Control who communicate with the astronauts onboard the mission. This mission was to be the first to land on a concrete runway. President Reagan was in the audience at Edwards AFB. It would be another critical first, as the wheels, tires, brakes, and nose wheel steering system would experience much more significant loads and use than during the previous lakebed landings. Since the long runway was much shorter than the lakebed, the crew needed to be right on the mark for energy control, touchdown location, and airspeed control to avoid the use of heavy braking during the rollout.

Being on the support crew as a backup entry CAPCOM was a great experience. As part of the Mission Control Team, CAPCOMs participated in many simulator runs with the crews. Simulator runs would test the crew and Mission Control Team's ability to diagnose anomalies and respond with appropriate emergency procedures. Only the last simulator run before the flight would be challenge-free. Occasionally, the simulated shuttle crashed. These were particularly great training events, as all participated in extensive debriefings to understand what had caused the crash and how to assure that it would never happen during the flight.

In addition to our primary duty to be well trained for entry, we also pulled on-orbit shifts during the mission with timing such that we would be on shift from orbit through landing on the final day.

The crew launched on June 27, 1982, and landed on July 4. It was billed as the final test flight of Columbia and the shuttle program. The plan was for the shuttle to be declared operational. The ejection seats would be removed before the next flight, and future crews would not wear pressure suits. Also, future crews would be larger than two.

The mission and landing were successful, and President Reagan and the First Lady welcomed the crew as scheduled. The president gave a speech declaring that the shuttle was now operational. The crew did a great job for the nation.

After STS-4, I became the primary entry CAPCOM and started training as the backup ascent CAPCOM.

Roy, as CAPCOM at the Johnson Space Center, next to Vice President Bush as he spoke to the crew of Challenger while in orbit on its first flight

STS-5, STS-6, STS-7

I was the primary CAPCOM for ascent and entry for STS-6 and STS-7.

Another interesting duty that fell on me as the primary CAPCOM for entry for STS-5 was as the primary support team member for the development of auto-land test procedures and training for the crew. I worked with the crew and engineers to develop training profiles for the simulator and the STA to include the down-mode criteria (when the astronaut might have to take over in the last few hundred feet if the automated system failed) and weather limits.

Astronauts are professional test pilots. They're very good. Whereas this auto-land system was not well designed. It had issues. Late in the game, if something went wrong, like a computer failure, the astronauts would have to take over the shuttle and complete the landing manually. And if you haven't had your hands on the controls all along, it can be hard to judge how to take hold of them and keep the shuttle smoothly on the same glide path. If you're only a hundred feet or so off the ground, you don't have time for trial and error. I had to make sure the crew was trained to handle this should the situation arise, as it did in STS-3 when the commander took over—and nearly crashed the shuttle.

There were two political sides to this argument. The program office consisted of engineers who were not pilots. They trusted their systems more than they did the pilots. If they could get this to be auto-land every time, it would take the human factors out of it. They were on the side of "Let's do this." And the astronauts were on the side of "I don't trust that system. I don't want to ever do an auto-land. Why am I in here if I'm not even allowed to land?"

At one point as the launch date for STS-5 approached, I became aware that my passion to get the crew well trained for an auto-landing was not appreciated by Captain Young or his boss, George Abbey. One of the senior astronauts told me privately that I was doing too good of a job with crew training, which was his not-too-subtle way of warning me about the office politics surrounding this event. I responded that I had no choice. If the crew was required to perform a manual landing, it was my responsibility to assure that they had excellent training.

The program office set up this mission to test the auto-landing capability. Not that they had committed themselves to doing it on every mission, but they wanted to try and see if it worked. So I had to get the crew ready to do that in case they continued with that decision. If they changed their minds, it would be fine with me to let the crew land manually, because I knew the crew knew how to land the vehicle well. I didn't know what would happen if they did this auto-land and it didn't work so well. There was no way to know until we tried it. The entire Astronaut Office wanted to land manually.

Every plane has a wind limit. If the winds are higher than that limit, you're not cleared to land because you can't do it safely. The Astronaut Office did not want to do an auto-land under any circumstances, ever. So to make it harder for us to actually do one, they set the crosswind limit unreasonably low—much inside what the shuttle was allowed to do.

To give one example of how hard it was to do my job in light of the Astronaut Office's reluctance to do an auto-land and the program office's determination to test it: I was asked by the Lead Flight Director to get an Astronaut Office buy-off on the crosswind landing limit for an auto-land. He knew that with this tight limit, the odds of us actually getting to use the auto-land on the flight were going to be minimal, and he asked me to go to John Young and see if I could get a little higher number.

I approached John Young with my recommendation, which was a slight compromise between what he wanted and what the Flight Director wanted. As I was explaining the rationale, he got up from his desk and walked to the restroom.

I didn't know where he was headed initially and, since I had not been dismissed or obtained a decision from him, I followed and continued my presentation even as he was standing at the urinal. He finally turned and said that he didn't compromise. I was to hold the line.

Eventually, the decision was made that it was not worth the risk to perform an auto-land. I was happy; it took a lot of pressure off of us. However, that decision came late in the training flow for STS-5, after the development and training had been completed.

At the crew party after the mission, the commander made some laudatory comments on my behalf as he gave me an autographed montage of mission photographs, which was a traditional gift from the crews to their support crewmembers. He specifically thanked me for my work preparing them to do an auto-land.

After getting my photo and walking back toward my seat, I passed by George Abbey, who said quietly and sarcastically just how much he appreciated my help with auto-land. I figured at that point that I might be last in line for a flight assignment, as George seemed to have his favorites, and I didn't appear to be one of them. I decided that I would continue to do my best for the crews and missions that I would support—and stay out of office politics.

My CAPCOM missions were exciting. For example, STS-6 was the first flight of Challenger. I was on the console when Vice President Bush visited Mission Control and sat down next to me to talk to the crew on orbit. That was somewhat of a historic photo op of me sitting next to the vice president. JSC had it printed on postcards and on a key chain, which were sold in the JSC gift shop. I received several of those postcards in the mail from friends who visited the Center afterwards.

STS-7 was the second flight of Challenger, and the crew broke the gender ceiling as Sally Ride flew to orbit as the first female US astronaut to launch and complete an orbit of the Earth. I was the voice of Mission Control when she described the launch as a real "E ticket" ride, which was the terminology for Disneyland's tickets for their most expensive rides.

For STS-6, STS-7, and subsequent missions, I purchased a radio for our home that had the correct frequency band to pick up retransmissions from Mission Control at JSC of all the communications to and from the space shuttle. This was a great help in preparing me for my shifts, as I could hear about problems while still at home getting ready.

Wheels, tires, and brakes

During these early missions there was another problematic issue, which was the braking system—wheels, tires, and brakes. The brakes were made of a lightweight alloy of beryllium with a carbon lining, and they were supposed to be good for five landings. With landing speeds of over two hundred miles per hour, the brakes could be subjected to high heat loads if applied too early and too hard at the higher speeds.

As the entry CAPCOM and support team member for many of these first missions to land on the concrete runway, I worked with the design engineers to develop braking procedures and crew training to minimize the potential for a mishap until the brakes and tires could be redesigned to absorb higher heat loads or be fitted with a braking parachute. This feature had been in the early design for the shuttle but was dropped.

As a result of my YA-10 brake failure accident, I was well aware of the danger. That motivated me to do everything possible to avoid one during a shuttle landing.

Despite our early efforts to minimize the potential for a mishap, we did encounter some close calls. STS-41B, the tenth shuttle mission, landed on the runway at KSC in February 1984 and had a brake failure near the end of the rollout, despite using only moderate braking. In April 1985, Discovery landed at KSC and had shredded tires and brake failure on the right side. The braking procedures, crew training, and conservative criteria for runway selection that we developed and employed helped us avoid more serious incidents until the systems could be improved and a drag chute added.

My brief career in television

For STS-8, the first night launch and landing for the shuttle, I was assigned to be a spokesperson for CBS. I provided the color commentary for launch and landing. This was an awesome experience, working with the TV anchor and production crew to make it interesting for the audience. Of course the audiences for this mission were somewhat smaller, as both events occurred late in the evening.

I didn't win any awards for my performance. I wasn't invited to continue in that role for subsequent missions, which was fine with me. A color commentator should have flown at least one mission in space to qualify.

Flight Data Files and Flight Software

After STS-8, I became the Astronaut Office lead for the Flight Data File (FDF). This involved the creation, validation, and publication of all the checklists and guides that would fly with the crew. The crews often wanted to personalize the quick reference guides that were attached to the instrument panels with Velcro, which often meant late-in-the-schedule changes that were tough on the crew of mostly women doing the production.

We were in the busiest time in the shuttle program as we built up the flight rate to 12 flights per year and made preparations for the first Western Test Range launch from Vandenberg AFB. Keeping up with demand was a monumental task.

I successfully assured that the FDF was accurate and met crew needs on time. This involved extensive technical knowledge of each mission as well as much time spent on coordination, persuasion, and attention to detail. Since there were multiple crews in training, this added complexity to what was already a gargantuan effort. A lot of the success depended on the production team, and they came through every time with flying colors.

During this period, I was also assigned to be the Astronaut Office lead for advocating changes to the shuttle software to enhance the software's capability to assist the crew during high-workload events such as aborts. This duty involved building detailed presentations for the Flight Software Change Board that would be convincing.

For example, I developed and successfully advocated a proposal for expanded flexibility in landing site selection and propellant dumps to the Astronaut Office and the Change Board. I also kept the crews well informed on flight software issues, problems, and nuances. This was another rich opportunity for me as an aspiring pilot, as I learned a lot more about the shuttle systems and software. The many crews that I supported commended me for my work in both the FDF and flight software areas.

Family Fun for the Holidays

For the Christmas and New Year holidays in 1983, we planned a family road trip to Tucson, Arizona. On the way home, we planned to spend a few days at the Angel Fire Ski Resort in New Mexico. The day before we were to depart, the weather forecast was for an ice storm in western Texas. I got on the phone and booked coach tickets on Amtrak, departing at midnight. We hustled to finish packing and get to the station in downtown Houston in time to catch the train. We made it.

It was a long night as we tried to sleep in the coach seats. We were ready to get off well before we arrived in midmorning. After celebrating Christmas with Benita's parents, we took an airline flight to Albuquerque for our ski trip.

It was the first time that Benita, Brian, and Tanya had skied. So all of us got into the beginner class. On the second day, Brian and I graduated to the intermediate level. And before we left there, Brian was skiing down blue and black slopes. Tanya and I were green and blue at best. Benita was crowned as "Queen of the Snow Snails," but she had fun, too, so everything was fine.

And Then...

In February, I had the privilege of being appointed as a family escort for the tenth shuttle mission, which was designated as STS-41B. The crew escorts accompanied the crew spouses and families to KSC for launch and, for the first time, to KSC for landing. This was an exciting mission. Bruce McCandless performed the first free flight in space using the new Manned Maneuvering Unit (MMU). He moved out 320 feet from the shuttle's payload bay. The crew performed the first landing at KSC on February 11, 1984.

In summary, the early days of the shuttle program were filled with opportunities to dig into the details of this immature and complex system, learn a lot about it, and find a work-around for problems while making improvements to fix them as time permitted. Every flight was new in many aspects. I learned to have a healthy appreciation for the limitations of our simulators and models that were used for designing and testing the shuttle and its payloads. I developed a reputation as a quick study of these complex details, as an effective spokesman for the office on flight software and procedural issues, and as a team player on a great team.

I enjoyed the technical and operational challenges immensely. Rather than being upset about being at JSC for many years and not being assigned to a crew, I found joy in my engineering and support roles. They prepared me well for a flight whenever that opportunity presented itself.

The one real drawback to being an astronaut who had not yet flown was trying to be effective during speaking engagements, since we had to pull our share of personal appearance requests. People really wanted to hear about flying in space from someone who had experienced it firsthand. Since I hadn't flown yet, I couldn't tell them what it was like.

But there were some special benefits that came with my astronaut status. For example, Brian and I were invited to visit the Houston Astros clubhouse and dugout prior to a home game at the Astrodome. We met many of the great players on that team. I was invited to pilot the Goodyear blimp with one of their IPs. Benita, who was a passenger, and I really enjoyed that unique experience. That was a nice add to the long list of aerospace vehicles that I had flown as a pilot. Now if I could just add the space shuttle, my dream would be complete.

Then one day I was summoned to George Abbey's office.

I had no idea why.

When I arrived, he said, "Roy, I know that you are really busy, so you probably don't have time for what I was going to ask you to do. I'm sorry that I called you over here. I'm just wasting your time. Why don't you just go back over to the office?"

I said, "George, wait a minute. I think I can work it out. What do you need me to do?"

He said, "Dave Griggs is on a flight, and the launch has been delayed. He can't train for his next flight on STS-51F, Spacelab 2. Would you be interested in being the pilot to replace him?"

All I could think was, *Oh, my God, I can't believe it's happening.* I was not the first member of my class to be assigned a pilot slot; many others had already been assigned. And I was not George's favorite. But by this little quirk, because this flight had slipped, I got to be the first of the pilots in my class to fly. This was like magic coming down from heaven.

"George," I said, "I would like to do that. Thank you."

I was finally on my way to orbit.

Christmas Letters 1981, 1984

1981: Yea! We made it for a whole year without moving. Some of you were probably wondering if Roy could keep a job anymore. Seriously, this has been a very intense, exciting year for Roy. He completed his "basic" training and became a full-fledged astronaut this summer.

Tanya, 11, is almost as tall as her mother and is going to Intermediate School (6th grade) where they switch classes just like the big guys and have a lot of homework, yuk! She plays a mean game of soccer—her team is in first place—and has shown a lot of talent with the piano. Between those, church choir, and ballet classes, she's a pretty busy lady.

Brian, 7, is in second grade. He doesn't love school nearly as much as catching frogs and lizards or going fishing. He also spends a lot of time practicing his soccer and baseball skills. Watching him really makes you want to be a kid again.

Benita is the glue keeping this critical mass from flying apart. She is active in both kids' schools. She has had her hands full getting us properly nested in our new (five yr. old) Texas house which has needed lots of tender, loving care. It is starting to shape up now, and we hope all of our friends and relatives will come see us in Texas.

1984: Last Christmas our family spent an exhilarating week at the Angel Fire Ski Resort in New Mexico. Everybody learned to ski, but we christened Benita the Queen of the Snow Snails. Brian was Mr. Hot Dog after two lessons. Tanya attracted a crowd of boys with her flaming red hair and black snow suit, and Roy kept a close eye on that situation.

This fall Roy was notified that he would be flying as pilot on the Spacelab 2 shuttle mission, scheduled for launch on July 9, 1985. Since the shuttle is having problems with its heat-protecting tiles, the flight may slip some. Benita is taking some special training at the church in preparation for becoming a Stephen Minister. After training, she will be given assignments to assist the minister in aiding those in the church with special needs.

Best wishes for a happy holiday season!

Chapter 31: STS-51F, Spacelab 2
October 1984–July 1985

Benita, Tanya, and Brian were all thrilled about my upcoming flight. Benita told me in later years that she'd had a promise from God that he would deliver me safely to and from orbit just as he had saved me in Vietnam. She even jumped on my commander once during training when he expressed some doubt about how successful we would be, given the problems in the program at the time.

The commander and crew welcomed me, and I moved into the crew offices. They were well along in their training, as we were only six months from launch. I had a lot of catching up to do.

Training

Despite my preparation, my initiation as a crewmember was tough. The simulator sessions were filled with multiple failures. Initially, I was overwhelmed. I would get behind doing the things to diagnose the failure modes and employing the emergency procedures. We crashed a few times as a result.

After a few of these debacles, our flight engineer, Story Musgrave, who sat in the middle seat, teamed with me. He would coach me on critical next steps for emergency procedures to keep me from getting overloaded. We jelled as a team and did well as we approached our launch date. I was comfortable working with the crew.

I started my training in the STA. Most of the missions were flown out of El Paso, Texas, to White Sands, but as we neared the launch date, we also flew missions at Edwards AFB and KSC. I liked flying the STA and got satisfactory grades from the IPs.

Gordon "Gordo" Fullerton, my commander, was an IP in the KC-135. He trained me in landing that aircraft so that I could add some large airplane experiences to my résumé. To make it as valuable as possible, he delighted in finding landing runways in the Texas area that had the toughest wind conditions for these practices. I managed to do okay with them. The KC-135 was tougher to land in these conditions than fighters.

Our launch date slipped three months, which gave us more time to prepare. One day, I was again called to George Abbey's office out of the blue. I hoped that I hadn't screwed something up. I was delighted when he assigned me to be the pilot of STS-61F, Shuttle Centaur, which would launch the Ulysses spacecraft on a mission to the sun in May 1986, less than a year after STS-51F. It would have a veteran crew of only four people.

I was on cloud nine.

Pre-launch quarantine

As the date for the launch on what I expected to be my first of two flights approached, my feelings of anticipation grew stronger each and every day. When we entered quarantine several days before flying down to the Cape, it began to feel like the flight was really going to happen. Our quarantine was in a modified warehouse on JSC, which housed several house trailers that we used for sleeping. There was a separate trailer for food service.

I was on the Houston night shift for the flight as the lead along with Mission Specialist Karl Henize and Payload Specialist Loren Acton. We were known as "the Red Shift," as signified by the red polo shirts that we would wear on orbit. We got up for breakfast when the other shift was having dinner. The Blue Shift was composed of blue-polo-shirted Mission Specialists Story Musgrave and Tony England and Payload Specialist John David Bartoe. Story led that day shift. Our commander, Gordo Fullerton, was in charge of the mission. He participated in activities where all crewmembers were required and kept an eye on our progress. He wore a blue-and-red-striped polo shirt.

Staying busy through the long nights was essential to staying in a good frame of mind. I spent every waking hour reviewing my "books" on shuttle systems and procedures and working

Official crew photo for the STS-51F
Spacelab 2 crew in front of the payload while it was
being processed before installation in the space shuttle

out to be sure that I was in top physical condition. I also did a lot of map study to practice spotting cues on approach to our highest-priority Earth observation targets.

On our last day of training at JSC, we did a final simulator run, which was typically a benign ascent, as we expected ours to be. Then we flew a four-ship—four T-38s flying in formation—down to KSC and settled into quarantine in the Astronaut Crew Quarters. The staff was great, and the food was delicious and plentiful.

My night jogging routine was frightening. I knew that the moonlight shadows of street lights could hide a rattlesnake soaking up the heat from the asphalt. Despite the low probability of danger, given what I was about to do, this fear plagued every run. I was relieved to complete all of my jogs without running into any snakes.

We enjoyed a nice cookout at the Beach House with our wives. Benita and I took a long walk on the beach and shared our thoughts about the mission. She had a lot of faith that everything would be great, just as she had when I was in Vietnam.

Eve of launch

The night before launch our families and launch guests were treated to nighttime viewing of the shuttle on the pad. I was in quarantine, so I had to observe my family from a distance. I noticed that my eleven-year-old son was sitting off to one side of the crowd on the ground, staring at the shuttle. This helped me to realize the enormity of the experience for my family. I have a photograph of that in my office to remind me of the many sacrifices that my family made in order for me to become and succeed—not only as an astronaut, but also in everything that led up to the selection process.

I spent some time during the last evening before launch day writing a letter to each of my children and to my wife reflecting on some last thoughts and words in the event that I did not return. These would be held in my personal gear that I left behind and given to my family at the appropriate time if needed.

I did my last STA ride practicing the Return to Launch Site abort (RTLS) profile on the Shuttle Landing Facility multiple times. Chief Astronaut John Young and Director of Flight Crew Operations George Abbey stood in the cockpit and observed my performance. I guess that I passed, because they allowed us to proceed to launch.

Finally, we had the last breakfast and departed the facility in the astronaut van for the launch pad. There was a large crowd as we exited the facility and walked to the van. We waved to them, grateful that they were there to see us off. I stopped at the restroom at the pad for one last bladder dump before being strapped into the shuttle by the close-out crew. None of us wanted to have to use the urine collection bladders strapped to our bodies before activating the Shuttle toilet on orbit.

Countdown

The countdown proceeded without any serious issues. Finally we got a "go for launch," and then it was totally quiet. Each crew member had specific tasks to perform just like they had practiced a million times, making sure to do them right on time. It was time for me to start the auxiliary power units. Then we waited for the countdown to shift to the internal computer at T–31 seconds. All continued smoothly. At T–7 seconds, the engines roared to life. Everything was looking good. Nobody was saying anything. It was *quiet*. Then the engines suddenly shut down at T–2.8 seconds.

We had just experienced a launch abort.

Brian looking at the Challenger on the launch pad
during night viewing before launch day

When I looked over at Gordo, I saw that he was looking at my hands instead of my eyes.

I quickly raised my hands and said, "Gordo, I didn't touch a thing. It was an automatic shutdown."

Looking back on it, I thought it was a humorous moment that he wanted to be sure that I wasn't the culprit, since I had the only throttle for the engines, and the engine shutdown buttons were on the center console between us.

Instead of going into orbit, we went to Cocoa Beach and spent the evening with families. I had a lot of disappointed family and friends on the beach. They weren't happy to see me there. And I certainly didn't want to be there. It was Benita's birthday, and I was supposed to have lit a big candle for her with the launch. My teenage daughter was mortified that perhaps her dad had messed up the launch in front of people watching, not only locally but also around the nation, on TV. I tried to reassure her that it wasn't my fault, but she wasn't in a mood to be convinced.

It was horrible. I had rented a bus to take all these family people here for the launch to the viewing site, and now most of them weren't going to get to see it. At the time, I didn't know if we were going to have another chance or when it would happen. This was a missed opportunity—for my whole family.

Brian, Benita, and Tanya on the roof of the Launch Control Center during the countdown for launch

Chapter 32: STS-51F, Spacelab 2 Second Launch Attempt
July 1985–August 1985

We all returned to Houston, and it was several days before we got the word that a valve on one of the engines had opened too slowly, causing the computer-controlled abort system to activate.

The next few days were troubling. We wondered if we would be able to reschedule the launch in the near term. There were some issues with the payload that had to be resolved, as well as fixing the engine. We practiced in the simulator and tried to make the best of it. Finally, we got the "go" for another launch attempt on July 29.

We repeated the routine of quarantine, flight to the Cape, and the other events leading up to launch. There were a lot fewer family and friends for this attempt, as many could not afford the time off or money for another trip to Florida so soon after our previous launch attempt. I had to max out my credit card to purchase the second trip to Cocoa Beach for my kids.

Go for launch

This time the countdown did not proceed as smoothly. There was a problem with the rate gyros on the Solid Rocket Boosters

Liftoff of STS-51F on July 29, 1985

(SRB) that had to be corrected. The delay was uncomfortable, with the afternoon sun streaming in through the front window, and the seats were hard on the back.

Finally all was fixed, and we got the "go for launch" again.

This time we got all the way to T–0 and *bam!* the solid rockets fired, and we were airborne and moving fast. I was thrilled. Because once those solid rockets fire, you're going to go for a ride.

We were moving more than 100 miles per hour as our tail cleared the launch tower. We completed the roll maneuver so that we were upside down and then completed the throttle down and throttle up to clear the max dynamic pressure region. At approximately two minutes into the ascent, the solids burned out and made a "whoosh" sound as they separated from the shuttle to parachute back into the ocean, where they would be retrieved by special retrieval ships and returned so that they could be reused.

You might say, okay, something could happen to us, for sure. But I wasn't thinking about that. I felt sure we would make it into space. This was the fulfillment of my lifelong dream. I was on top of the world.

The ride during the first two minutes was somewhat rough, with considerable vibration. Imagine a cat trying to hang on to a window glass. That's kind of how it felt. We were getting jostled around. It wasn't uncomfortable, but I'd never felt anything like it. None of the simulators did that, of course. So this was an unusual feeling that I had never experienced before. You were just hanging: you had a tiger by the tail, and you were just trying to hang on.

But once the solids separated, everything smoothed out, and the only noticeable feeling was the steady increase in g-forces through the chest as we accelerated.

As we approached 2 g's, I explored the overhead panel. I wanted to see if I could reach the overhead switches easily under g-loads, as this condition could not be simulated on the ground—simulators can't simulate 2 g's or 3 g's, like we were going to experience. So I was trying—could I reach that switch if I had to get to it?—and as I reached over my head for the last row of overhead switches, I felt the g-load suddenly decrease, accompanied by warning lights and sounds.

When this happened, Gordo didn't have time to look at my hands.

I knew he'd seen me do something, so if he'd had time, he probably would have looked over at me with a look that said, *What did you do?*

Engine down

Then we got the call from Mission Control. "Challenger, Houston. Abort to Orbit." (ATO)

We started an emergency procedure to respond to the loss of one of our three engines. Gordo turned the abort switch to ATO and pushed the button to activate our guidance system for ATO. We started a fuel dump of our orbital maneuvering system fuel to reduce our weight and give us a better chance of making it into orbit.

Now we had to hope that we would achieve sufficient velocity before running out of fuel to be able to stay in orbit. If not, we would have to Abort Once Around and land at Edwards AFB without achieving orbit.

Since we were the first (and ultimately the only) shuttle to lose an engine going to orbit, we were now into the unknown. Would the fuel line low-level sensors work as designed, as we would surely deplete all of our liquid propellants? If not, the

turbo pumps would cavitate, overspeed, and likely destructive-
ly fail. So we were all busy—and we were all mortally worried.

After getting the necessary actions underway after we began the ATO, Story and I simultaneously said, "This is starting
to feel just like another sim. They're not supposed to be doing
this stuff to us."

We had lost the engine approximately thirty seconds after
passing the last chance to land at the Transoceanic Abort Landing site (TAL) in Spain. Had it happened thirty seconds sooner,
we would have set a transatlantic speed record of thirty-seven
minutes from Florida to Spain.

Thankfully, we left that record for someone else to set.

"Challenger, Houston"

Then we got another troubling call from Mission Control. "Challenger, Houston. Limits to inhibit."

This was a terrifying radio call.

It was definite, clear, crisp.

"Limits to inhibit" was a switch on the center console that
would inactivate our engine safety shutdown software. We had
never used that switch in our many simulator sessions.

Gordo threw the switch. Now we were unprotected from
overtemperature and other serious conditions in the remaining two engines.

After the flight we learned that our Booster Officer in Mission Control, Jenny Howard, saw a troubling signature in one
of our remaining two engines that matched the signature of the
failed engine. She told the Flight Director and CAPCOM to go
Limits to Inhibit to avoid another engine failure.

The failure was in an over-temperature sensor that failed
hot, sending a signal to the computer that the engine had
reached the temperature that is too high for safety, causing the

engine protection software to shut down the engine. When two of three sensors voted hot, the shutdown was activated. One more failing and we would have another engine down. Fortunately for us, Jenny Howard saved us from a bad day, as we had not yet reached a velocity where we could get to orbit on one engine. That caused other concerns for me.

Before the flight, I had approached our lead flight director on behalf of the crew to request permission to schedule a simulator session to validate a downrange abort-landing site. He asked why.

I said, "It would be needed in the event of a two-engine failure before we reach a velocity where we can get to orbit on one engine. All previous missions launched into a 28.5-degree inclination orbit. We are the first to use a 49.5-degree inclination orbit. The previously validated downrange abort site will not work for our inclination."

He said, "That's an unrealistic failure scenario. Get out of my office and quit wasting my time."

But my granddaddy and an alligator had taught me to always have a backup plan. I scheduled the simulator session anyway. I validated the computer code to enter in the event of this failure: we would have guidance to land at Souda Bay Naval Air Station on the Greek island of Crete.

I had the hexadecimal code written on my kneepad.

Now I might actually have to use it.

As we neared orbital velocity, the shuttle throttle automatically moved from full thrust to a value that would sustain a maximum of 3 g's. We all nervously watched the velocity indicator, as the value at Main Engine Cutoff (MECO) would determine our fate—enough to stay in orbit or an Abort Once Around.

"MECO." Then the shuttle main tank separated, and *bam!* *bam! bam! bam!* the attitude-control jets in the nose and tail fired to separate us from the tank.

STS-51F crew on orbit (left to right from bottom row: Loren Acton, Roy Bridges, Karl Henize, Story Musgrave, Tony England, John-David Bartoe, Gordon Fullerton)

Orbit

We had enough velocity to stay in orbit, so we prepared to fire our Orbital Maneuvering System engine to achieve a stable orbit. We ended up a few miles lower than the planned orbit, but it was high enough to salvage the mission. The planners would need to plan our activities again and send us new instructions via teleprinter each shift to assure that we pointed the shuttle correctly and at the correct times to achieve the science results, given that the timing would now be off slightly because of our lower altitude.

I was overjoyed that we didn't need that downrange abort site. After the flight, I shared the story with Lead Flight Director Jay Greene, and we both had a belly laugh over it.

The effects of zero gravity

Shortly after arrival on orbit and activating the on-orbit systems, such as opening the payload bay doors and activating the toilet, the Red Shift had to turn in for a short nap for a few hours and then work the night shift. We three crawled into our bunks and tried to sleep, but it was fitful as we all adjusted to the sensations of zero gravity. I was in the bottom of a stack of three bunks. My shift mates did not fare too well on that first orbit sleep shift. I heard a lot of bumping around and noises indicating gastric distress.

After our alarms sounded to alert us to arise and prepare for our shift, I exited my bunk, took a birdbath, and donned my on-orbit clothing. I felt a little hungry and decided to have some oatmeal and a glass of juice. That was a big mistake. It turns out that my particular symptom of space adaptation syndrome was that my stomach had ceased to function at all. The food that I ate stayed painfully trapped just below my esophagus. I finally picked up a barf bag and stuck my finger down my throat to relieve the pain.

Arriving on the flight deck for crew shift handover, we learned that all was going well with Challenger. Our shift was all set to activate the rest of the payloads that had not been activated on the first shift. As pilot, I took charge of the care and feeding of shuttle systems, including pointing the shuttle to the correct attitude per the mission timeline. This involved getting a teleprinter message that had to be cut and pasted into each crewmember's checklist for activities on our shift. We did that and began work.

The view out the windows was absolutely stunning. The Earth is so beautiful from space, and I never tired of looking at it. At our speed of almost five miles per second, the view of the surface changed rapidly. Sunrises or sunsets every forty-five minutes presented their own majestic beauty.

Payload of STS-51F from the aft cockpit window

Our adjustments to zero g continued. As my shift mates made progress with payload activation and checkout, they were in frequent contact with the mission control center while we were within range of ground stations. When we went out of range, I would often hear sounds from each of them as their gastric distress continued. We all wanted to keep these adjustments to ourselves for the time being. Mission Control couldn't help us adapt. We just needed to be patient.

I stuck with fluids all day and never experienced the nausea. I found zero-g to be at once both exhilarating and disorienting. Coming up from the mid-deck, the shuttle could be moving upside down, sideways, and canted with respect to the Earth, which made the idea of up or down irrelevant, and that was a strange feeling. Clearly, my body's sensors and brain were straining to sort these feelings out. The primary symptom for me, other than not being able to eat, was feeling tired and lethargic. I didn't know whether this was from lack of sleep, lack of nutrition, or another variation of space adaptation syndrome.

At the end of our first shift, we were exhausted. Skipping dinner for obvious reasons, we prepared to float into our bunks for our first full night's sleep. I had been provided, and had tested, a sleeping tablet on the ground to make sure that there would be no adverse side effects. I decided to take one before going to bed to assure some badly needed rest.

After taking it, I realized that I had forgotten to perform one final housekeeping chore. I needed to unscrew the cover of a ventilation duct on the ceiling of the middeck and clean the filter.

As I completed this relatively simple task, I became disoriented. I felt lost in space and was not thinking clearly about how to navigate to my bunk. In retrospect this sounds so silly, but it happened. I eventually figured it out and found my way to bed. I determined that it was a side effect of the fast-acting sleeping pill that had not revealed itself during ground tests. I resolved to never take another pill on orbit, and I didn't.

After waking up for the second shift, I felt much better. Nevertheless, I skipped the morning meal, as I didn't yet trust that my systems had adapted. After a few hours of work, I felt hungry and could tell that my stomach was doing its normal things. I made a cup of consommé soup and enjoyed it. After being sure that all my internal systems were working well, I went to the mid-deck and made some scrambled eggs. They were great; things were back to normal.

Experiments and an extra day

The only significant problems with the Challenger were with two of the payloads, the Instrument Pointing System and one of the solar telescopes, which were all on their first flight. After much work and discussions with Mission Control, software updates were implemented to get the Instrument Pointing System working well. One of the solar telescopes refused to open its door to allow checkout. Mysteriously, this problem eventually corrected itself. As these problems were corrected, payload observations began in earnest.

The Red Shift and Blue Shift teams performed all mission activities superbly, and all was well with the mission.

On the evening of the second shift, the Red Shift enjoyed dinner together, as would be our habit for the rest of the flight. That was a great time for sharing our insights and experiences on this great adventure. We sang songs and told jokes and participated in some zero-g experiments, including body acrobatics that were not possible on Earth. What fun!

The mostly rehydrated food was good enough. It was complemented with thermally stabilized and irradiated food in pouches for items such as grilled steaks and spaghetti and meatballs. Gummier food stuck better to our spoons. Food producing a lot of crumbles was not appreciated, as the crumbs floated in the cabin, irritating our noses and eyes.

One of our many duties was particularly enjoyable: looking for our preplanned Earth observation targets. We spent as much time as possible viewing the many special targets and photographing them. This had required a lot of study on the ground before flight. We needed to be able to judge when we were approaching the target so we could be ready for the short window of time we would have over the target to get good photographs. Over the course of the mission, the crew took over 2500 photographs.

As the mission progressed, I got a feeling that I was one of the most fortunate people on Earth. I had been born in a great, free country; raised by loving parents, relatives, and friends; enjoyed one of the best possible educations, despite humble beginnings; and survived several harrowing events on the way to orbit, not to mention the many other operational events during my career that could have ended tragically. As I looked down on many desolate places on the planet, I knew that millions of other humans were not nearly as lucky. I resolved to do as much as possible to improve the human condition during the rest of my life.

In addition to our four solar physics experiments mounted on the Instrument Pointing System that we used to observe features such as sunspots, we had other interesting payloads, including an x-ray telescope, an ultraviolet telescope, and a cosmic ray detector.

I knew that we were recording data on cosmic rays. I had noticed that in the darkness of my bunk, I often had fireworks shows in my eyes. I asked the doctor about this phenomenon. He said that these were the result of cosmic rays coming through the shuttle and hitting my optic nerve. I thought that this was somewhat destructive but was informed that I shouldn't worry about it. Not too reassuring, but I would just have to wait and see—nothing could be done to stop it.

The most exciting and demanding experiment was flying in proximity to the free-flying Plasma Diagnostics Package (PDP). First we attached this small payload to the end of our 50-foot long Remote Manipulator System and precisely surveyed the electromagnetic atmosphere surrounding the shuttle. We were flying through a region of the atmosphere known as the ionosphere, which has enough electromagnetic particles to interfere with some current and future experiments. Our mission was to gather data around the shuttle that would inform future scientific experimenters.

After completing the Remote Manipulator System survey, we released the PDP and maneuvered 1500 feet away from it. We maintained a precise position such that the PDP and the shuttle would be on the same magnetic field line once every one-half orbit. At the correct time, we fired an electron gun in the payload bay. The electrons spiraled up the magnetic field and were received by detectors on the PDP.

We needed to be in precise position for this part of the experiment to be successful. As a visual cue, we released a small bar magnet in the shuttle and could see that it lined up precisely on the PDP. Gordo did a great job of precisely maneuvering the shuttle, and we got direct hits.

During normal operations on the shuttle we used small attitude-control jets in the tail to maintain our attitude. Those were silent and unobtrusive to us in the cabin. For Proximity Ops we used the larger attitude-control jets in the nose and tail. When these fired, it was similar to a large-caliber cannon going off in the nose of the shuttle with bright flashes of flame. A spectacular light and noise show!

After several successful orbits, we closed on the PDP with plans to capture it with the remote manipulator system. Karl got it and returned it to the payload bay holding fixture. Mission success!

In addition to being the only shuttle mission to lose an engine on the way to orbit, we scored another first. Because we ended up at a lower altitude resulting from the engine failure, our planners had to prepare new flight plans for each shift and send them to us on the teleprinter. As a result, our mission was the only one to have the teleprinter run out of paper. Story and I had trained only once during our pre-mission training to replace the roll of paper. It was a complicated operation. Working together, we managed to get the job done, but it could have easily gone badly.

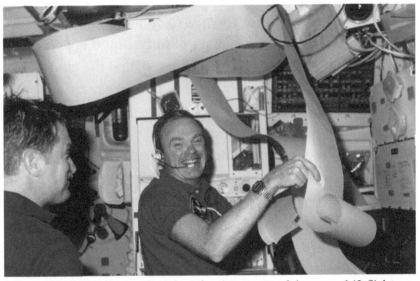

Roy and Tony England collect the teleprinter copy of the next shift flight activity schedule. The schedule had to be planned and sent to the crew before each shift due to the lower orbit caused by engine failure during ascent.

Our thirteen major science experiments were the heart of our mission, but we had another special reason for flying. Coca Cola had invented a high-technology Coke can that we had to test in zero-g. Bubbles of gas in a regular can would cause the liquid to spew out too fast to drink. The special can was designed to dispense the fluid in a controlled way. And they had taken a lot of the carbonation and separated it from the liquid, so it didn't fizz as much. Pepsi got wind of this and, late in the flow, asked us to test their can as well. It was much less sophisticated.

We divided the crew into Coke and Pepsi teams for the test. I am a native of Atlanta, Georgia, the home of Coke. Alas, I was assigned to the Pepsi team.

Bummer.

None of us were impressed by the taste test, because we had no way to cool the fluids. Hot Coke and Pepsi are not so great. The Coke can worked well. Pepsi was still too fizzy.

But we had a lot of fun with the fizzy balls. After completing the test, we created a little galaxy of fizzy, liquid Pepsi planets. By gently blowing on them, they rotated, and the gas bubbles migrated to the poles and looked like polar ice caps. After playing with them and photographing our galaxy, we cleaned up by swallowing them. Karl was the master of this game.

All too quickly, our planned seven-day mission was approaching an end. Then we got a one-day extension as a result of our being miserly with the use of electricity. The liquid hydrogen and oxygen feeding the fuel cells to generate electricity were the limiting consumables. Gordo was relentless in turning off lights and other equipment when it wasn't needed, so we had him to thank for our extra day. His leadership in all aspects of the mission was superb.

Entry

After our extra day on orbit, it was time to pack up and make our entry. We secured our payloads, closed the payload bay doors, donned our G-suits, and guzzled the required amount of water and salt tablets to help us increase our blood volume to counter the return-to-gravity effects, which in the worst case could cause us to black out.

Entry began with a short burn of our Orbital Maneuvering System engine over South Africa, a half orbit from the landing site in California. This lowered the perigee of our orbit so that we would hit the top of the atmosphere approximately over the western Pacific Ocean.

We maintained a high angle of attack as we entered the atmosphere to use the heat shield on the belly of the shuttle to create a lot of drag. We made several turns about the centerline of our trajectory to reduce our energy in a calculated way to arrive over Edwards AFB at precisely the right altitude and speed. I could already see white caps in the sea as we flew over Guam. It looked to me like we were too low.

Challenger lands on the lakebed at Edwards AFB

Through the rear cockpit overhead windows, Story and Karl could see the plasma trail that we were generating. They reported that it was spectacular!

As we approached Edwards, events seemed to speed up from the initial slow ballet to a frenzy of activities. We crossed the California coastline over the Harbor Freeway in Long Beach going Mach 3.5. We flew over the bay area, the mountains to the north, and into the Antelope Valley, the home of Edwards AFB and its dry lakebeds. We were landing on one of the dry lakebeds to reduce the wear and tear on our tires and brakes until a planned upgrade could be completed.

Gordo did an expert job, and we ended up on final approach with the right energy. I managed to lower the landing gear at the right time. Gordo performed a perfect touchdown and rollout.

We did it.

Home again.

Defying gravity

After coming to a stop, we completed the checklist items to shut down and safe the orbiter systems. Then it was time to get up and out of my seat.

That proved to be difficult. My legs wouldn't move; I had to manually lift them over the center console and use the back of the seat to pull myself into a standing position. I felt heavy and immobile. Readjusting to gravity was not instantaneous.

After stomping around for a while and getting our balance and mobility systems engaged again, as a crew, we felt we were ready to go. We exited the orbiter and greeted George Abbey and John Young at the bottom of the mobile stairs.

We did a short visual inspection of the orbiter, which was in great shape, and then went to the facility to meet with the doctors, take needed showers, and change clothes. Then we gathered in a reception area, greeted our spouses, and ate some great finger food. I was hungry. After I finished my food, I attempted to float over to the table to deposit my empty plate. Fortunately, Benita noticed my unusual attempt to float and grabbed the back of my shirt to keep me from falling on my face.

STS-51F crew departs Challenger after landing

We flew home to Houston in the G-2 with our spouses and entertained them with our stories on the way. Arriving from the airport at Ellington to our home in Clear Lake about 10:00 p.m., I was surprised to find all of our neighbors standing in our yard, waving little flags to welcome me home. It was great to visit with our kids and neighbors in such an unplanned, impromptu fashion.

After saying good night to our friends and neighbors, we went into our house. We visited a little more with our kids, then

I finally flopped into bed. By that point, I had been awake for almost 24 hours doing rather intense things. I was exhausted.

I was surprised that gravity was so strong. I felt like I would suffocate as gravity sucked my face into the mattress. I seemed too weak to roll over. I woke up every time that I tossed and turned over the next few nights because of the tremendous effort required to make the moves. Transitioning into zero-g and back both had their moments.

We had to go through a period of debriefing, more medical tests, and talking about everything that happened on the flight, so they could make a record of it. There were some days spent doing that. And then we had a party to celebrate our successful mission and got on with life.

At our party, we all shared our gratitude for the help given to us during the mission, and especially for the great call by Jenny Howard and Mission Control that probably saved the day. The ATO was clearly a close call, but we survived it. We completed all other aspects of the mission successfully. I felt good about how well the whole team had performed. Victory seems even sweeter when you have to overcome significant obstacles along the way.

Down to Earth

After my flight, I had many speaking engagements to show photos that we took on our mission and tell about our adventure. I was sometimes asked if I had found God in space.

I responded, "I highly recommend that a person find God before strapping into a rocket and launching." I also shared that my studies of our amazing universe pointed to a magnificent creator.

I quietly advocated for some changes in how our families were transported and supported during launches. I didn't believe that everyone should have to max out their credit card to enable their family to be at the launch. My little paper on that was greeted with hostility. But, after the Challenger catastrophe, it turns out they implemented everything I had suggested. People realized that they couldn't split up the family of the crew and send kids back home on a commercial airline, after they just lost a wife or husband or parent. They realized they had to keep these folks together and take care of them.

I had been selected for a second space mission that was scheduled to launch in less than a year. I felt a little selfish, as many of my 1980 classmates had not had a chance to fly yet. Of course, I was not going to bow out, as the opportunity to fly more was just too enticing.

Now I was ready for more.

Christmas Letter 1985

From Benita: We have enjoyed a very special year and have so much to be thankful for. Roy finally got his space flight out of his dreams and into orbit. And let me tell you about my trip to space: I was transported to the Challenger during the mission in one of the first TV pictures to be received aboard a spaceship and retransmitted to Earth.

From Roy: Benita has been in charge of everything around our house this year since I have been absent a lot (in mind and body). She has been very active as a Stephen Minister in our church and has been blessed with a unique talent for this work. She regularly walks 3 miles at 5:30 a.m. (ugh!) and plays in the local tennis league.

Tanya is an A student at Clear Lake High School. She has continued with her piano studies and is an expert with the difficult but lyrical Scott Joplin compositions. She still does aerobic dance exercise and jogging, is active in the church choir, and plans to go skiing with the youth group over the Christmas holidays. She is an excellent babysitter and has made enough money to finance her trip.

Brian is also having a good year in school. He is doing so well with tenor sax that he was selected to participate in the Christmas program orchestra. He is a Boy Scout. He would love to go skiing also this Christmas, but he will settle for a ticket to the Bluebonnet Bowl on New Year's Eve to watch a great Air Force Academy team whip up on the Longhorns of the University of Texas.

All of your letters and prayers sustained us through the special but tense time this year. God bless you in 1986.

Chapter 33: Training for STS-61F
August 1985–May 1986

When we landed STS-51F, I was within ten months of the targeted liftoff for my second mission on Challenger, STS-61F, Ulysses/Centaur. It was a complex mission with the new high-energy upper stage needed to put the spacecraft we would deploy into a polar orbit around the sun, which had never been studied before from that vantage point. Adding to the complexity, a sister mission was to launch just weeks after our launch date to put the Galileo spacecraft on the way to orbit Jupiter, using another Centaur upper stage. We had a four-person crew led by Commander Rick Hauck—navy captain, flight officer, a very, very good guy. I was the pilot. Mission Specialists Dave Hilmers and Mike Lounge rounded out the crew.

Normally the Mission Specialists trained to do any contingency Extravehicular Activities (EVA), but one of our Mission Specialists was needed inside to manage Centaur operations along with the commander for some off-nominal conditions. That meant that I would train to do an EVA should one be needed to handle an emergency. That exposed me to some exciting new training.

Our crew members were veterans of a space flight, and we got to work quickly, given the unique challenges of our mission.

One of my duties was to learn as much as possible about the Centaur and make sure that our crew procedures were adequate to handle any contingencies. I engaged with our systems engineers to develop an expert understanding of the Centaur and its integration with Challenger. Since the Centaur was still in development, a lot of new insights came to light as testing progressed. There wasn't much time to work out any problems because of the tight launch window for our flight.

Official crew photo for the STS-61F mission, which was canceled after the Challenger accident (left to right: Mike Lounge, Roy, Rick Hauck, and Dave Hilmers)

Safety issues dilemma

I was surprised at the safety issues surrounding the integration and operation of this new upper stage. After sharing the issues with the rest of the crew, we quickly surmised that we were on a combat mission with a high probability of a serious mishap. Rick raised our concerns with the Chief of the Astronaut Office, John Young.

John called our mission "Death Star." He thought that it was going to be the highest-risk mission ever flown.

John and Rick met with program officials about the risks. The management of the space shuttle program did not agree and decided to continue with Centaur.

At a meeting of the crew members, Rick told us, "NASA is doing business different from the way it was done in the past. Safety is being compromised, and if any of you want to take yourself off this flight, I will support you."

We closed the door of the office for some of these meetings with nobody but the crew in attendance. We needed to speak frankly about exactly what was going on. We were upfront with each other. We knew exactly what we were getting into.

One of our concerns was that the Centaur used liquid oxygen and liquid hydrogen as propellants. The bulkhead between the tanks was shared, meaning that any breach of the bulkhead would result in the mixing of these propellants and a catastrophic explosion. The thin-walled propellant tanks were structurally stiffened by pressurizing the tanks with helium gas under high pressure. To handle the liftoff loads, the pressure had to be increased just before launch. The mechanisms for maintaining pressure were quad-redundant sets of electromechanical relays to activate valves. We learned that these relays had a high failure rate during testing. Design engineers weren't that concerned because similar shared bulkheads had been used in other rockets.

We weren't as confident.

There was no emergency egress capability for the crew of the shuttle should there be a catastrophic event. There probably wouldn't be enough time to activate one even if we had it.

Another safety concern was the ability to dump the propellants should we have an ascent abort or on-orbit abort that would precede the release of the Centaur. I worked with the engineers to make sure that our procedures were adequate for these emergencies. Testing and engineering calculations suggested that there would be a high probability of a less-than-complete dump of the hydrogen tank during a Return to Launch Site (RTLS) or Transoceanic Abort Landing (TAL), which would present the real possibility of an explosion in the payload bay after landing at the abort site.

For an on-orbit abort requiring a Centaur dump, engineers calculated that the dump would result in spinning the shuttle because the oxygen and hydrogen dump ports were on opposite sides of the shuttle, with some impingement on the wings. This would torque the shuttle into a roll, and we would have to use our attitude-control jets to stop the roll. Unfortunately, that would deplete our attitude-control fuel needed for entry.

As a crew we all recognized the importance of the mission from a scientific point of view. NASA had committed the shuttle to perform all needed military and science missions, and all expendable vehicles had been sidelined. The program managers were under tremendous pressure from a lot of different directions; they were not going to be able to meet the schedule for some of these national security payloads. If they killed the Centaur, that would mean a slip of years to get something else that would be capable of doing this job.

Combat mission

We determined that we could probably be successful, despite the chances of failure, with all hands on deck in Mission Control and on board; however, we did not regard the Centaur as a good match for the needs going forward. Given these design characteristics, there would never be a "routine" Centaur mission.

Yes, this was going to be a combat mission.

Given the nature of this mission, it was appropriate that I deepen my spiritual journey.

Benita had attended a Bible study called Bible Study Fellowship for several years. She encouraged me to attend, and I began to attend weekly sessions in Houston. I invited a neighbor and astronaut classmate to go with me. The course was comprehensive. I enjoyed it, and it helped me grow spiritually by gaining new insights from the scriptures on how to live my life more consistently with my beliefs. I didn't do it out of fear, as I had already faced death many times during my aviation and astronaut career and had come to terms about the risks in my chosen career.

Benita had shared with me her strong feelings that I would survive my space mission, just as she knew that I would return from the war in Vietnam. Her faith led her to that conclusion. It helped her to share in the preparation and execution of my mission with the same awe and wonder as I felt, rather than being lost in anxiety.

Disaster

On January 28, 1986, the date of the STS-51L launch of Challenger, I was representing the STS-61F/Ulysses Centaur crew at an Ascent Flight Rules meeting. We were developing the rules that would guide us in the event of any emergency during ascent. Obviously, the main topic was how to handle any contingencies involving an ascent abort and a Centaur dump.

During the meeting, we took a break to watch the launch of Challenger.

Like the rest of the country, we were stunned and horrified when the Challenger exploded on its way to orbit, killing all on board.

It was deathly quiet in the room. Nobody said anything.

Everybody knew exactly what had happened and what the results were going to be: there were not going to be any survivors. This was going to be the blackest of black days for everyone concerned. Not just in that room, but the whole Center, and the other centers that were involved in the shuttle program.

This was the worst.

The meeting never resumed. We all quietly left and communicated with our family members about the tragedy. This was a life-changing event for everyone in the Astronaut Office.

The human costs

And it was terrible for my wife before I got home. There were reporters knocking at our door. The pilot on this flight, Mike Smith, lived only a couple of blocks away. He and I had been officemates for a while; we spent a lot of time together.

We were close.

At home that night, I gathered my family in a group hug in the kitchen. I tearfully said that I wanted to stay in the program and help get the shuttle back in flight again. Benita, Tanya, and Brian all voiced their support. We were committed as a family to that quest.

We all grieved the loss of our friends on the Challenger. My wife and many others volunteered to help the families of the Challenger crew respond to the many letters of condolence that they received.

As we worked to return to flight, there were a lot of concerns about what needed to change with the shuttle and how we operated it. The Challenger Accident Board concluded that the O-ring in the Solid Rocket Booster (SRB) had failed, resulting in hot gas entering a joint in the SRB and causing it to fail structurally. The O-ring stiffened because the extremely cold temperature on the day of the launch prevented it from functioning as designed.

Data revealed that some partial failures had occurred on previous launches, but nothing was done about it. Although the Astronaut Office was informed and consulted on many potential shuttle safety issues in these early days of operations, we were stunned that no one in the office was aware of the series of partial O-ring failures.

After the funerals, everyone in the office focused on the return-to-flight efforts. Our STS-61F crew members all committed to assuring that our concerns with the Centaur were addressed satisfactorily.

It would be a year or two before another shuttle would be launched; we had time.

Fate comes calling in Arizona—again

I was sitting at my desk one day a few weeks later, working on a briefing that I was preparing on our Centaur concerns. I got a phone call from the Military Personnel Center. They talked at length about a new position that they wanted me to take as Wing Commander for the 6510th Test Wing at Edwards AFB, California. They spelled out the number of aircraft and test programs that would be under my command as well as several locations that would be under my charge.

I said, "My name is Roy Bridges. Are you sure that you have the right person?"

They responded affirmatively.

I said, "I am flattered to be offered such a position but cannot accept it. I am extremely busy assisting the Astronaut Office in the return-to-flight activities. I cannot desert my duties to take a plum job."

That night I informed my family. We did another standing group hug. My family expressed their support for me to stay at the Johnson Space Center and fly a future shuttle mission. "Dad, we want you to stay and fly again," said my daughter. I was moved to tears.

I continued to deflect calls from the Military Personnel Center on this subject over the coming weeks. Each time I said, "No."

At spring break from school, Benita and I took the kids to visit her parents in Tucson, Arizona. While there, I got a call from Admiral Truly. He was an astronaut who had recently been reassigned to NASA Headquarters as the Associate Administrator for Space Flight and would eventually become the NASA Administrator.

I was outside, painting my kids' grandparents' home. I'd rented a paint gun and scaffolding, and I was out there when this call came in. I had to get down and go in and talk to him. I didn't even know how he found me.

"Roy," he said, "I was at a social function last night, and this four-star air force general took a bite out of my butt. He said, 'You've got a hundred astronauts and no shuttles to fly for years. I just want this one officer, Roy Bridges, to be my Wing Commander at Edwards AFB.'"

Truly continued, "That is going to be a fun job. Why don't you get yourself out to Edwards AFB? Do that job for a couple of years. If you want to get back in line for a shuttle flight, I'll make it happen."

I said, "Okay sir, I'll pack my bags."

My fate was sealed.

Given my rank as Colonel and my age—43—it would be unlikely that I would be able to secure a future flight, given all the people who would be in line in front of me. And turning down the chance to be the Wing Commander at a place I loved? I couldn't do that, either. There were many talented astronauts in the office, and they would do a fine job of getting the shuttle back in flight. Time to move on.

That is how I found myself at a change of command ceremony at Edwards AFB in May of 1986.

The "Death Star" mission was initially delayed after Challenger instead of being cancelled. On May 22, 1986, Rick Hauck briefed the program again about the risks of flying with the Centaur. On June 19, 1986, the concerns were presented to the NASA Administrator, and the Centaur program was cancelled. A high-energy solid-propellant upper stage was eventually used to propel Ulysses into solar orbit from the shuttle. It launched on October 6, 1990.

Christmas Letter 1986 Excerpts

Edwards AFB, California

7 Dec.—the 45th anniversary of Pearl Harbor—coincidentally the morning I began this annual summary of our family's odyssey. Looking back, one can see that the worlds of 6 Dec and 9 Dec. 1941 were separated by a chasm in time, not just a day . . . 28 Jan. '86—a chasm in time for our little world—the world of space explorers. Your heartfelt prayers for us were much needed that day and in those following as we all tried to come to grips with our deep grief.

11 Apr.—It's official. We're moving. The commander of Systems Command has decided to recall Roy to the air force involuntarily. The good news is that his new command is a good one—commander of the test wing at Edwards AFB. Life has been rich in Houston, and a large part of our hearts will live there forever with our friends who continue with the shuttle program, our church, and our neighbors. But now it's time to look ahead.

May—Tanya does well in a Texas state music competition. Brian becomes a First Class Scout.

Late June/July—Roy returns to help with move, and 1 July we hit the road with two birds and a cat. The cat tries to get the bird and is banished to the other car. Visits overnight with friends in three cities were great and made the long trip so much more pleasant. Edwards...Desert Villa transient quarters. Better than they were in 1970, but.... We narrowly missed having a blowout on the front wheel of the car Tanya was driving. We are all thankful for the safe trip.

August—House is finally ready. Shopping here is a pain. The nearest town is 30 miles away and small. LA is 80-150 miles —it's big!!! School starts. Tanya is a junior, will take a college-level music class at the local junior college and accompany both junior and senior high choirs on piano. Brian is in 7th grade and will play tenor sax in the marching band.

November—Everybody but Roy travels to Tucson for Thanksgiving. Roy has to stay home and present 24 debutantes at a ball. (Nobody told me about this piece of work when I signed on!)

December—After Christmas, Benita and Roy took off for a two-day "fourth honeymoon" in San Diego at the restored Hotel Del Coronado!

Book 3: Leadership

Section 1: USAF Command & Staff

**Chapter 34: Commander, 6510th Test Wing
at Edwards AFB CA**
May 1986–March 1989

Some people achieve their dream relatively early in life—Olympic gold medalists, Football Hall of Famers—and end up having to reinvent themselves. I would have been happy remaining an astronaut until they kicked me out for old age. But that wasn't to be. My first post-dream reinvention was going back and trying to figure out how to be a commander at Edwards AFB.

Having left Edwards in 1975 as a new major, I was as surprised as anyone that I would return as the Test Wing Commander. I thought that maybe I would enjoy being the boss, but it was going to take a lot of adjustment from my previous jobs of doing my individual duties to the best of my ability.

Soul-searching

Reflecting on this sudden turn from my dream job of being an astronaut to something that I had never aspired to be brought a flood of thoughts. Could I do all that was needed as the leader of a large organization to help them be successful?

To me, the essence of leadership is this: As your people are getting the work done, what is the biggest challenge facing them that they can't do? That's the thing that I need to take on. So I tried to look for those big rocks in the road that maybe other people couldn't see yet, and tackle those, rather than micromanaging really good people doing really good work every day.

Given how few people had ever orbited the Earth, how many times did I have to fly to space to be satisfied? My goal had been several times. Could I be happy with just one exciting mission?

It occurred to me that USAF leaders at the four-star level had handpicked me to lead the USAF's largest flight test wing. I wondered why I was singled out of a large group of highly qualified officers for that plum job, especially since I had never lobbied anyone for it. Could I get past my disappointment and give it my best? After all, the nation was trying to win a multi-generational cold war with the Soviet Union. Our airmen needed the best warplanes in the world to win it, and I could help make that happen.

At the time, I had never considered attaining a higher rank to be on my dream list. This position was a stepping-stone to becoming a general officer. Since that wasn't on my bucket list, could I step up and do that well?

Eventually, I settled this internal debate by remembering my granddaddy's advice: Do your duty and work hard to do it well. That advice had helped me be an "improbable astronaut" and pilot the Space Shuttle Challenger on a great mission. It was time to savor the success of my prior achievements, accept this turn of events, and do it to the best of my ability. If the unit succeeded, I could be happy with my contribution and not look back.

Challenges and joys

The position proved to have unique challenges. First and foremost of them was figuring out how to build up the capability of the wing in response to President Reagan's defense buildup. We had more mission than capability, with much more to come. At the Flight Test Center level, there was a process called Countdown to outline the increases that we would need to field to handle the present and coming workload. How many more control rooms and test pilots we would need were just two of dozens of items on the needs list. I personally worked with other members of the wing to identify test pilots who would be eligible to return to Edwards over the next few years and began a personal recruitment campaign. We were successful and managed to staff up for the coming challenges.

The Flight Test Center Commander was Major General Ted Twinting. He had held the position of Wing Commander earlier in his career and had definite ideas about how I should command the wing. He felt that I should be able to figure it out on my own, so his technique was to not tell me what to do but to increase the pressure on me until I arrived at the same answer that he would have selected. This made life difficult, to say the least.

Things were also tough for my wife. We had been out of the air force base structure since 1975, so all of a sudden being the Wing Commander's wife was somewhat of a shock, complete with new challenges. Being a leader for the Wives' Club was just one example. Some of the other colonels' wives seemed jealous and argumentative. She hung in there and made lifelong friends before our tour ended.

One consolation for me was being able to continue to fly. I was checked out in the F-15 and worked with the F-15 Combined Test Force (CTF) on occasion to assist with test and chase duties. In addition to it being a real Cadillac of a fighter airplane, it was also excellent as a cross-country vehicle. I had to visit other units in the wing, such as the test squadron in Utah that operated the Utah Test and Training Range (UTTR) and performed tests on drones. Flying the F-15 was one of the joys of command. No matter how tough things were, my spirits soared during every flight.

Leadership: Decision and discipline, risk and reward, trial and tribulation

The days began early with "rounds" to the test squadrons and CTFs at 0630 every morning to be briefed on all the test missions that were on the schedule for that day, with an emphasis on any that were categorized as hazardous. For that category, I got a full briefing on the tests as well as actions that were planned to mitigate the hazards. At the end of every day, we had a stand-up briefing to the Center Commander on the results of the day and plans for the next. Over time, I became an expert at the workings of the wing. All of my CTF commanders and squadron commanders felt a mutual respect for each other.

One day on rounds, I was briefed on an F-16 hazardous test mission. They planned to do a low-altitude structural loads test over the ocean. The test would result in nine g's. The engineers wanted them to perform the test using a descending turn so that the airspeed could be maintained.

"No," I said. "You will do a pull-up maneuver."

I'd learned from my mom and grandfather that testing boundaries was fine, but learning to do it safely was important.

The pilot passed out doing the maneuver and woke up passing 17,000 feet. Had I not insisted on a lower-risk maneuver, he would have died.

There were opportunities for me to fly a test mission with one of the test forces to observe them in action. When the B-1 was ready to begin night low-level tests (tests very close to the ground), I was tasked by the Center Commander to fly on a daytime mission with them while they were under the hood to certify their ability to do the night tests safely. I sat in the center seat in the B-1's cockpit and observed the crew fly at 540 knots at 200 feet through the rugged terrain of the Mojave Desert and foothills of the mountains. They performed in an excellent manner, and I certified them as ready to begin the hazardous night missions.

Another time, I was flying in a helicopter on the UTTR, snagging a drone with a special rig, reeling it in, and returning it to base safely. I also flew an early test mission on the new F-15E Strike Eagle as well as sorties in the F-16 and other aircraft to observe the progress in developing new capabilities.

One of my F-16 missions was flying at low altitude through the mountains near Edwards to test a new night-vision system. It turned night into day on the Heads Up Display. What an amazing capability. It would have made a huge difference in our ability to interdict truck traffic at night in North Vietnam.

An additional interesting set of missions was to fly chase on cruise missile tests, either launched from land on the range, dropped from bombers, or fired from submarines off the coast, and fly with them to targets on the UTTR to assure no danger to other traffic. These were long missions requiring a lot of attention to detail, and the wing performed them well.

The most difficult situations were the accidents, particularly those involving the loss of life. The worst of these was a midair collision between a T-38 and a civilian aircraft doing air-to-ground photography of roads in the nearby area, which killed the four people onboard—two in each aircraft.

In this case, my wife and I had to find the visiting fiancée of the pilot and break the news to her. We learned that she was staying at a hotel in Lancaster, so we set out to find her. On the way to Lancaster, we spotted her car heading to Edwards. We turned around and met her just as she arrived at the test facility to pick up her soon-to-be husband. What a wrenching and heartbreaking conversation.

The other situations involved the disciplining of pilots when they violated procedures and created unsafe situations.

One such situation involved a routine night-training sortie. Before the sortie, friends at nearby George AFB, where an exercise to simulate enemy attack was in progress, called the aircraft commander and asked him to fly a low-level pass down the runway to kick off the exercise. Unfortunately, the aircraft commander recklessly flew a little too fast, exceeded the speed of sound, and knocked the windows out of many businesses in a nearby town.

This caused a lot of excitement.

I was in an executive development program at the University of New Hampshire when I got the call about, *Oh my God, what have they done now?!?* And I'm going to be out of town for another week or two, so people want me to tell them *what are we going to do?*

After the investigation was completed, I had the unhappy duty of establishing a flying evaluation board to remove the wings of the aircraft commander. Needless to say, this was an unpopular exercise for fellow pilots, but it had to be done to assure that we acted professionally at all times when in flight.

I always tried to be fair when exercising my duty to discipline pilots who committed unprofessional acts, and these incidents were rare.

For example, my investigation of the incident above showed that the pilot in the rear seat, a junior pilot to the aircraft commander, had no role in the unfortunate incident other than being aboard when it happened. He was an exceptionally gifted junior officer. Later in his tour, I asked the Center Commander to endorse his performance report with a top rating. The general called me to his office and said that my recommendation was noted, but he rated the person as someone who, with additional training, might be qualified for his current rank.

His recommendation would prevent the officer from ever being promoted again.

Fortunately, the incident had occurred in the previous report period by a slim margin. Although I knew that, I didn't object to the recommendation. Several years later, the officer appealed that performance rating, and I was able to point out that the incident occurred outside the period of performance and got it removed from his record. The person eventually became a colonel and a NASA astronaut.

One memorable moment in my tour as Commander was welcoming the crew of the Space Shuttle Discovery when they landed at Edwards AFB on the Return to Flight Mission, the first mission after Challenger, on October 3, 1988. The crew was the same as my STS-61F crew except that Dick Covey had replaced me as the pilot, and Pinky Nelson was added as a mission specialist to increase the crew size to five. The crew presented me with a memento—a crew photo and photographic montage of their mission. They inserted a photo of me in my air force uniform into the crew photo. I was honored.

Summing up the trials and tribulations of wing command, I experienced a third accident during my tour. This was not a fatal crash, but the crash destroyed the helicopter flying a mission on the UTTR.

General Twinting called me to his office and said that I needed to check out an F-15 and configure it with external tanks so that I could fly non-stop to Andrews AFB to meet with the Commander of Air Force Systems Command (AFSC) and explain how I ran the wing.

He also said that I should pack a set of civilian attire in case they fired me on the spot and sent me home in a commercial aircraft.

With my stomach knotted up, I did as instructed. I had a set of viewgraphs explaining how I managed the wing's affairs. I met with the AFSC Commander, Vice Commander, and Deputy Chief of Staff for Test and Resources and presented them. They asked plenty of tough questions but at the end of the session allowed me to fly home in my F-15.

Welcome changes

A family event of significance occurred in 1988 with the high school graduation of our daughter, Tanya, at Desert High. She did well in school and was accepted into Austin College in Sherman, Texas. She began with the intent to be in premedical studies and go on to medical school as well as to study under a piano concert artist-in-residence to obtain a minor in music.

Near the end of my tour at Edwards AFB as the Wing Commander, General Twinting retired and a new boss, Major General John Schoeppner, took command. He had some interesting ideas about how the center should be organized and asked me to set up a study to determine the feasibility of reorganizing it. The gist of it was to reorganize the CTFs into squadrons like the rest of the air force. Instead of reporting separately to the center commander, the Aircraft Maintenance Group and Test Engineering Group would be reorganized into the wing.

At the conclusion of the study, we determined that it was feasible. After getting approval, we had a change of command ceremony for the new squadron commanders. We also changed the name of the wing to a historic counterpart, the 412th Test

Wing. The 412th Fighter Group was activated at Muroc Army Airfield CA on November 29, 1943. The dry lakebeds at Muroc were the test sites for the first jet fighter, the XP-59A, which made its first flight on October 1, 1942.

Not long after this event, the general called me to his office and asked if I would be interested in a new assignment as the Commander of the Eastern Space and Missile Center at Patrick AFB and Cape Canaveral Air Force Station in Florida.

After checking with my wife, I said, "Yes. I would be honored to lead that outstanding unit."

It would be great to be a part of our space program again. Little did I know at the time how important the assignment would become in qualifying me for future assignments to support our nation's space program.

I moved to Florida in March 1989. The family followed after the school year was over, and we moved into the commander's home in Satellite Beach.

Christmas Letter 1987

It's Beginning to Look a Lot Like Christmas
16 December 1987
Here we are at Edwards and it's snowing—already a couple of inches on the ground. Roy just left in time to make it through the mountain passes to get to LAX International for his flight to Washington DC this morning.

This past year we have been blessed with many visitors—relatives and friends. Even some childhood friendships have been re-established after more than 20 years. (Guess these Xmas letters pay off after all!)

Brian is in 8th grade, wears size 11 shoes, is taller than Benita, and will probably pass Roy up by the time this letter goes to press. Benita no longer mows the grass or rakes leaves—Brian's job and spending money. He's still playing the tenor sax.

Tanya took ceramics at AV College with Benita's old teacher (1970-71) and friend, Rich Sim. She was inducted into the National Honor Society and her piano teacher offered her the chance to teach her beginning students. The pay is sure better than minimum wage.

Tanya got busy applying to colleges. Roy helped get all those applications out and Benita saw that all the checks were included and deadlines met.

Benita spent most of her summer taking Tanya, Brian, and their friends special places all over southern California. (You know her—she refuses to grow up.) Hopefully, we will be here next summer to see the safe completion of the 26th shuttle mission with a perfect landing on our lakebed with our NASA friends.

Last week, Roy and Benita drove to Hill AFB just outside Salt Lake City to check on his troops. We made an outline for this letter as we drove home. The West is beautiful and the mountains relaxing. Benita says the mountains make her feel secure, reassured of God's presence and promises.

This Christmas will find us here at Edwards for a relaxing, safe holiday. This snow is great. There is a real live roadrunner on our patio porch, hiding from the storm. He looks like he'd like to come in. Will Roy be able to make it home Friday and back to DC on Monday and return in time for Christmas??

Chapter 35: Commander, Eastern Space and Missile Center at Patrick AFB FL

March 1989–January 1990

Patrick AFB is located in Cocoa Beach, which is on a barrier island on the Atlantic Ocean. The area is spectacularly beautiful. I settled into my one-bedroom guest quarters temporarily while our base house was being renovated. After finding my way to the office, I learned of some complications that would occupy me almost full time in the coming months.

We were halfway through the fiscal year and did not have enough funding remaining to complete the year without drastic action. My new boss informed me that the previous commander had been fired because he threatened to close the range in August as leverage to obtain additional funding.

He advised me to select a different approach.

I'd done everything I could do at Edwards. I thought I'd done well enough to get promoted, but I had not been promoted, so I'd kind of given up on that. And when the boss said, "Hey, would you like to have this new command assignment, launching rockets?" all I could think was, "What? Are you kidding me? I would take an assignment launching firecrackers."

And then I got down there and found out that the guy who preceded me got fired because he didn't have enough money to keep the range running the rest of the year. What??

On the plus side, I found the command and community to be welcoming, which was nice. One immediate problem threatened that relationship. Prior to my arrival, a lot of palm trees had been planted to replace losses over the years from storms and other natural circumstances. They were dying because of a lack of water. People driving by the base on the main coast highway could easily see the distress and were complaining. I ordered them watered regularly to avoid a "Palm Tree Gate" scandal.

Why the previous commander had used money to plant palm trees was a mystery, given the dire situation with the budget. No wonder he was fired.

Range safety and other responsibilities

The mission at Patrick was to operate the Eastern Space and Missile Center (ESMC). ESMC supported all space launches from Cape Canaveral Air Force Station and the infrastructure located there. We also supported NASA's Kennedy Space Center for space shuttle launches and landings and navy launches of Trident missiles from submarines off the coast.

The range had tracking radars and telemetry receivers that were used to determine that launch vehicles were on proper trajectories and were healthy. Range safety officers were empowered to destroy any vehicle that was off course and a threat to the launch site or downrange areas, using range safety transmitters that set off explosive charges on the boosters.

That was an especially sensitive function for NASA's space shuttle launches with human crews on board. We had a Range

Safety Office, which was run by some people who were conscientious about planning for this unthinkable scenario in minute detail, preferably by doing everything possible to prevent it. But getting that plan approved, particularly for a new vehicle, could be tedious. People hated my Range Safety Office, because they put them through their paces to make sure that everything was going to work. The Range Safety Office never wanted to have to destroy a vehicle. So they scrupulously analyzed the overall safety of each and every operation.

The range had sophisticated weather forecasting capabilities to assure that launch site and upper altitude winds and weather on the planned trajectory were safe. This area of Florida is known as the lightning capital of the world, which was a threat to both personnel and launch vehicles.

Downrange sites on the islands of Antigua and Ascension tracked the rockets when they went out of sight at the Cape. Ascension Island is just south of the equator in the Atlantic, approximately halfway between Brazil and Africa. It is administered as part of the UK's overseas territory of St. Helena Island. We had support contractors manning these downrange support sites with regular military transport flights to provide supplies, replacement equipment, and personnel support. I visited each of the sites and found them fascinating.

I was also the only air force officer with responsibility for a ship, the USNS Redstone, which was a tracking ship in use since the Apollo program.

In addition to running the range, ESMC also operated and maintained the launch and payload-processing facilities for the Titan, Delta, and Atlas launch vehicles.

Reviving the budget

We had a busy launch schedule, hence the sensitivity over the threat of a shutdown because of budget problems. I convened my leaders, and we developed a plan to make it to the end of the year without shutting down the range.

It was March, and we didn't have enough money, given our current commitments, to operate until the end of our fiscal year, September 30. No new money was going to come in, and we couldn't shut the range down. We needed to find some way to free up money to do the things that absolutely had to happen. So we were identifying anything discretionary and not spending money on it.

The easiest things to identify were the minor construction projects—where we had planned to contract something out and hire a contractor to do it. We set those aside. Then we eliminated stocking extra inventory ahead of time. Unless it was a critical part, we were not going to keep it in the warehouse. We kept a list of what we weren't buying and let people know that at the end of the year, if we had some money, we would put in an order to get them back up to where they should be.

Although complex in its full detail, in essence it was fairly simple: delay the purchase of anything we didn't need right now. Since our support contractor did a lot of these purchases and activities on our behalf, I discovered rather quickly that supervisors from our air force warehouse, as well as civil engineering supervisors, were threatening them with low award fee evaluations if they delayed purchases for them, because they were getting complaints about the understocked shelves. The terms of the support contract specified that they were to be graded at the end of every year. Basically, they had a scorecard. People like the supply warehouse guy would give them a score for how well they kept his warehouse supplied. The only way the contractors got paid was through the awards fee. With a low score, they would lose money—they could even lose their contract.

So what we had to do was to get everyone on board. Hey, look, guys, we can't buy that right now. Because it could mean that launch that's supposed to go off in September is going to be delayed, and then we're screwed. Or we run out of money and we go to jail because we're spending money we don't have—that's a violation of the Antideficiency Act, and it's a criminal offense.

I worked with both sides. I communicated with my people, explaining our plans in more detail to encourage their full support and to make sure that they understood that their people needed to quit threatening the contractors.

Then I called a meeting with the support contractor leader to win his confidence and support so he could get his people on board. I said, "Yeah, I know, you're getting all these little threats for low-level stuff. But let me let you know: if we run out of money, you ain't getting *any* award fee. You got that?"

Once everyone was on the same page, we put together a list of purchases and contractual actions that we fully prepared and put on the shelf. In the last days of the fiscal year, some commands were not able to use all of their funding. That excess funding was advertised and made available to others who had immediate needs and could obligate the funds before the end of the year.

Who knew that the budgeting skills I learned in high school would come in so handy?

Bottom line: we made out like bandits. We got our entire wish list funded in the last days.

To celebrate our victory, Benita and I hosted a "get out of jail" dinner party. We wore black-and-white striped outfits and had a bread centerpiece made for the table that was crafted into a ball and chain.

I also visited with the general in charge of the Air Force Systems Command financial community to assure that he had a full understanding of the root cause that had led to the budget shortfall. We reached an agreement on the funding needs going forward so that the situation would not reoccur. The future looked much brighter.

Scuba and surprises

During the summer vacation from school, I signed up Tanya, Brian, and myself for a scuba diving certification course. I had thoroughly enjoyed scuba diving at the USAFA and wanted them to have an opportunity to try it. After we completed the academics and pool training, we went on an open ocean dive off the coast of Palm Beach and had fun.

Later in the summer, after Tanya had returned to college, Brian and I completed an advanced course where we learned undersea navigation and went on a night dive again off the coast of Palm Beach. That was a special experience for both of us. The colors of the fish and coral formations were much brighter and more colorful when they were illuminated with our flashlights than in the ambient daytime illumination.

I was surprised to get a call from the Commander of the Air Force Space and Missile Center in December 1989. He congratulated me on how we had solved the budget issues and how well that we had performed during the year. He followed those kind words with a big surprise announcement: I was on the promotion list for Brigadier General.

That was the good news.

The bad news was an order to move to Andrews AFB, Maryland, in January to take on a new position as the Air Force Systems Command Deputy Chief of Staff for Test and Resources.

I was going to miss the excitement of running ESMC, where I participated in leading the busiest launch command in the nation and got to do things like ride in a nuclear missile submarine for a test missile launch and visit our people at such exotic places as Ascension Island. We would also miss the many friends that we had made in the community.

Maybe we would get to return someday.

Christmas Letter snippets 1989

Greetings from Florida 1989

It is the night before Thanksgiving and suddenly we have much more for which to be thankful. We just watched some of our dearest friends successfully go to Earth orbit aboard Discovery, STS-33. It was a night launch, and a spectacular one. Roy was in the Range Control Center, on duty, watching over the crew: Fred Gregory, John Blaha, Kathy Thornton, and Story Musgrave. Brian and I were at the viewing site with their friends and relatives. This part of our new assignment at Patrick AFB, Florida, is the most enjoyable.

Brian misses his special best friends at Edwards. The scuba diving is great, though! Tanya, Brian, and Roy are now certified divers. We all miss the mountains and the snow skiing as winter approaches. This has been a topsy-turvy year.

During spring break for Tanya and Brian, we all drove to Florida with Roy for his Change of Command, visited my folks in Tucson, and picked up Tanya as we traveled through Texas. Tanya and Brian were soon playing in the warm waters of the Atlantic Ocean in March—another nice feature of this place.

We left Roy at Patrick AFB, Florida, where he launched right into being Center Commander of the Air Force's Eastern Space and Missile Center, and we went back to Edwards/college until late June. I returned to my favorite, tho' temporary, job at the Palmdale City Library, and worked until we moved. Roy, conveniently busy launching rockets, left us to pack up the house and drive to Florida again. I-10 is a long road and we know it well.

We're relaxing in the base's beach house this weekend. Those waves make a nice, relaxing noise. We hope next year is more stable—but probably not—the A.F. keeps us guessing.

Chapter 36: Air Force Systems Command Staff at Andrews AFB MD
January 1990–August 1991

Tanya was in college, but we would have to move Brian in the middle of the school year to a new school in Maryland. I tried to talk him into letting us register him in a private school because I was concerned about the quality of the public school that he would attend, but he adamantly refused. After the change of command at Patrick AFB in January 1990, Brian and I drove to Maryland to get him into his new school. Benita stayed behind to supervise the packing of our household for the move to a home on Andrews AFB.

Reinvention: from Commander to Deputy Chief of Staff

My dad demonstrated remarkable resilience through his long lifetime, reinventing himself again and again while staying deeply devoted to his family. I am grateful to have learned from his example—and I needed it, time and time again.

I already knew from experience that being a commander was a better fit with my personality. It would allow me to make a larger impact on an organization and would be more fulfilling than being in a staff position. I would just have to evolve to handle it. Another reinvention was required.

My new position as Deputy Chief of Staff for Test and Resources had a broad range of responsibilities. These included organizations for test, manpower, logistics, and civil engineering. As I had to reinvent myself to take on these responsibilities, I would also need to steer the reinvention of those under my command.

The Cold War was winding down. The air force leaders knew that budget cuts were on the horizon. They wanted the majority of those to come from the tail rather than the spear. We were clearly in the tail as an organization responsible for acquiring new weapon systems rather than operating them.

Some thought that we were too fat. They saw the problem as a zero-sum game.

I had to travel often to the Pentagon for meetings with high-ranking officers and civilians to explain our progress and problems in meeting their objectives. Everyone on my staff felt the pressure to perform miracles to achieve savings. I had a senior lieutenant colonel break into sobs in my office because of the pressure that we were facing on a daily basis.

One example of the pressure was a sudden initiative by the Department of Defense (DOD) to put the laboratory and test agencies from all the military services—air force, navy, and so on—into a new defense agency. I was given orders by my boss, the four-star commander of AFSC, to find an alternative, as the impact on our effectiveness would be too significant.

I began meeting with my counterparts in the other services and with a group of DOD leaders who were forming the new agency. There was a trust issue among the services about getting their testing or laboratory work from some other service. We came up with a counterproposal and offered it to the DOD senior leaders. The essence of it was to create a joint service process that we called "Reliance." It involved a service relying on the test capabilities of another service and eliminating duplicate capabilities to reduce the budget. After some extensive maneuvering, the concept was accepted in lieu of the proposed new DOD agency. Now we had to deliver a working process and some near-term results.

RELIANCE

My staff and I took the lead in producing a workable set of procedures. We established a joint team to flesh them out. I was the air force voting representative on a joint service group called the Joint Group-Test and Evaluation. I took the concept and procedure to them and asked them to take ownership of the process. My Reliance staff, supplemented by a member from each of the other services, would train study teams and manage day-to-day execution of this effort.

My concept was accepted, and we began a series of technical benchmarking studies at the affected ranges to decide which service would become the lead service in each Reliance category. My Reliance staff trained each of the teams and facilitated the review and approval of the study results through the joint group to the top level of DOD's test organization. Everything had to also be approved by headquarters.

As you might imagine, this was an emotional set of studies.

Results were to be audited at the DOD and Congressional levels. The services were expected to return savings to their headquarters.

While this was to take place over several years, we were under intense pressure to produce early successes. I personally negotiated with each of our air force–affected ranges and each of the other services to deliver some successful early win-wins. I narrowed down the candidates to the air force organization responsible for the ground testing of turbine engines and developed a proposal that we took to the navy. We recommended that the navy consolidate turbine engine testing at Arnold AFB, Tennessee.

It took a lot of work on a person-to-person basis to convince the heads of these operations and bring them to the conclusion that, "Oh, well, sure. I'll just do all my jet engine testing at your place and I'll close my place. I'll give the money back to the navy." Some people would lose their jobs. Some people would have to move from New Jersey to Tennessee. You can imagine how emotional all these changes might be for somebody who's kind of attached to his facility.

Fortunately, the facility in Tennessee was much newer and had a good reputation. The navy was struggling with their jet engine test facility because it had been around a long time; it needed a lot of work. It was tough getting them to trust us that this was going to work for them. But after much discussion and inspection of facilities and capabilities, the navy accepted the proposal and eventually closed their facility. We added the navy's logo to the sign at the front gate and accepted a senior navy officer as Deputy Commander of what now became a joint facility for this function.

This was a huge early success for Reliance, but it was not easy. It was not enough to satisfy the critics of service test duplication, but it was a concrete, major victory.

Standardized studies led to new relationships among senior service test personnel. These relationships led to a period of much better cooperation. Cooperation led to increased understanding. Understanding led to additional Reliance successes for sled tracks, environmental chambers, chemical and biological warfare, and more.

Complicated reorganization

Another tough nut to crack was my appointment as the co-chair of an executive steering group charged with reaching an acceptable agreement to transfer command authority of the

AFSC launch and range complex at Cape Canaveral Air Force Station and Patrick AFB in Florida and the units of the west coast launch and range complex at Vandenberg AFB, California. Authority for all of them would move to the relatively new Air Force Space Command (AFSPC) at Peterson AFB in Colorado. The commanders would now report to the AFSPC instead of to the Air Force Systems Command (AFSC). Giving Space Command the launch ranges would be a logical move on the surface, but there were complications.

The steering group was composed of general officers from Systems Command, Space Command, the Space and Missile Center, and the Special Projects Office. The commanders as well as the Assistant Secretary of the Air Force for Space chartered our group. We were given a short time to complete the task.

As a former commander of the Eastern Space and Missile Center (ESMC), this was an emotional undertaking for me—this was my former launch command being transferred to another command. It was a big technical challenge as well.

My concern was: How could we split the responsibility for manufacturing and launching spacecraft without breaking the process? The contracts to get the spacecraft built had been written by the Systems Command. Part of that responsibility was being given to a separate command. Since the manufacturing process was being completed on the launch pad at that time, this transition made it a little dicey: Once a spacecraft shows up at the launch site, who's really in charge? With part of the authority changing hands, how could we avoid a conflict of ownership during the transition?

I suggested a breakthrough technique based on my experience in the aircraft flight test community, where we used the concept of a Combined Test Force (CTF). There, the CTF consisted of a prime contractor and two government teams in separate commands all working together with one leader toward a common objective. In the CTF, work moved from an initial intensive prime contractor developmental test effort, to a government developmental test team, and finally to a government operational test team.

I advocated the use of this concept to transition over time from the current arrangement under Systems Command to a final arrangement under Space Command. We also advocated for a payload mission director who would have the final veto for launch as well as insight into the total process that supported it. When the spacecraft shows up at the launch site and is getting ready to be integrated onto the launch vehicle, we wanted the contractor working under contract with Systems Command to be in charge of completing the checkout and integration of the spacecraft with the launch vehicle. All we wanted Space Command to do was give us access to the pad, and all the machinery that we needed in order to get the spacecraft checked out and integrated onto the launch vehicle. Once that was done, the Space Command launch team would provide launch services.

This concept and detailed plans for the transition were eventually accepted and the transfer was completed. My co-chair and I did a lot of work building trust and cooperation at many levels in the two commands and in the classified space community to make this happen.

Today, everyone considers the resulting transfer a great success. In the air force, operational commands are in a better position to advocate for requirements and resources. Moving the launch ranges from a research and development command to an operational command helped to secure top-level support for needed modernization and upgrades. It also gave Space Command much greater insight into requirements for improved spacecraft and launch vehicles. We took an important first step toward a Space Force for all of DOD, which is now a reality.

To close or not to close?

Another sticky problem was pressure from many to close the AFSC base in Los Angeles, which hosted the Space and Missile Center (SMC), and move it to Kirtland AFB in Albuquerque, New Mexico, which was underutilized. Given the high cost of living in Los Angeles, it was difficult for SMC to attract and retain a significant number of junior military officers; consequently, SMC was supported by a large number of expensive contractors. I put together a team to see how we could make this happen.

I worked closely with the commander of SMC, a three-star general, and the Air Force Director of Special Projects, a two-star general, who was also located in Los Angeles. Once when the two were visiting AFSC Headquarters at Andrews AFB, they dropped by my office for an update. When the time came for their transport to leave, we were still deep in important negotiations. We would lose too much ground if we were interrupted at that crucial point. On the spur of the moment I decided to go with them and continue discussing the issue during their flight to California. This was difficult for me. I would have to fly across the country, from Maryland to Los Angeles and back, and return home late at night, to avoid destroying my busy schedule for the following day. But I desperately needed them to understand what had to be done to bring this thing to a conclusion, because it was driving me crazy. There were people in Washington, DC, saying, "Get that damn base in California closed," and two California generals predicting their—and my—imminent demise if we closed it. This needed to be decided, and fast.

Ultimately, the move never happened. We convinced the Pentagon that the cost, both financial and in the loss of brain-power, would be too high. Our progress in space would have suffered.

Brigadier General

In the midst of this work, I learned a few days in advance that I would be promoted to general in July 1990. My boss, General Ron Yates, would be officiating. He and Benita pinned on my stars. My parents attended along with the rest of the family.

It was a great day. I never aspired to be a general officer, but getting such a coveted promotion felt great and would allow me to contribute more to the air force that had done so much to help me achieve my dream of flying in space. My parents had so enjoyed my time at NASA, as it gave them a lot of recognition in their community. They were not happy when I went back to the air force, but my promotion helped them overcome their disappointment. They were beaming with pride as they watched the ceremony. Benita and my kids were thrilled as well.

To add to our workload, the US went on a war footing after Iraq invaded and occupied Kuwait in August of 1990. While troops from AFSC weren't likely to be deployed, we did have a lot of things in development and test that the operational commands wanted completed right now. In some cases, we would need to deploy a limited number of logistics personnel and engineers to support these efforts. We set up a command post to stay in touch with everything that was going on and to organize any required support.

The air war began on January 17, 1991, with attacks on Iraqi forces and facilities in Iraq and Kuwait. The ground war began on February 24 and concluded with President Bush calling a ceasefire on February 28 after the Iraqi army was defeated. Our troops and our allies performed superbly. The F-117 was a significant factor in reducing our potential losses and limiting the ground war to four days.

Volunteering and family activity

Until the war was over, Benita monitored CNN around the clock at our house. When injured service personnel were airlifted back to the US, many of them were routed through Andrews AFB. The base turned an indoor tennis complex into a field hospital, which was named the 10th Aeromedical Support Facility. Benita had been active as a Red Cross volunteer at Edwards AFB and jumped into action to support the facility and its work.

She met most of the transports to greet our returning injured servicemen and servicewomen. Many of them arrived in the middle of the night. Then she made rounds at the hospital to help with connections to family and arrange help when needed. She solicited donations for flowers and treats to help them feel special. She transported injured troops for trips to the Base Exchange in her car. She was passionate about making sure they were well cared for and had a shoulder to lean on.

Brian adjusted to his new school well and made a lot of friends. We had a recreation room in the basement along with his bedroom. He often had friends over. He also started working at the local Burger King during the summer. Tanya continued to do well in college. She stayed with us for summer vacation and took a summer course in physics at Georgetown University.

During the winter, we traveled to ski resorts in Virginia, West Virginia, and Pennsylvania. When one planned trip during spring break was rained out, I quickly arranged for round trip tickets to Salt Lake City for Brian and me for a long weekend of skiing at several of the nearby ski areas. We stayed in inexpensive military guest lodging at Hill AFB and had a great time.

As the workload continued unabated to do even more to help the air force reduce its "tail," my boss informed me that the chief of staff and secretary of the air force had made a decision to merge AFSC with the Air Force Logistics Command (AFLC) at Wright-Patterson AFB, Ohio. The new headquarters would be in Ohio. He formed working groups and joint sessions of the staffs and installation commanders in the two commands to organize the new command, develop a detailed plan for the staff organization of the new headquarters, and detail the resources to support each of the staff units. In the new command, the several directorates under me would become separate organizations that would be merged with similar organizations in AFLC. With several units in my organization affected, and given the difference in duties and cultures, I had to work hard to protect the important work going forward.

The dark before the dawn

At some point in the summer of 1991, I reached a low point in my career. The unrelenting workload was the primary cause—moving testing centers to Tennessee and launch sites to Space Command, Reliance, finding solutions to meet future budgets that were being cut severely, being the face of the Pentagon telling folks they had to cut their budget by 20%, all of those meetings at the Pentagon about how many people we were going to have to give up. People were not happy with me. I was tired, and depressed that I couldn't find a way to cut any more people and still protect the quality of our work.

One weekend, I sat down and wrote a letter of resignation to General Yates. When I arrived at work on Monday and set out to hand-deliver it, I discovered that he would be out of town for a few days on business. I put the letter in my desk drawer. Before he returned, I had a couple of "wins" and decided to leave the letter in my drawer.

One day in August 1991, General Yates called me to his office and said he was sending me to Edwards AFB as the Air Force Flight Test Center Commander.

That was welcome and exciting news—and a great relief.

It would be our third assignment in the California desert to a unit that was close to my heart. I would also have a much bigger staff to assist me. I would be able to fly again, although this time always with an IP, which was mandatory for generals.

I was grateful General Yates picked me for this opportunity. He is the best boss I ever had.

We had worked with each other several times before. He was an IP at ARPS when I was a student. He was the A-X/A-10 Director of Test and Evaluation in the System Program Office. As the operations officer of the CTF, I worked closely with him. He was in the Pentagon as the F-16 PEM while I was there working the F-15 and A-10 as a PEM. He was already a full colonel by then.

Now he had given me the plum of all senior test pilot positions. I was thankful for his confidence in me.

My family again made plans to pack and move quickly, as there was not much time before the change of command ceremony. At least this time, we would move before the start of school for Brian.

Christmas 1989, continued, and Christmas 1990

1990 Happy Holidays from DC (and some further notes on Christmas 1989)

This year had an auspicious beginning with the December 1989 announcement of Roy's promotion to Brigadier General. This was an event we felt had passed over him, so it was a nice surprise. The bad news was an immediate reassignment. Roy had three weeks to close out his affairs at Patrick AFB, Florida, and report as Deputy Chief of Staff for test and resources at Air

Force Systems Command Headquarters, Andrews AFB, MD, about ten miles from the capital.

We hated to leave Patrick. It was a fun "job" for both of us. Launching rockets and space shuttles, a lot of visitors, "life on the beach," tennis, and great people on the base and in the community. I guess someone knew we were having fun and felt obligated to stop it.

Brian was the one dissenter to a happy life in Florida. Some things were great, like scuba diving with his dad. But gregarious Brian didn't find any new friends at that school. He was homesick for his good buddies at Edwards and was ready to get out of town—even to DC. Roy took Brian with him to DC while I faced another move alone.

Brian immediately liked the new area. He found a lot of friends with common interests. Brian still likes to skateboard and is a master ramp builder, but he took a fall and broke his ankle just as school got out. This delayed him getting his driver's license till August. He made a trip to California to visit friends and also spent a week building picture frames with his Grandpappy Bridges in Georgia.

Benita's dad, John Allbaugh, died unexpectedly in April. He was 85 years old. Benita's mom is still in Tucson at Santa Rosa Health Care Center.

Tanya was home for the summer. She took a complete college physics course at Georgetown University. A chapter a day plus two lab sessions each week kept her busy. Between her two sessions, we went to New York City for a weekend. We had a great time—stayed across the street from Carnegie Hall, saw *Cats* on Broadway and a lot of sights.

Roy's job is tough. Services are cutting back a lot and very quickly on top of the activity in the Persian Gulf. He pinned on his star officially on the first of July, with only a few days' notice, but enough for his folks to come. John Blaha and Story Musgrave came up from Houston for the ceremony.

Roy and Benita took a very short vacation—more a drive away from DC in any direction than a planned activity. Neither of us had ever toured much in New England, so we took off for Maine, determined to avoid anyone we knew or any organized activity. We spent two nights in Bar Harbor, Maine, where we did a driving tour of Acadia National Park. Wow!! it was a great escape and helped us survive the hectic fall.

It was great that Roy got to be off to attend the reunion in Colorado. Almost all of his squadron returned for the event, and we spent three nights and days renewing friendships. Later in October, Roy was invited back to Purdue for Homecoming to receive an astronaut engineering alumnus award. He got to march around the field with one of those scantily clad golden girls again (he did a similar thing in '85) and had a great time.

Hard to believe that Christmas season is here again! We've been in a different house the last three years. Wonder where we'll be next year! (??) Stay tuned!

Chapter 37: Commander, Air Force Flight Test Center at Edwards AFB CA
August 1991–June 1993

The change of command occurred in August 1991, and I began my dream job for a test pilot at Edwards AFB, California. As commander, I would be in charge of the premier flight-test facility in the USAF. I never expected to be the commander. Now that I was, I intended to do everything in my power to support the mission and the people who performed it.

Edwards AFB hosted the largest test organization in the USAF, with over 7000 military and government employees and support from over 1000 contractors. In addition, there were over 5000 aerospace contractors and operational test personnel working in partnership. Test programs were in progress for the C-17, B-2, F-15E, and advanced models of the F-16, plus many other smaller efforts. Edwards AFB was located on a 300,000-acre installation and operated two other off-site ranges and activities. NASA's Dryden Flight Research Facility was also located on Edwards AFB, and Air Force Flight Test Center provided support for space shuttle landings.

Since I had been the Wing Commander for several years in a prior assignment as well as serving as a test pilot student and working test pilot for five years in my first assignment at

Edwards, I was well aware of the culture and challenges involved in the job and looked forward to doing my part to improve and strengthen the command in strategic areas.

We moved into the commander's home on the hill adjacent to the Officers' Club. Our backyard faced the golf course. We lived in a small community of senior officer housing with mature shade trees and well-maintained homes. We had a large living and dining room that opened to a long, enclosed veranda, which was ideal for entertaining. The home came with an enlisted aide who assisted with cooking for dinner parties. We could also arrange catering from the nearby Officers' Club when that was needed. Trustee prisoners from the Boron Federal Prison maintained the landscaping. They were an interesting group of men who had been convicted of a variety of nonviolent crimes. We were happy to have their help, and they seemed pleased to have some days outside doing relatively light yard work.

I inherited a great staff consisting of an administrative assistant, an executive officer who also served as my IP for T-38 flights, a deputy commander and his administrative assistant, a chief of staff, a command enlisted advisor, and two protocol officers. They were all immensely helpful in handling the day-to-day work. The rest of the staff offices, such as public affairs, finance, and others, plus the military flight test units and base support units, were all led by talented men and women.

We still had challenges and problems, but I had great help to tackle them.

Combined Test Force

The scope of operations at Edwards was big and complex. We flew 115 aircraft consisting of over thirty different models on demanding test and support missions for over 20,000 hours per year with crews from many organizations. There were always over a dozen test units, with many having multiple projects underway and in planning. On a typical day, we scheduled over one hundred sorties and flew over eighty. We worked hard to create a system to manage this well but without making it too manpower-intensive.

I believe that the combination of a strong team of government and military flight test engineers working with a great group of military test pilots who were competitively selected and trained made it possible to delegate a lot of the task of management to Combined Test Force (CTF) directors and other senior leaders. Partnership in the CTF was crucial to success.

One of the problems we tackled was the flight test program for the new C-17 transport aircraft. The contractor was saddled with an unrealistic test schedule and tended to ignore the inputs of our C-17 CTF Director. As a result, we noted several incidents that did not conform to best practices to maintain a safe test operation.

That got my attention.

I launched a more intense investigation into their daily planning and scheduling.

I learned that the contractor had several incidents whose root cause they did not fully understand, and they rushed to schedule additional flights before investigating thoroughly. When I learned of these I would consult with the Wing Commander and the CTF Director.

I learned that the contractor leadership would ignore the protestations of the CTF Director to slow down and investigate. For instance, I found out that they blew a tire on an aircraft on a test flight. Rather than investigate to see why it failed, they just changed the tire and scheduled another flight. After my experience with a blown tire on the YA-10, I didn't think that was such a wise idea.

"Why weren't you curious enough to try to figure out what caused this failure?" I asked them.

And their response was, "We don't know. We just changed it out. And we'll fly another sortie tomorrow."

What? You don't know why it happened? Then how can you make sure it doesn't happen again?

Well, now all my hackles were up. My hair just stood up on the back of my neck. Because that attitude is exactly what caused me to have an accident in the YA-10. After this happened a number of times, I began to have nightmares about an out-of-control test program driven by a schedule that was being forced on the contractor by the government program office.

One day they were doing so-called high-angle-of-attack tests. This is where you're near a stall in the airplane. Once that airplane stalls, you lose lift on the wings, and it starts sinking out of the sky.

While doing these tests they got into a stall. But the people in the control room—senior management level and experienced engineers—including the people flying the airplane, for some reason, assumed they were having a flight control problem. Meantime, this airplane was sinking out of the sky, and they're working a flight control problem. Finally, a junior controller, who could see that they were out of configuration, said, "Flaps!" They had forgotten to put their flaps down. Then the airplane was doing just fine again.

You would think, when they almost crashed this airplane, that they would stop and try to understand: What is it about our flight crew and our control room, that they're not able to see that we've exceeded the stall angle of attack, and put us in a safe configuration? They could have crashed this airplane and killed people.

It became obvious to me that this junior controller who properly analyzed the problem didn't feel comfortable saying something until it was almost too late. Why was that? Did he feel like his input would not be appreciated?

That's how it is in some organizations—people often suppress opinions that don't appear to agree with what the big guys are thinking. But fortunately, he spoke up, and people realized, "Oh, this guy's got a point." There is a program called Crew Resource Management, which tries to get crusty old commercial airplane captains to allow their junior officers to speak up and to actually appreciate their input. After the flaps incident, we started teaching that program in our control rooms. If you see something wrong, say something!

As a result of my interest (primarily my perceived interference in their test program by suggesting that they were rushing rather than taking time to investigate incidents thoroughly and fix root causes), a retired four-star general who was now working for the prime contractor visited me often. He tried to get me to give them a free hand at running their developmental test operation so they could meet their schedule commitments. In my assessment, they were running an unsafe operation, and I told him that at the end of the day I would be held accountable for safety for all test programs, including the C-17. I insisted on improvements that would give the CTF Director more insight and influence in planning and executing the test schedule.

I learned that the CTF Director had been offered a good job at another base. I privately encouraged him to take it, as it would be good for his career. It was also a miracle for me; I could have the Wing Commander appoint a new director who would insist on the right way to respond to these types of incidents.

When the prior director left to take a new assignment at another base, I recommended a new CTF Director in whom I had a lot of confidence. Working as a team, he, the Wing

Commander, and I won approval for a new schedule and set up a good system to track and report progress. After these two things happened, the program began to respond to incidents correctly and everyone breathed a sigh of relief.

The workforce responded well to the new schedule as something that was achievable but still challenging. We saw an almost immediate improvement in productivity, teamwork, and safety. The team finished the test program with flying colors despite the rough start.

I was convinced that, had the prime contractor not been in a CTF environment, we would have eventually failed to bring this program to a successful conclusion. The government team added tremendous value and stability by influencing the planned program and the daily execution of it.

The bottom line is that the men and women of the Air Force Flight Test Center were proficient in the best practices for running test programs. That is all that they do. A prime contractor could go years without a new military aircraft to test.

As a result of the reorganization that I had led in my previous tour at Edwards, the CTFs were now Flight Test Squadrons. Before that, when a promotion board would see "CTF Director," they would say, "What is that? I don't have any idea what a CTF Director is." Unless you're in the test business, you would have no clue. So we reorganized the CTFs into squadrons so that we could make them squadron commanders. Promotion boards understood the position of squadron commander; it was part of their familiar hierarchy. This benefited our talented leaders as their careers advanced.

Safety first

As the installation commander, I had the final say on the numerous hazardous test flights that we performed on the programs.

It was my responsibility to assure that the test team had thought through the reasons for the test, the hazards and how to mitigate them, and whether the benefits of getting the information justified the risks involved. After my review and approval of the hazardous test plan, the test team was empowered to execute the tests and be accountable for the results.

This was much more than the average flight safety program. The Wing Commander was briefed every day in the morning on any hazardous tests to be flown on that day during his early morning walk-about. I was briefed with the results at the end-of-the-day stand-up. I was also involved when there were surprises or deviations. In general, the process worked great. There were complaints from prime contractors regarding the time to do the homework and get started, but it paid off over time.

An improvement in the hazardous test planning was made because of the A-10 crash in the late 1970s. They had forgotten the importance of having the APU running during gun tests. I required our system safety office to set up a more rigorous "lessons learned program" and repository. Those responsible for preparing the hazardous test plan had to do a thorough review and incorporate mitigations for any risks that had caused previous accidents or incidents. The thoroughness was assessed during their review of the plan with me.

During my tour as installation commander, we had some accidents and incidents, but none were attributed to a failure in our process. *Incidents* refers to something potentially bad—a minor difficulty this time that could be disastrous another time—for example, minor damage to an aircraft. *Accident* means loss of some kind—equipment, aircraft, injuries, or lives.

We did not have accidents during a hazardous test mission. Unfortunately, though, there were some accidents, and they occurred during the most routine operations. Therefore, we took action to extend the thinking process of test safety to other areas of our operations to find and mitigate hazards.

One tragic accident involved a helicopter on a routine parachute training mission at Edwards AFB. Several of the crew and parachute test personnel died when the main rotor blade separated from the helicopter.

After an extensive review and discussion with accident board experts in maintenance, logistics, and operations, we decided to tear down our remaining helicopters to look at all potential failure modes and associated parts and equipment. We never did find out what caused the accident, but we wanted to make sure it was not something hiding in our other helicopters. We then reassembled them under the supervision of experts. We did not have a recurrence and were able to establish renewed confidence in the safety of our helicopter fleet.

Total Quality Management

I spent a lot of time implementing a Total Quality environment with its concepts of continuous process improvement and empowerment to assure that we continued to get better at this demanding business. I started by attending a training course in the philosophy of Dr. W. Edwards Deming, the pioneer of what came to be called the Total Quality Management system. Deming believed that there was no such thing as a perfect process; there is always something changing that can affect it. Everyone involved, at every level, from the top down, needs to continuously assess their work—to achieve the best possible quality at every level and every step of every process.

His philosophy was basically "if you don't measure it, you can't fix it." And we did. I kept a lot of data, charting where we started and where we ended. Implementing a set of meaningful and useful metrics proved to be one of the most difficult things in my career. People are reluctant to have something that might be critical of their leadership so they want metrics that are always green or good. I insisted on useful ones. We kept at it until we got it right.

One of the most significant improvement initiatives that resulted was a comprehensive strategic and facility plan based on Total Quality principles.

First, we performed an in-depth assessment of our progress, which included a no-nonsense review by a group of middle managers based on their survey of our people. We scored only 18%, so we had a long way to go.

We followed that with a series of off-sites—meetings some-where away from our usual hierarchical office space, where people would be more apt to speak up and engage—to build our Total Quality Road Map and its specific improvement goals. These were all tied directly to command and USAF goals and objectives so that everyone could see how they fit into the big picture and how their efforts could make a difference in the outcome. We took abstract principles and made them specific and relevant to the work we were all engaged in.

The plan itself was a short, loose-leaf document because we wanted a living process rather than a phone book that would always be out of date.

We also developed a set of metrics to help us measure our progress and put them into practice all across the flight center. These were difficult to create and implement, but we stayed the course and made slow progress. The board met regularly to re-view progress and fix things as needed. Major subordinate unit commanders were members of the board. Tiers One, Two, and Three were included so they could see what was really causing some upper-level problems, because they were on the forefront of it. They were accountable for their supporting objectives and processes.

Our process was cyclic—we scheduled periodic updates on an approximately annual cycle. We completed another in-depth assessment and off-site prior to my departure. Our score had improved to 30%, which, while it wasn't where we wanted to be, was significantly better than it had been. There were also many indications of significant cultural change reported by the team, which were encouraging. The workforce scored our leadership at 52% versus the previous 23%, which was positive feedback for the leadership at all levels. We had a much easier time making difficult resource decisions now that we had a good corporate framework. Cooperation and teamwork to help the entire center succeed were now in vogue versus the overfocus on internal competition and equity that had existed previously.

Comprehensive facility plan

We also worked to improve our comprehensive facility plan. A lot of good work had already been done to document failing infrastructure, and significant resources had been allocated for repairs and replacements. I saw a lack of cohesiveness in the overall effort and tendencies of falling back on the previous crisis-management mode of operation. Our environmental responsibilities were buried under the civil engineering bureaucracy and were not getting enough priority. Finally, many projects to fix occupational safety and health problems were not completed expeditiously.

These conditions were not acceptable. They needed to be addressed, immediately.

I decided to hire a facilitator to help us prepare a comprehensive facility plan for the key area of our base's dormitory, housing, office, and maintenance complexes. The people who lived on base had a lot to say on the matter, and we listened. The plan made the health, safety, needs, and preferences of our resident workforce, who used the facilities and infrastructure on a daily basis, a top priority. As a result, I made major changes to our priority list of facilities and won top-level support for new housing and dormitories, which were our top priorities.

I initiated a program to move us out of the dark ages in our ability to keep track of the extremely large base with its hundreds of facilities and thousands of miles of support infrastructure such as our roads and utility systems. First, we mapped the entire base using aerial photography and documented the results in a Geographical Information System (GIS) database. We populated that database with our infrastructure information (plumbing, electrical, communications, environmental monitoring data, etc.) for a 450-acre section of the base in the heart of our industrial area as a pilot project.

The project was successful, and its utility expanded to all types of planning activities across the entire center in subsequent years. For example, the army used the database and its accurate maps to save money on navigation tests for a new helicopter system.

The air force chief of staff visited early in my tour to review the B-2 program. While I was driving him to his meeting, he made critical comments about our lack of a good architectural and paint-color scheme for the base. I learned from others that he was notoriously passionate about that subject. They weren't wrong. There I was, driving him through the campus while he chewed my ear off about my ugly paint scheme and how it was not consistent from one building to the next. "Is that pink? You painted every building pink?"

So, it became clear to me that because of this Total Quality Management thing, some people in the Tactical Air Command, where he came from, had applied the Total Quality philosophy even to paint on the base so that everything was consistent from one building to the next—sort of a paint architectural scheme that everybody was going by. And I knew that before he came back again we had better have that pink gone.

As it turned out, he wasn't wrong, either. As a result of his lecture, I implemented and enforced new architectural guidelines for painting and other highly visible structural details, which made an almost immediate difference in the appearance of the base that was amazing to our frequent visitors. I created the concept of an "atomic paint chip" to use as a reference, much like the atomic clock is used for time in applications requiring high accuracy. This stopped the use of off-brand and off-color paints, which had contributed to making our facilities look poor, especially considering the large size of some of them. I approved a lot of facility redesigns using the new standards, which gave the base a needed facelift that would last for many years into the future.

Environmental priorities

While I was training for a marathon during my weekly long-distance jog, I explored out-of-sight shores of the dry lakebeds. I discovered a lot of 55-gallon drums and other abandoned debris. There were large storage tanks for jet fuel, sitting on a hill, overlooking the base, and there was a pipeline that ran from those tanks down to the flight line. At some point in its past, it had leaked, and now the groundwater under the dry lakebed's surface was contaminated with jet fuel. It was not feeding water going to a community, but it obviously needed to be cleaned up.

I created a new environmental management office that reported directly to me and gave a higher priority and management emphasis to safety and health initiatives. Since we were a Superfund site and home to several endangered species, these deserved more attention. I conducted regular performance reviews for these projects with the environmental office manager. We quickly worked through the backlog of quick kills and began to make real progress on long-term efforts. Stakeholders and regulators at all levels noticed the changes almost immediately, and we benefited from their new spirit of trust and cooperation.

As another example of results, I was awarded a national-level leadership award for implementing new criteria for office furniture to reduce the potential for injury in our workforce.

I also initiated a corporate report to document and celebrate our progress on an annual basis. We published our first report for FY92 using a desktop publishing program to keep costs down. The combination of periodic Total Quality assessments and annual corporate reports was helpful to me in sustaining our efforts to make cultural changes and major improvements in results for our customers. We made a lot of progress in a short time.

I also led a few test range improvement efforts. For example, our team advocated the replacement of the F-4 cruise missile chase fleet with a much more versatile F-16 fleet with a 59% cost savings in mission costs and much greater flexibility in scheduling our resources. We won approval for the effort and laid out design criteria to assure the instrumentation package would fit in a pod on the F-16 rather than internally as we had done on the F-4. This assured greater operational flexibility and efficiency. The design work was done in-house, using Total Quality techniques as an early demonstration of the value of concurrent engineering. The system was successful and allowed us to retire the entire F-4 fleet early. Since we had the last F-4s in the air force inventory, this was well received at higher levels.

Another range improvement project was focused on the safety of the airspace used for our mission at Edwards AFB. The airspace at Edwards was jointly managed with the navy and army. The FAA provided air traffic control services with an approach control located at Edwards AFB. We needed to replace the software system, which was used to process and display the radar data. The system in use was becoming unsupportable. I started a local effort with support contractor assistance to redesign it and kept the local FAA controllers and managers totally in the design loop. I advocated and supported this program at every phase of its development and assured resources were available.

We developed a system for a small amount of money, and it worked so well and was so impressive that we invited the administrator of the FAA to come and see it. He and his staff were also impressed, which helped us get it verified and online. The software allowed us to select and use the radar data from multiple radars in a high-speed tracker algorithm. The system being replaced had used information from one radar at the time. With the new system we could see changes in the flight path of dynamic targets (9 g's at 500+ knots) quickly. The system greatly enhanced the safety of the airspace on the range, which was one of my top safety initiatives.

We began a program at Edwards to upgrade our large anechoic chamber to perform some of the electronic combat and integrated avionics system tests on modern aircraft. The program kickoff was political since some people wanted to build a large chamber at Naval Air Station Patuxent River and have everyone use it. I worked the politics hard at all levels and obtained the go-ahead to start a modest program before I departed. We had to survive several attacks by the DOD Inspector General to get the approval, as well as other ambushes. The capability is needed for modern aircraft development at the primary test sites to avoid a fly-fix-fly operation, which is costly. We formed a small program team and had a good plan in place to execute the effort before I departed. The effort continued to compete well for resources and to enjoy top-level air force support.

Given my efforts while at AFSC headquarters to work across services to encourage less duplication and more cooperation, I wanted to reduce some destructive competition between the ranges.

At lower levels, there were attempts to bring aircraft development work to Eglin AFB, which was not their core mission. Eglin was supposed to focus on the development of armament for aircraft, which included qualifying the new weapons for safe carriage and employment on aircraft. Working with the commander of the Air Armament Center at Eglin, a two-star general, we set up a small office that we called the "single face to the customer" office. The office jointly reviewed customer needs and recommended the most optimum place to perform the test. The two commanders reviewed any disagreements or objections to the recommendation for resolution. This created more cooperation within the air force flight test community.

International hospitality

We hosted a lot of visitors from around the world during my tour at Edwards AFB. These ranged from a plane full of senior NATO commanders to Congressional delegations. Benita and I entertained general officers—high-ranking visitors—from other nations at our home when they came to the base for events such as a Test Pilot School graduation of an exchange student from their country.

We learned to stock the bar with a large selection of alcoholic beverages, as they did enjoy a little alcohol during our dinner parties. We loved hosting them and enjoyed hearing their stories.

I was invited by my counterpart in the French air force to fly to Paris for a week-long tour of their test ranges and bases plus a couple of flights in their newest aircraft. I had a great time.

I invited him to visit our bases and arranged to meet him in Washington, DC, and fly him to Edwards AFB on board the chief of staff's personal transport aircraft, which was a modified four-engine jet transport aircraft. After touring Edwards, we hosted him and his staff at a dinner party at our home. Before leaving for his next tour stop, we took them all for a weekend gliding outing and picnic at the glider base in Tehachapi. They traveled on the chief's aircraft to our other test bases and were hosted for tours and socials at each of them.

I also attended many general officer meetings and often was transported to them in the small transport jets the air force used for that purpose, since the T-38 wasn't a great cross-country aircraft, with its short legs and my limited time to devote to making the trips. Once when returning from a command conference, which Benita also attended, we were chatting with each other and the other passengers while on final approach to Edwards late in the afternoon. I happened to glance out the window as we neared touchdown and didn't see familiar terrain. I yelled at the pilots to "go around." They did and we avoided a near tragedy. They had lined up for a landing on the short runway at the old South Base adjacent to the main base at Edwards with its super long runway. The setting sun in their eyes had partially blinded them. The South Base runway would have been way too short.

1992: a year of milestones

There were a lot of promotion parties and retirement/farewell parties, given the large workforce. Benita was active as an advisor with the Officer Wives' Club and its philanthropic activities, such as a scholarship fund for military children.

Tanya graduated from college with a double major in biology and music in 1992. I picked her up after graduation in a U-Haul truck and transported her and her belongings to our home at Edwards AFB. She then traveled to Germany to take a summer job as a tutor for military children attending secondary school there. She returned home after that tour and began volunteering for companies doing wildlife and environmental work on base and in the surrounding area. She did it as an internship to help her qualify for a full-time wildlife biologist position, which was one of her passions. It was great to have her living with us again.

Brian graduated from Desert High School in May of 1992.

I got a pleasant but unexpected surprise for Christmas in 1992. I was promoted to Major General.

General Yates showed up on New Year's Day of 1993, and he and Benita pinned on my second star.

Like my first promotion to general officer, this one came with a price.

On the road again

A few months after my promotion, I got a call from General Yates. He said that he needed me to join his staff at Wright-Patterson AFB as the Director of Requirements for the Air Force Materiel Command (AFMC). He needed me there in June.

I had hoped to stay at Edwards until my retirement, since I was not expecting to be promoted beyond my two-star rank. To qualify for one of the three-star positions in AFMC, the person needed to have a strong acquisition background, which I lacked. Since I needed to serve three years in my new rank to be able to retire at that rank, I would have to move at least one more time. I didn't want to retire at the lower rank, nor did I want to desert the air force that had done so much to make my career dreams come true.

Benita and I made arrangements to pack up and hit the road again.

It is no wonder that the skit that would be the highlight of our going-away party was a takeoff on the musical *Camelot*. The plot showcased the change at Edwards AFB from "Fly-a-Lot" to "Plan-a Lot." Of course we still flew a lot, but we had also improved our strategic planning with visible results.

I "laughed-a-lot" during that skit.

I knew that I was going to miss the thrill of flying jets. I certainly would not be able to get the same satisfaction out of flying civilian aircraft, nor could I afford the cost of doing it as often as I needed to keep up a safe level of proficiency. Just before the party, I flew my last flight as pilot during my air force career in the T-38 and endured the ceremonial fire hose shower after climbing out of the cockpit.

Even dripping wet, I would miss this.

Christmas Letters 1991-1992

Merry Christmas from California

It's a good thing that we are "desert rats," because we are back again in the Mojave—and love it. Our spirits breathe a little better in the wide-open West.

Roy took command of the Air Force Flight Test Center at Edwards AFB, CA, on 30 August in an impressive ceremony that included him strutting around and inspecting the troops with General Yates, his four-star boss. "Roy looked just like he did as a cadet," said one of his friends. From afar, of course. Up close, he's added some creases and lost a lot of hair. Roy is happy with his job, to say the least.

Benita had an exciting time at Andrews AFB as a Red Cross volunteer at the welcome-home point for all the troops that were sick, injured, or wounded in the Gulf. Most of the flights arrived in the middle of the night, and it was a great feeling to help put a big smile on their faces. In addition to handing out coffee, hot chocolate, sodas, cookies, and American bubble gum, she procured red-white-blue ribbon and dressed up every flower vase and bed in the 250-bed facility, a converted gym and indoor tennis courts. She has lasting memories of a significant event in our nation's history—the war in the Gulf.

Brian likes being at Edwards and has several good friends here as well as his best friend. He and Roy went to Utah last spring for four days of skiing and look forward to trips to nearby ski areas this winter.

Tanya is a senior at Austin College in Texas and will graduate next spring with a double major in biology and music.

Tanya is the only one that had no misgivings at all about leaving DC, since she was away most of the time. Brian left his girlfriend as well as many special friends behind. Roy and Benita had many wonderful neighbors and friends both on staff at HQ Air Force Systems Command and around the area.

This is a very turbulent time for the world with the collapse of the Soviet Union and the resulting rapid reduction in our armed forces. Everything is changing all at once, which keeps us all hopping. We hope to be at Edwards for a few years, but given the circumstances, we are staying very flexible. At this Thanksgiving moment we're quite happy to have our health, a nice family, and a job. Many don't have the latter, and our hearts are heavy for them.

We're celebrating Roy's folks' 50th wedding anniversary this Thanksgiving weekend, and it is so special to be around our loved ones. We all flew to Georgia and had a great time.

May the Lord bless and keep you in a peaceful 1992!

Christmas 1992: Some Blessings

1- Roy has a job.

2- We didn't move this year and like where we are now.

3- Tanya is safely home after a three-month trip to Europe.

4- Brian made a B in English.

5- Roy's group hasn't had a fatal accident this year.

6- Our country isn't at war, and we're feeding the hungry in Somalia.

7- Russia is friendly this year.

8- We're all healthy.

9- The election is finally over. (& we live in a country where political transition is peaceful.)

10- There is hope for a better future for many. (Look at all the advances and initiatives to improve health, education, safety, and the environment—although having that for all is still elusive.

Roy's official photo as a USAF Major General

Chapter 38: Air Force Materiel Command (AFMC) Staff at Wright-Patterson AFB OH
June 1993–July 1996

I departed Edwards AFB on my way to Ohio and my new assignment in June 1993. Benita followed later after she supervised the packing and moving of our household goods, which we set up to match the availability of a home on base in Ohio. Our kids rented a small place in Lancaster, as they wished to stay in the area and continue with their jobs, at least for the time being.

A dubious start on the road to Ohio

On the way I stopped overnight at a motel in Clovis, New Mexico. The next day, as I departed, I ran into severe thunderstorms just across the Texas border. I noticed that people were pulling off the road and stopping on the shoulder of the highway. I wondered why for a few moments before learning the awful truth. A hailstone the size of a softball hit my front windshield with a loud thud. I slowed and planned to stop on the shoulder of the road. As I was doing so, another softball hit my driver's side window, shattered it into hundreds of pieces, and hit me in the left elbow. After stopping, I grabbed my cardboard sunscreen and held it up to the now-open driver's side window to protect myself. Several more large hailstones struck the cardboard and partially penetrated it.

When the barrage finally stopped, I had no choice but to return to the motel. I got permission to park the car under the portico for rain protection. I found a nearby junkyard that had a car like my model with an intact driver's side window. After I had it installed, I resumed my trip.

My car had many dents in the hood and roof, but it got me to Ohio. I had the cracked front windshield and broken windshield wiper fixed after arriving in Ohio. Over the next several years, the freezing and thawing weather cycles during the winters removed most of the dents.

We moved into one of the generals' quarters on base. It was an older brick home with two stories plus a partially finished basement. It was historic; generals much more famous for their contribution than I had lived in it. While it was somewhat dated, it was well maintained and quite adequate for us.

New ground

I began work in my new position, which was truly new ground for me and well outside of my experience. As the Director of Requirements, I served as the senior corporate staff director for the acquisition and sustainment business areas, which were the heart of what the command did for the USAF.

Acquisition is the act of purchasing airplanes, missiles, spacecraft and satellites, armaments and other supporting equipment, things like radars, computer systems, communication systems—developing your specifications, bidding it to contractors to supply it. Then you have to test it.

Once a plane has been declared operational comes sustainment, taking care of those things—repairs, minor upgrades, periodic depot maintenance for more detailed inspections and repairs, avionics upgrades—over its lifespan. These used to be two separate entities, separate cultures that didn't necessarily talk to or trust each other.

With AFMC, we had combined those two commands, bringing the logistics sustainment people into the process from the beginning, so that, given the benefit of their knowledge and experience as to what would make their job easier, we would *build* an airplane that was easier to sustain throughout its life cycle in addition to performing well.

We were working through these difficult mergers of two very different cultures, trying to get people to learn to trust each other and, frankly, *depend* on each other to do what's right at each step. In that role, I was now in charge of A to Z—acquisition *and* sustainment—providing functional staff support for the 100+ program managers who acquired and sustained the USAF's weapon systems.

I chaired the corporate board for that business area, which was made up of four product and five logistics center commanders who were all two- or three-star generals. The board had responsibility for strategic planning, policy, resources, and training support to program managers across the air force. My staff and I also served as an extended staff to the air force acquisition executive at the Pentagon for creating and implementing acquisition reform initiatives.

We were under constant attack to reduce manpower and bases to meet future budget commitments. I put these attacks into a category that I called the "peace dividend."

Defense budgets were being trimmed, and those of us in the "tail" were paying the price. We were still under great pressure to reform how we did acquisition and sustainment, to save cost and reduce manpower. Congress was cutting the budgets of the services as the Soviet Union disintegrated. The operational air force wanted to retain as much force structure as possible. They put pressure on the "tail" of the air force, us, to preserve more of the "spear," them. The point of the spear is the entirety of the protection of the United States. But it can't survive without the support provided by the tail. Finding the balance without losing effectiveness was crucial.

The acquisition and sustainment workforce of 57,000 people was reduced by 53% between 1989 and 2001.

Our efforts to reengineer the processes and implement many reform initiatives helped us continue to be successful despite these significant reductions. Given the high stakes in question, this was essential.

In order to get to this Integrated Product Development process that would flow through the whole command, we had to answer some questions. What is the headquarters doing to make this work? Was this going to be performed down in the program office? What do we need to do to foster and guide this to completion? It was an oversight process—almost a primer to help the guys in the program offices come up with one process that worked for all the programs.

Progress was reported through a comprehensive series of action plans and metrics, which we created. They were maintained online instead of on paper. I used these to guide the agendas for board meetings and my report to the command at the periodic Horizon Conferences. I also hosted semi-annual training and feedback sessions with our primary internal customers, the program managers. Although they did not report directly to me, I was responsible for how they did their business in some kind of consistent way.

Each program office was doing something different—some were buying weapons, some were buying airplanes, some were buying spacecraft—but whatever program office you went into, you would see a similar process as far as how they organized and managed their programs, with variations as necessary because of the different lifecycle processes. Obviously, spacecraft don't go through periodic depot maintenance like aircraft and jet engines. We were providing the blueprint for processes that drove the work of the program managers.

The AFMC Commander described our results as a "watershed" for the business area. An unprecedented spirit of corporate teamwork in tackling the difficult and painful resource decisions and culture-changing reengineering projects moved the formerly divided command to an integrated process for acquisition and sustainment, versus the ages-old transfer of responsibility between the old AFSC and the Air Force Logistics Command at some rather arbitrary calendar date in the life of the program.

We pioneered the implementation of the management philosophy of Integrated Product Development in our program offices and in teams with industry to execute our programs. This new process focused on assuring that our new systems not only performed well but could also be sustained well: wins at both ends of this previously divided process. We were gaining control of the process up front, rather than somebody having to pick up the pieces somewhere down the road.

We had great success, which we advertised widely to build recognition and support. I did a lot of missionary work to spread this concept to higher levels. For example, I presented a proposal to apply this approach at the Pentagon to the USAF Chief of Staff and Secretary and their key staff in a briefing.

We also populated the key Process Action Teams being formed on acquisition reform in the Office of the Secretary of Defense with articulate spokespersons who would push this reform idea.

We even persuaded the DOD to get on board. Their slightly revised version of our program was called Integrated Product and Process Development. Historically the DOD was filled with people who viewed their success in terms of picking out problems in our programs and spreading criticism throughout the department, as opposed to helping solve problems. This resulted in a system of program managers presenting their programs with the most positive spin rather than asking for help and getting the resources needed to move their programs forward.

Added to the problem was extensive bureaucracy at DOD. Before this change of philosophy, a Program Manager had to navigate through many different offices and get the resources and approvals that they needed to take the next step before getting a senior official to let the program move forward. Now, Program Managers had a single focal point for all oversight activities, which significantly reduced the amount of time and effort that they had to devote to satisfy stakeholders and obtain milestone approvals for their programs.

More importantly, the Office of the Secretary of Defense staff was told they would be graded on how well they helped program managers succeed with their programs rather than the number of obstacles that they could put in their paths. Instead of finding fault with the programs, they are instructed to help program managers navigate and quickly get everybody on board with what needs to be done. This helped build transparency and trust there. And again, you don't need as many people if you're not having to fight the Pentagon in depth to get your program to move forward.

Our program managers perceived this as a major victory.

The DOD goes green

The DOD was charged with eliminating all atmospheric pollutants that were destroying the ozone layer. This led us to create a joint service group to be the single focal point for "greening" up our manufacturing processes in our defense plants. I created and chaired this group, which consisted of one- and two-star generals and admirals from each of the services. The joint group was chartered by the Joint Logistics Commanders, the four-star commanders from each of the services, who commanded the acquisition and sustainment activities in DOD. The charter gave my group the authority to perform this function by the highest-ranking officer in each service who would be affected by the changes that we would recommend. I formed a small part-time staff and created and developed a process to do this job, which was to find an easy way to move to less-polluting and less-expensive manufacturing processes for all contracts in a plant simultaneously. We called it the Block Change/Single Process Initiative.

BLOCK CHANGE/SINGLE PROCESS INITIATIVE

The paperwork processing savings alone generated by this initiative was over $5 million. This doesn't even begin to account for the personnel and hours previously required to service hundreds of contracts. But the up-front investment in time, negotiators, and negotiations was considerable—and ultimately worth it.

Take Texas Instruments as an example. Texas Instruments produced avionics for many programs and the Department of Defense—army, navy, air force, and marines. They were each controlled by separate contracts that also listed all the specifications that they had to meet. Changing these one by one was impossibly expensive and time-consuming. Because the manufacturing processes were identical, nothing could be done until all were changed and approved.

So, say for instance that Texas Instruments was producing chips. These chips might be used in an army system, navy system, and air force system. They've each got different contracts and different specifications laid on there. Now, how do you get 151 contracts changed easily?

That was the essence of this Block Change/Single Process initiative. We would say, "Look, guys, in order to reduce this particular ozone-depleting chemical, we need to change that chemical from X to Y. You need to allow us to change the contract to allow this chemical change from X to Y." And so we'd list all these contracts on a page and list all the specifications that were requiring X. Then we would specify that we were changing those contracts so that they require specification Y, which was a different chemical. And we could get one signature on there that would allow Texas Instruments to make that change for all the relevant contracts. Therefore, you just eliminated tons of ozone-depleting chemical—and tons of paperwork.

Getting the army, navy, air force, and marines to agree to let you pick an official to make this change meant we had to go convince people that changing from chemical X to chemical Y was a good thing and would allow us to meet our goals of reducing or eliminating the ozone-depleting chemicals.

That was what was happening behind the scenes. There was a lot of work done before you allowed this one person to sign to make sure all parties understood exactly what we were doing. I organized and ran that Joint Service Group to make this happen.

The group was organized with a general officer in each of those other services, and we would meet regularly. I had an expert, a colonel who came up with the idea for doing this. He had an informal team of folks like him from the other services. They would go in and look at what Texas Instruments said that they could do for us to get rid of a particular ozone-depleting chemical. The burden was on Texas Instruments to describe how this other chemical was going to work as well as, or better than, the one we wanted to eliminate. They would have to convince this working group and then they would make a presentation to convince the general officers that this new chemical would work just as well as the current chemical and not deplete ozone. All of that happened behind the scenes. The general officer group would then agree on the one person to sign for all of the affected contracts.

Another example: Say every airplane produced at Boeing was found to have a primer paint that was very bad in terms of environmental pollution. We would need to have Boeing come up with a new primer paint for these airplanes and convince our team that this primer paint was just as good as the other but it wouldn't be a pollutant. And then we could have one single contract signing with Boeing, the same thing we did for Texas Instruments, to change out the paint for every airplane that they will produce.

The initial results won a lot of recognition and were significant over the long run. We won recognition for the first use of the Block Change/Single Process Initiative in DOD. We used it to change 151 contracts and over 3000 drawings with one signature at Texas Instruments. The paperwork processing savings alone was over $5 million. DOD's top officials and local regulators attended the award ceremony at the plant.

I was invited to showcase the project and the technique at a White House Conference on the environment. The project moved into full-scale deployment using a decentralized approach in every region of the Defense Contract Management Command to accommodate as many projects as industry could push our way. This helped us to meet a command goal of being an environmental leader and helped the USAF meet its objectives of reducing pollutants (yearly goals) and operating expenses.

Balancing the human cost

In summary, the results of our reform and reengineering activities enabled the continued downsizing of the workforce. Developing and implementing successful downsizing was a key initiative of the command and the USAF and one of my key responsibilities.

In addition to the 53% reduction from 1989 to 2001, we were able to reduce the acquisition workforce in our program offices, a subset of the total reduction, by 33% from 1995 to 2001. These program office cuts were made possible by the acquisition reforms we had created that made our processes simpler, improved communication, mandated teamwork and cooperation, and required fewer people to do the streamlined work.

The USAF was judged by an industry association as having made the most progress in acquisition reform of any service. Many felt that the best indicator of our progress was what industry saw as a customer of our processes for acquisition and how many people we had on the payroll in this area.

My staff had been under great pressure even before I arrived, and the pace continued unabated while I was there. They were also under a mandate to reduce the staff by 50% over the three years from 1992–1994. As a result of the merger of Air Force Systems Command and Air Force Logistics Command, they all had new duties. Their morale was low.

The staff resented what had happened to them and were under tremendous pressure to perform well since we were leading big changes for the USAF. Many eyes were watching us from the highest levels of the service.

I led my division chiefs through a series of off-sites to develop a clear understanding of our mission, exactly how every one of their groups contributed to the mission, and how that fit into our upper-level goals and objectives. Our office was in a converted warehouse. There was a recreation area where they would have picnics, and a hall if the weather was bad. We would have our meeting, then we would have lunch and a social activity—maybe play a softball game, or, if it was late in the day, have some finger foods and drinks and conversation. A chance to work in a casual setting, have a nice lunch, and play for a while.

We documented this, and I explained it to our people until they all understood it clearly. Then we surveyed our people to find out how we could help them do their jobs better—what could improve our morale, make people more productive and happier. We settled on a few high-payoff internal improvement projects, which we committed to completing.

It turned out that one of the number one complaints was our horrible computer system. So we got a better computer system and set up training so people had what they needed to do their jobs. We spent a little more time up front making sure new hires understood their new job, how what we did was different from what anyone else in the air force did, and how it fit in. And the results were amazing—overnight. We established an on-site training center for our unique needs and trained our new hires to orient them to our business, quality system, and tools.

We also reviewed, prioritized, and documented our processes. We discovered that many were common across the divisions, which helped us standardize them. This also helped us move our people to the most important functions and balance workloads. The visibility into our processes and workload helped us learn to work together as allies instead of competitors.

The previous director had placed a large golden hammer inscribed with large letters that read *No Whining* in the conference room. He wasn't known for being helpful.

I ceremoniously retired the golden hammer.

It has been in my tool shed ever since.

The measure of success

To help us measure our success as a staff, we developed service standards and metrics, which were deployed down to each individual. We used this technique to find out what our internal customers, the project managers, needed, our commitments to deliver on their needs, and customer feedback on how well we were meeting their needs. This was a groundbreaking technique for them, but it worked wonders. I began to get calls from the field and have people pull me aside at meetings to tell me how much they appreciated the help they were getting from my staff.

We shared our success stories at our monthly "brown bag" lunch sessions focused on quality, and they continued to increase in number.

Over the three years that I led this staff, we exceeded our original downsizing goal of 50%, grievances were low, and none ever rose to my level. Equal-opportunity complaints were zero, and morale rose to a high level despite the continuously high workload.

Our people were known for what they had accomplished with us and were frequently recruited for other positions. Talented people volunteered to come and serve on the staff when we had vacancies. You know you're doing something right when people want to work for you—and when others want to steal your people away. Word got around: this was not a dead-end job. You could go places.

Thorny issues

My staff and I set up meetings and videoconferences with customers in the operational commands of the acquisition and sustainment services provided by our program managers. We stayed in touch with our program managers about key issues and progress on our top programs to help us prepare agendas and briefing materials. We coordinated agendas with the operational command staffs to make sure that we covered the points they wanted to discuss.

I have often described my role in these sessions as being the "whipping boy" for the command. We wanted full and open discussions of any issue or complaint, and initially we got an earful. As we worked hard to resolve them, our relationships improved, although I wouldn't go so far as to describe them as pleasant.

One of the thorniest issues was that commanders of both the Air Force Space Command (AFSPC) and Air Force Materiel Command (AFMC) made it clear that they wanted to develop a standardized process for developing and maintaining software systems. At the time, there were many different systems and many different approaches. And the two commands had different functions. It was somewhat like hiring two different contractors to come into your place of business and simultaneously begin upgrading the operating system of your computer (AFMC) and fixing minor maintenance issues that inevitably crop up during daily use (AFSPC)— while you are using it. Only a crazy person could think this would result in smooth and error-free operations. Our job was to find a way to consolidate all these variables into a standard system under one umbrella, making their work simpler for all concerned.

Most of the effort came to a focus in the Cheyenne Mountain complex of national warning systems. These systems all belonged to NORAD and AFSPC, and they were in charge of notifying the national command authorities—the president, as commander in chief, and his highest-ranking advisors—who make final decisions in regard to our response to an early warning of any missile launches, etc. that threatened the country. They were built at various times by various contractors, hence the multitude of entities updating or maintaining them.

The complex was fed and served by numerous space- and ground-based sensors and systems. At the time, AFMC was doing major development through contractors to upgrade and modernize the Cheyenne Mountain complex, and AFSPC was doing routine software maintenance and operational reconfigurations. There were no off-line systems for checkout of new or modified capabilities; they had to work on the real thing, in real time—and shutting the system down for maintenance was not an option.

This community of 19 systems—radar systems, satellite controls—all have computer systems that are controlling and keeping track of all this. The community served the national command authorities. In the case of such a national emergency, they would have only minutes to warn them. And no false warnings or significant interruptions in service could be tolerated.

Military commanders at NORAD did not want to wake up the president for a false alarm. Nor did they want to be blind while some system was being upgraded or fixed. A transfer of control to a single command was essential to develop a standardized process for upgrading and maintaining/sustaining these systems, some of which were pretty dated and needed a lot of help. When two entities are both making changes, accidents are bound to happen that can take a system off-line. Clearly, universal processes, standardized protocols, and one go-to office were in their best interests.

This new organization would set this group up to become integrated, use more modern process-control techniques, and do a better job. We could show our customers—primarily NORAD and AFSPC—that all of these units were doing a better job than they'd ever done before. That would make it easier for them to give all the sustainment business to us—to the AFMC— instead of just a little bit of it. That was the essence of our initiative. One command would be in charge of making modernization upgrades as well as routine maintenance of the various systems in use.

The initiative to transfer the sustainment responsibilities to AFMC stalled. The AFSPC didn't trust AFMC and felt there was too much risk to them to turn all this over to us without a better understanding of how things would work. Senior officials at AFSPC feared loss of control and potential lack of responsiveness, and they refused to continue the process of transferring the manpower and responsibility to us.

My boss told me to get this back on track within six months.

Applied Diplomacy

There was an additional complication to solving this problem quickly. The chief of staff of the USAF, who was personally reviewing the USAF's organizational structure, ordered us to combine our nineteen separate detachments and operating locations in Colorado Springs that were supporting AFSPC into one unit. There was a fight between our product center and logistics center commanders over who should own these resources and how they should be organized.

I needed to solve this problem before going to AFSPC and trying to resurrect the software maintenance initiative in Cheyenne Mountain. It was another tough nut to crack.

We couldn't change the fact that there would be 19 different pockets of people doing this. But maybe we could organize them differently. If I could provide a support staff for all of them, instead of every one of them having to scrape and fend for themselves, and we could implement some Total Quality Management to make sure they're doing their business well, we could improve it.

First, I needed to build an alliance with our AFMC field commanders strong enough to convince our customers that we would always bring the full resources of our command to bear on their problems. I began by bringing the involved field commanders—the generals in charge of the commands to which the 19 units in Colorado Springs currently reported—together for a face-to-face review. After my presentation, they agreed that I should lead the effort to solve the underlying problems. They also agreed that we had to succeed with both efforts and gave me their support. Many people in their organizations continued to do battle with me as we proceeded, but having top-level support from the general officers allowed my team to make progress.

Next, I created the Space Systems Support Group, which would report directly to me and be the single focal point for our business in Colorado Springs. The 600+ people in the unit who were supporting program managers for acquisition and sustainment efforts would take their operational direction from their program managers. I proposed a small staff of about twenty-five people to provide facilities and support services to the program managers and a new effort to support cross-cutting improvements—continuous improvement in our processes as a result of the Total Quality approach—that our customers wanted. This unit could now be the repository for the manpower that we wanted AFSPC to transfer to us. The commander of the unit would assure that we were delivering services that met the needs of the operational command customers and could work any problems if we were not meeting their expectations.

This unit proved to be successful.

I set up a group to work with the program managers to develop a set of metrics and improvement initiatives that the top customers and I would review to make sure that we kept our commitments on service and cost. I completed two reviews before I departed, and we were on target. Service was better across the board. We had saved over $200 million and avoided many future problems by consolidating development and sustainment efforts into single contracts. The customers were pleased and even transferred some additional work to us.

Finally I made a series of presentations to the customers with the full support of the field units on our commitments to deliver them better service than they were currently getting and at a lower cost if they would transfer the sustainment responsibilities to us. Eventually, the customers agreed, and we completed the transfer within the time frame that my boss had mandated.

Family troubles and triumphs

Living at Wright-Patterson was tough on my family. We didn't enjoy the more than 250 gray days per year in cloudy Ohio. We purchased some bright halogen lamps for our so-called sunroom and that helped a lot. Winters were challenging; temperatures plunged well below zero, and I found that I was traveling to work in the dark and coming home in the dark because of the short daylight hours at that latitude.

Staying physically fit helped us beat the blues. Benita joined a walking club and walked every day that weather permitted. We had a good gym at work, and I worked to heal my knee, which I had injured while training for a marathon during my Edwards AFB tour. I also had a cross-country ski machine in my basement at home that I used on weekends.

There were a lot of social activities that we had to attend at the Officers' Club. We also had good friends on base that we liked to visit. Benita and I learned to play mah-jongg with them and still enjoy it today on occasion. There were good restaurants in the area that we liked to visit.

Benita and I traveled to Vienna, Austria, to attend the Association of Space Explorers Congress for a week in the fall of 1995. We went sightseeing around the area, including a cruise on the Danube. Benita stayed for an extra week. Her German friend traveled by train to Vienna and escorted Benita to her home in

Germany. They made sightseeing trips around the area. While I was attending pilot training, Benita had traveled from Indiana to California with this same German friend to show her many special sites in the western United States.

Brian joined us in Ohio and started going to the local community college and working at a good restaurant as a cook.

Tanya got a job with the Bureau of Land Management in Barstow, California, as a wildlife biologist. She broke her leg while doing fieldwork. We visited her in California as she was recovering and helped her buy a truck with an automatic transmission to replace her VW with a manual transmission, to assist with her healing process. She met her future husband, who also worked as a wildlife biologist at the Bureau. They became engaged and then married in a gorgeous ceremony on an American Indian reservation near Palm Springs in March 1996 in a "ring of palms." We were happy for them.

Another special occasion for us was attending the ceremony where I was inducted into the Georgia Aviation Hall of Fame. My parents attended. Admiral Truly, who had become the NASA Administrator before he retired from NASA, introduced me at the ceremony.

What an honor to be recognized in such a special way. Given my humble beginnings and difficult early experiences with flying, being elevated to join the famous aviators of Georgia was amazing.

Retirements

General Yates retired after my second year at Wright-Patterson and requested that I stay at least one more year since the new commander had most of his experience running a logistics center and knew little about the acquisition side of our business. My civilian deputy and I visited the new commander before his change of command to give him some insights into how we were doing acquisition as well as our progress and challenges with acquisition reform. Our relationship with him was good, and he gave us a lot of rope to do our jobs as we felt best.

We did not fare as well with the Air Force Acquisition Executive at the Pentagon. When she originally rolled out her acquisition reform initiatives that she named "lightning bolts," she surprised General Yates and me with the announcement at one of our periodic program manager conferences. Both of us were shocked that she had not bothered to consult with us on the practicality of these in advance.

She also continued to ignore our concerns during our attempts to implement them, which caused us to fear that we were on the verge of breaking our well-tuned acquisition system. I became so frustrated with her imperious and dangerous direction that I wished for the end of the year that I had promised General Yates so that I could retire.

Because the new commander had little understanding of the acquisition system, he was not supportive on pushing back on her directions. He once told me that in his opinion, all that he would need to pursue the acquisition of a new weapon system would be a yellow pad of paper, a pen, and access to a contracting officer. This lack of understanding was shocking.

I became depressed.

Out of the blue I was called to his office one day. He said that he expected his deputy to depart for a new position within a few months and asked me to consider becoming his deputy, which was a three-star position.

I said, "Thank you for your confidence in me. May I discuss it with my wife tonight and give you an answer tomorrow?" He was okay with my suggestion.

That night Benita listened as I did my best to present the pros and cons of accepting the position. She said that she thought that our commitment of three years at Wright-Patterson was enough. She would pick up a lot of social responsibilities as the Vice Commander's wife, and didn't look forward to performing them.

I thought about it overnight and reported to him the next day. I said, "I am honored that you offered the position to me, but I am at a place in my career where I want to retire from the air force gracefully and make room for new blood in the acquisition community."

I felt that I had contributed my best ideas during my three-year tenure. Privately, I didn't want to be on point to support the Air Force Acquisition Executive's continued push to implement her "lightning bolts." I also had concluded that if I couldn't support her policies that I should step aside.

He was not pleased with my answer but granted my wish, and I retired on July 1, 1996, after thirty-one years of service, at fifty-three years old. The retirement ceremony was in the Air Force Museum with a lot of the planes that I had flown and tested as a backdrop.

At the reception for friends and family afterwards, my kids put a big photo of me on an easel with the caption, "The Real Roy Bridges."

There was a spoon hanging off my nose.

Benita and I scouted some locations where we would like to live. We both decided that Colorado Springs would be a great place. Brian also agreed. We purchased a small home there with a great view of Pikes Peak from the kitchen windows and deck.

Christmas Letter 1993

In June, we moved to Wright-Patterson AFB near Dayton, Ohio. Tanya and Brian stayed in Lancaster, California, so we have an "empty nest" for the first time.

We do miss Edwards AFB, our air force home. We had such fun on this last tour. It was hard to leave—the place, the mission, the people. But mostly the people.

In July, John Blaha, Roy's best friend and our best man, retired from the air force and invited Roy to officiate in Houston. John and his shuttle crew just landed from a historic flight of two weeks duration. We still miss NASA and our friends there. It is fun to go back for visits, but these days most of the people we see there look too young for the job.

Fortunately, there is a place where "older" space folks go, and we went there for the first time: the Congress of the Association of Space Explorers, held in Vienna, Austria this year. The Association is composed of about 250 people from 26 countries who have flown in space. We had a great time getting to know everybody and touring the beautiful country.

Section 2: NASA

Chapter 39: Retirement in Colorado
August 1996–March 1997

I had a big adjustment to make in the first few days of retirement. After thirty-five years in the air force, counting my four years at the academy, I was used to structure in my daily activities. Now there was none.

I would wake up in a sweat over the lack of any structure or near-term goals. I worried about whether we would be able to survive financially. After Tanya's wedding and the expense of buying a home, I had only $4000 in my savings account. I felt like I was too young to retreat from an active work life.

I was already failing retirement.

Slowly, I managed to make the shift. My first goal was to plan a vacation with Benita. We wanted to see some of the West that we'd never had time to explore. We planned a driving trip to Yellowstone National Park and invited my mom and dad to accompany us. I researched the cost of renting a bigger car to accommodate the four of us but quickly determined that we could not afford it. We crammed into our little Saturn sedan for the trip.

We made stops in Steamboat Springs, Dinosaur National Park, and Jackson Hole, Wyoming. We toured Grand Teton National Park and picnicked at a beautiful spot, String Lake. Then we spent several nights in Yellowstone National Park and saw all the famous sights.

It was tough coming home after such a wonderful trip. But we weren't finished yet. Benita and I wanted to share a previous experience and take my folks on one of the "million dollar" drives in the country. That was a trip from Colorado Springs to Durango, Colorado. The drive from Ouray to Silverton on the way certainly rises to that level of spectacular beauty.

In Silverton after lunch, my parents and I boarded the Durango & Silverton Narrow Gauge railroad for the trip down the mountain. Benita volunteered to drive the car down and meet us at the station. She doesn't like railroad travel, but my parents and I really enjoyed that unique trip through the wilderness of Colorado. This vacation helped me to begin to enjoy the respite from the daily struggles of my previous duties.

My other favorite activity in Colorado was skiing. When the first ski areas opened late in the fall, I was ready. Every day that Brian had off from work, we went skiing at one of the nearby areas. We got a lot of visiting done on the ski lifts, and I believe that renewed our friendship, which had been strained during the past several years. I'd had little time for family activities during my tours at Andrews, Edwards, and Wright Patterson. Bonding with Brian again was my biggest achievement in retirement.

Job-hunting

I was too young to retire and needed some stimulating activities that I couldn't find sitting at home. Skiing was fun but wasn't enough to fill the void. The $4000 in my savings account was not enough of an emergency fund to handle life's inevitable setbacks. I needed to look for a job.

First, I had to learn how to compose a résumé, since I had never prepared one. I got into some books at the library and worked to translate my military experiences into something that would be meaningful for a private sector hiring manager. I also began to work my network of friends and acquaintances to look for something appealing in the aerospace industry. Eventually, I was invited to interview for several positions and received three offers.

Much to my surprise, I was called by friends in NASA to gauge my interest in the Center Director position at NASA's John F. Kennedy Space Center in Florida. I interviewed with the NASA Administrator, Dan Goldin, and was offered the position.

I looked forward to rejoining NASA in such a responsible and exciting position.

I accepted and began the process of planning a move to Florida to take the leadership position in March 1997.

At the time of my acceptance, I had less than six weeks to find a home in Florida and make the move. Benita and I traveled to Cocoa Beach to look for a home. After much searching, we settled on a two-bedroom condominium apartment on the fourth floor overlooking the beach. We were thrilled to have the opportunity to live in the Cocoa Beach area again.

We liked our little home in Colorado and decided to keep it. Brian agreed to be our house sitter. After a short while living in a temporary apartment while we waited on our new condo to close, we moved into our home on the beach.

Christmas Letter 1996

1996 was quite a year! On March 16, Tanya and Tom shared their marriage vows in a natural palm tree grove in the foothills above Palm Springs, CA. Their parents are thrilled for them.

They work in California as biologists for the Bureau of Land Management.

Roy retired from the air force on 1 July. The really neat thing about retiring is you get to pick a location. We chose Colorado Springs and have enjoyed six months here. Brian has a job at Office Max and lives here, too. He bought a snowboard and Roy bought skis. They have already been to the slopes several times. Benita works out at her favorite gym. Before the snow, we all got in a few long hikes in the beautiful mountains, and Roy and Benita played a lot of tennis.

Roy has discovered that looking for a job is a full-time job! He has a few interesting prospects. We'll know more by the New Year.

**Chapter 40: John F. Kennedy Space Center—Living on the
Beach and Launching Rockets**
March 1997–August 2003

In March of 1997, I was appointed as the NASA John F. Kennedy Space Center (KSC) Director. I had always admired the people of KSC for their dedication to the mission and flawless performances day after day, doing hazardous processing of launch vehicles and payloads as well as running the almost equally hazardous supporting infrastructure.

As I took charge, the Center was facing monumental challenges to remain relevant for the future. At the same time, the team was busy supporting multiple space shuttle and expendable launch vehicle launches per year along with preparing their payloads, such as the complex Spacelab missions. In short, KSC was a busy and exciting place to work.

Living on the beach in Cocoa Beach, Florida, was the realization of a lifelong dream.

When I used to visit the seashore on Jekyll Island as a youngster, I noticed that some of the caretakers lived in homes on the island. I thought to myself *that would be my dream home.* Now I was realizing it.

Xanadu Condo was ideally located on the south end of Cocoa Beach and just a few steps from the ocean. Our apartment was on the fourth floor, facing the beach. Our family room was equipped with a wall of floor-to-ceiling mirrors on the north wall. The visual effect was stunning. Opening the front door and stepping into the apartment was like being transported to the deck of a cruise ship.

Many mornings I would run on the beach in the dark or early dawn. Sunrises were often spectacular. The cumulus clouds over the ocean were dramatic. They looked like mountains rising out of the ocean. Aquatic birds were abundant. Large sea turtles crawled out of the surf to the sand dunes to dig nests and lay their eggs. Because of the constant sea breeze, biting bugs, such as mosquitoes, stayed away from the beach.

The noise from the surf provided a sleep-inducing lullaby at night. When storms were forecast, we just rolled our steel hurricane doors on the balcony closed and retreated to a safer place such as a friend's house in Orlando.

There were no yard work or other time-consuming household chores to do. Our two kids were adults and doing well on their own. We put most of our "stuff," which we had moved around to every one of our previous homes, in storage. I learned that I didn't miss it.

Living on the beach and launching rockets for a living proved to be an ideal situation for Benita and me. We were happy.

Faster, better, cheaper: transitioning KSC

I began to focus on the challenges facing KSC and its workforce right away. I was blessed by having a great team of leaders reporting to me who not only took care of the day's mission, but also were willing to tackle larger, immediate, existential challenges with me.

The situation that the team faced was dire. NASA and the administration were committed to reducing the size of the government workforce and refocusing on research and development as a core mission.

KSC was an operational center with minimal research and development content.

NASA adopted the motto: "Faster, better, cheaper." To achieve it, NASA planned to transition operations to contractors and reduce the size and importance of the federal workforce in accomplishing operations. Since many in the KSC workforce were directly involved with oversight of space shuttle operations, the outlook was demoralizing. They were directed by headquarters to transition to an insight as opposed to an oversight role.

In an oversight role, they were in charge, 24/7. So they were responsible for anything that happened, and the contractor took direction from them.

Once they transitioned to an insight role, the contractor was in charge. And KSC was reduced to looking over the contractor's shoulder—basically acting as observers. They could step in and speak up if they saw something out of kilter, but, except for launch and landing, they would not be in charge.

And, to add insult to injury, when NASA consolidated the space shuttle operations contracts into a single contract, they gave the control to manage that single contract to the program office at Johnson Space Center, as opposed to the Kennedy Space Center.

These people had been in charge. They built the space program at KSC. They *owned* it. Suddenly they were hearing, "Hey, you civil servants at KSC, we don't need you anymore because we've got these contractors. We just need some federal oversight," or as they called it, *insight*, because they didn't want them intruding. Now these folks who created this industry were going to be relegated to looking over somebody's shoulder, being very careful about ever saying anything.

Before arriving, I called the senior KSC leader for space shuttle operations and asked whether he thought that the Center could make this transition while maintaining the safety of operations. He thought that it was doable but would be difficult. The goal they'd been given was to make this transition and reduce the size of the government civilian workforce from 2498 in 1993 to 1490 by 2003.

The essence of the issue was how to make this transition without losing our best and brightest in the workforce.

Thinking and acting strategically

We decided the best way to approach this critical issue was to think and act strategically as opposed to a lot of tactical actions. We needed to convince our best and brightest that KSC had a bright future. All the messaging from the HQ was that NASA is a research organization, and KSC was operational. After the HQ took actions to move operations to a contractor and gave the leadership of that contract to Johnson Space Center (JSC), Kennedy Space Center was just an insight organization with an uncertain future.

As I'd learned in Key Club many years earlier, I enjoyed being a project leader.

A lot of people never have an opportunity to think strategically. Thinking strategically means asking what we want to accomplish, recognizing what steps need to be followed in order to achieve it, and methodically going about getting those things done. As opposed to having an emergency today, emergency tomorrow—doing little things to keep the railroad running without having any idea where the train is going.

I asked an expert, a professor who taught strategic planning at the University of Central Florida, to come in and be an advisor. Then we did some off-sites with him. He would recommend things that we ought to think about, and then we would fill in the details.

There were long days of discussions. And in holding these discussions, the whole idea was that we all come together on a certain focus rather than knocking heads, because I needed everybody pulling on this stalled-out big wagon in order to get it moving—and moving in the right direction. We needed to come up with a plan that everybody could relate to and be interested in seeing come to fruition.

In this kind of business, there are fires burning—and new ones starting—every day. So it's easy to get wrapped up in that and forget about the bigger picture.

We held a strategic off-site. The team developed a detailed road map for how to make the transition and how to message it to the headquarters and the workforce. The essence of it was that the people of KSC had critical knowledge of how to develop new space vehicles. They could assist with the design of them so that the lessons learned about launch site processing and infrastructure could be incorporated to reduce costs and assure safety. We also envisioned a future of many spaceports. All of them would need new technology to operate effectively. KSC developed a line of research to develop those spaceport technologies and got bright people involved in performing the new work.

Another key idea was to develop and implement a concept to manage the infrastructure jointly with the air force's Cape Canaveral Air Force Station just across the Banana River Bridge from KSC. This was a stretch, but we believed it could save a considerable amount of money. In addition to having fewer people in the contractor workforce, we could also reduce the federal workforce overseeing several contractors who were performing the work currently.

The NASA Administrator was not convinced that it could be done, but he called me with an interesting proposal. If we could do it, he would allow KSC to keep the savings and invest them in projects that would assist us strategically. I enthusiastically agreed!

After some key meetings to flesh out the concept, I was able to convince the air force that this idea was a win-win, and we set up a joint office to manage it and proceeded with an acquisition. We called it the Joint Base Operational Support Contract (JBOSC). The first indication that we had made a good call was that, on day one of the contract, the new contractor hired 500 fewer people to do the entire job, saving millions of dollars.

We encountered problems with the financial accounting to assure the right customer was charged for the appropriate services, but we eventually succeeded. Over the first five years, from 1998 until 2003, KSC saved more than $70 million, which was invested in strategic projects. We also were able to reduce the civil service workforce supporting these functions by 67%. We were awarded the Vice President's Hammer Award for this innovative partnership.

The transition of the space shuttle contract from a civil service to a contractor operation succeeded.

The civil service transitioned to insight versus oversight of day-to-day operations. Full civil servant control was maintained for launch and landing operations. Civil servants were moved to strategic projects.

Two of those strategic projects proved to be beneficial to both KSC and NASA. One was to obtain approval to process the International Space Station modules using a Multi-Element

Integrated Test process as opposed to the original concept of "ship and shoot." KSC engineers and technicians were critically involved in the design and execution of these more comprehensive tests. Some of them moved over from the shuttle program, where they were no longer needed.

The other big project was convincing the HQ as well as the Goddard Space Flight Center and Glenn Research Center to transfer the acquisition and operation of NASA's expendable launch vehicles to KSC as a program, as opposed to simply providing limited operational support during launch campaigns. NASA HQ agreed that this made great sense strategically. Again, we were able to attract a lot of our best and brightest to transfer to the new program.

We were able to reduce the shuttle workforce by 63%. The civil servant headcount declined from 1075 to 354 for the shuttle, and most of the best and brightest moved to the new programs and activities. The shuttle contractor headcount also decreased by 10%, from 7299 to 6557, over the FY 93-to-FY02 time period.

Overall, KSC achieved a 29% reduction in the civil service headcount from 1993 to 2003, dropping from 2498 to 1773. If we had reached the target of 1490, we would have had to achieve a 40% reduction. After much discussion and deliberation, HQ realized that KSC needed to stabilize its workforce at this higher number, given the contributions being made on programs critical to the agency and to avoid further critical skill challenges stemming from a longer hiring freeze.

We developed a core leadership team that learned to think and act strategically despite the challenges that we faced along the way. Many of the key leaders moved to other critical, top-level positions within NASA and mentored many others over their careers, creating even more win-wins for the agency and KSC.

NASA has had a superb safety and customer satisfaction record with its expendable launch vehicle program, proving the wisdom of making this strategic move. The International Space Station program achieved a successful 20-year anniversary in 2018, and many credit the Multi-Element Integrated Test program as one of the key factors in its success over the years.

KSC focused on other key issues such as safety, one of the guiding principles in our strategic road map. We were awarded the Occupational Safety and Health Administration (OSHA) Voluntary Protection Program Star Flag for our achievements in safety across the Center. Both KSC civil servants and major contractors were awarded this rating.

We created many activities, projects, and metrics to guide us to these achievements. I personally led projects such as mandatory safety walk-downs of all work areas by supervisors. Many improvements were recommended and funded as a result.

I started a simple award program. The award committee consisted of only me.

Anyone could be nominated for recognition for suggestions to improve operations, health, and safety. If approved by me, I would take a photographer and go down into the workforce and award a "Gold Dollar" to the awardee inscribed with his/her name and date as well as a citation citing the details.

Every year we had a "Gold Dollar" breakfast for all awardees. We raffled off door prizes donated by businesses and individuals to all attendees. We also established an "Ace" program for all who were awarded five Gold Dollars. This proved to be a popular program to get all involved in making key improvements.

Florida invests in the future

One other notable achievement was our success in engaging the State of Florida to be our supporter and advocate, given the importance of the space program to the economy. Jeb Bush paid me a visit in my office at KSC to tell me of his personal support for KSC while he was running for election for governor, which he won. I used that promise to engage him with my ideas of how to help us.

We wanted the legislature to pass a bill funding the basic infrastructure for a space industrial park and the first building in the park, a Space Experiments Research and Processing Laboratory that would replace a dilapidated facility currently used for that purpose at Cape Canaveral Air Force Station. Part of the funding would be used for a road through the industrial park outside the security gates to KSC.

As a first step we successfully convinced the leadership of the wildlife refuge that this park on disturbed land, used in the past for orange groves, would be a win-win. It would not damage the refuge that included the undeveloped land at KSC.

While lobbying for this initiative, Governor Bush assigned the Lieutenant Governor to escort me personally and introduce me to key legislative leaders. Over $30 million was provided for this strategic project. Today, industry is building rocket and satellite manufacturing factories in the park, creating many high-technology jobs for the area.

People thought I was crazy; they thought the government would never give me $30 million. Then they thought that was a waste of money because it would take twenty years—*twenty years*. Now they have two spacecraft factories there, and in September of 2021, they announced that they're going to build a third one and will hire over 2000 people in addition to the several thousand that are already there.

There were some in the community who were supporting the development of technology for high-speed trains. They approached me about granting them a route through KSC to the port at Cape Canaveral. I explained that would be tough to do since we were located in a wildlife refuge. Sometimes, you just have to say, "No."

We also made many improvements for the workforce at KSC that had been neglected over the years. Many of our employees' workspaces were housed in dilapidated house trailer parks and railroad boxcars that were far beyond their design lives. These were not only expensive to maintain, they were also unsafe, given the hazardous weather environment at KSC. Tropical storms and hurricanes were always a threat.

We were able to replace these inadequate facilities with new construction over the years. Trailers and boxcars were removed.

So those old orange groves have now brought in multiple thousands of jobs to this area, which helps make up for the very large contractor workforces that used to be there. Now, a lot of the risk in capital is coming from companies like SpaceX and other folks, and NASA doesn't have to spend so much money keeping everything going.

The full story of the strategic transformation of KSC is in the book, *Transforming Organizations—Strategies and Methods* by Timothy G. Kotnour. Tim was an associate professor in the Department of Industrial Engineering and Management Systems at the University of Central Florida. He was our consultant for strategic planning and transformation during the KSC transformation and was invaluable in that role, and his consulting relationship with NASA continues, more than twenty years later. As of this writing in 2022, he is a tenured professor and the Director of the Engineering Leadership and Innovation Institute at UCF.

Benita and Roy welcome President Clinton upon his arrival at the Kennedy Space Center to observe the launch of Senator Glenn

Hospitality, celebrities, and world travel

Benita, like me, thoroughly enjoyed our time at KSC. She was the First Lady and took part in escorting our many launch-day guests. One of the most memorable launches was John Glenn's shuttle mission in October 1998, when he was 77 years of age. As they disembarked from their airplanes on the runway at Cape Canaveral to attend his launch, Benita and I welcomed many members of Congress and President Bill Clinton and First Lady Hillary Clinton.

As John Glenn was training for the flight at JSC, he made several trips to KSC for that portion of training. He made it a habit to stop by my office during these visits. One evening, I was working late and had gone for a run around the Center. I was still in my running clothes, answering email at my desk, when he stopped by the office. He made light of my attire and brought me up to date on his experiences.

Later in my career, I had several opportunities to meet with him in his office in Washington as well as follow-on visits by him and his wife to KSC. He was always gracious and helpful—truly an American hero.

Roy as Center Director of the Kennedy Space Center (KSC) presents a memento to former President Jimmy Carter and Mrs. Carter during their visit to KSC

We had the interesting opportunity to welcome and support the shooting of several movies and TV shows at KSC. One of my guests for lunch in my conference room in the headquarters was Tom Hanks, who wanted to secure our approval for filming the *Earth to the Moon* series about the Apollo Program. I joked that I had just had lunch with Forrest Gump. After the series was completed, the world premiere was hosted by KSC. I had an opportunity to meet John F. Kennedy, Jr., who spoke at the premiere.

Another movie shooting that we hosted was *Space Cowboys*, which was directed by Clint Eastwood. When he visited my office, I had the entire complement of headquarters females in my outer office waiting for a sighting.

I had many opportunities to travel to other launch sites. I took a delegation on a trip to visit the European launch site in French Guiana. We enjoyed an in-depth tour and a traditional dinner of South American food.

On a great visit to Japan to deliver a speech at a community event and tour their launch site at Tanegashima, we were treated to a traditional meal as well. My intern, who was traveling with me, nudged me when one dish was served. He said that his lobster just blinked at him, which is just how fresh the raw lobster tail was.

I made two trips to Russia to tour their space facilities and observed the launch of one of their elements of the new International Space Station from their Baikonur launch site in Kazakhstan. During my first trip, I visited Red Square and the Kremlin. As I first saw the picturesque square, I was struck by how amazing it was to be working a great space venture with the Russians instead of worrying about a nuclear war. I was also able to visit Star City, where the cosmonauts and astronauts flying to the Mir Space Station trained. While there, I visited with astronaut and my former Purdue and UPT roommate, John Blaha, who was training for a flight to Mir, and his wife in their temporary home.

We launched a rocket from the new Alaskan launch site on Kodiak Island. I made several trips there, including a trip in the KSC airplane to pick up our crew, who had been stranded after the airlines were grounded for a while after 9/11.

On one of those trips my daughter arranged an introduction to the Wildlife Refuge Manager on Kodiak Island. He took me on a seaplane trip to the remote side of the island. I saw all sorts of wildlife in that pristine wilderness, including dozens of bears lined up in the river to catch salmon.

Honors

I was honored to make a trip to West Lafayette, Indiana, to attend the graduation ceremony at Purdue University and be awarded an honorary doctorate in engineering in 2001. I had enjoyed a previous trip to Purdue University in 1999 for an astronaut reunion organized by the university. I recall standing at the bar at an evening reception and being sandwiched by the first and last men on the moon. Neil Armstrong and Gene Cernan wanted to hear about happenings at KSC from me.

Before departing KSC I was awarded an honorary doctorate in science from the Florida Institute of Technology. I also received the Kurt Debus Award in 2001 from the Florida Committee of the National Space Club.

Rumor has it...

Being Center Director had its share of special challenges. One of those was keeping our customers at other NASA centers happy with our performance. I spent a lot of time visiting with the program directors of the key programs with activities at the centers and had good relationships with them during my tenure.

One notable exception came up because our leadership team in 2000 decided that we needed to reorganize the Center, given the many strategic changes being implemented. I traveled to JSC and briefed the Center Director on our plans and process. I agreed to keep him well informed about any changes that might affect JSC key programs. Despite that visit and several others, I learned in a roundabout way that JSC was unhappy with what we were attempting to do.

I went to the annual Goddard Dinner in Washington, DC, and ran into a friend from my days in the air force. He said that he had heard that I was leaving KSC. After returning to Florida, I had an opportunity to meet with my boss face-to-face about this information. He said that the JSC Director was unhappy with our reorganization plans and had complained to the NASA Administrator, who had started searching for a replacement for me.

I said that I couldn't run KSC effectively without the full support of the NASA Administrator. I also explained that I could easily get another job if they wanted me to leave. I gave my boss a deadline to either convey to me the full endorsement of NASA or I would leave. I had stated these and other things in a letter, which I hand-delivered to him at this meeting. Among other things, the two-page letter said,

> Nothing else I will ever do in my professional life will be able to compare with my current experience [as director of KSC]. ... However, I can not function as a leader in an environment where the Administrator is not supportive of my continuing. If, as rumor has it, he is also actively recruiting my replacement, my situation is untenable. ... I hope that I can continue here at KSC, but I must have clarification on this issue immediately.

A few days later, he said that the Administrator had second thoughts and fully endorsed what I was doing at KSC. Interestingly, the JSC Director who had complained, George Abbey, was removed not long after that because of NASA's unhappiness with the cost growth for the International Space Station.

After the JSC Director's firing, the NASA Administrator invited me to breakfast in Cocoa Beach during one of his visits and offered me the job of JSC Center Director. I was flattered, as JSC was an important center, and it would be a great experience to lead it. After much deliberation over the next few days, I arranged a meeting with my boss, and subsequently the Administrator, and declined the invitation.

My primary reason was that the timing was not auspicious, as the administration was changing and a new NASA Administrator was going to be appointed. Given the nature of the improvements that the current Administrator wanted me to make at JSC, I felt that I could not be successful in the remaining time of his tenure to win the support of the workforce and community at JSC. Clearly, an acting center director for JSC would be the best for the agency, given this timing. This would allow the new NASA Administrator to pick someone who would enjoy his or her full support for the important position.

Family life

We celebrated several significant milestone family events while living on the beach. We became grandparents in January 1998 with the birth of our granddaughter, Kynna Egan. We celebrated a family reunion in Florida with our entire family, including my mom and dad, our kids, their spouses and significant others, and our granddaughter in December 1998.

Our son, Brian, announced his engagement to Jennifer during a spring break visit in 1998. They married in Colorado Springs in June 1999, which was another great family reunion

Family reunion in Cocoa Beach, Florida, in 2001, while Roy was serving as the Kennedy Space Center Director (clockwise from left: Tom Egan, Benita, Elizabeth, Roy Sr., Roy Jr., Kynna Egan, Jennifer, Brian, Tanya and Kiley Egan)

opportunity. We attended the wedding and had a wonderful time welcoming Jennifer into the family. In July 2001, we celebrated the birth of our second granddaughter, Kiley Egan.

Benita continued attending a special Bible study called Bible Study Fellowship that she had begun several years earlier. The course required daily Bible study, followed by probing questions about the meaning of the verses for each student and how to apply the lessons to our everyday lives. Once a week she would attend a small seminar of 15 students led by a volunteer discussion-group leader. The students would share the answers to their questions and discuss them. This class would be followed by a lecture for all of the students by a teaching leader. After the lecture, notes were distributed to summarize the main points of the week's lesson, along with blank questions for the following week. The lessons covered major sections of the Old and New Testaments over the course of a dozen years.

My wife had encouraged me to attend the men's Bible Study Fellowship course when we were living in Houston. I did, along with an astronaut neighbor, and enjoyed it. After retiring from the air force, I started attending again in Colorado and continued to attend for the six and a half years that we were in Florida. In Florida, I encouraged three other friends to carpool with me to Orlando for the evening classes.

I was also extremely active in our United Methodist church in Florida, including accepting a leadership position as the chair of the Pastor-Parish Relations Committee.

Tragedy: 9/11

There was tragedy as well. On the morning of September 11, 2001, my senior staff and I arrived at Dodger Town by bus for a several-day off-site to review progress and make mid-course corrections to our strategic road map. As I was hanging my clothes in my hotel room, I noticed that the TV news was showing a smoking skyscraper in New York City. Then a second one was hit.

I was stunned and grieved about the loss of innocent lives in New York as well as at the Pentagon and the airplane crash in Pennsylvania. After meeting at lunch to review the situation, we abandoned our off-site and headed back to the Center to prepare for the aftermath of this attack on the nation.

In the days after the attack, details about the hijackers started to become available. They had trained to fly. We didn't know if there were more lurking in the shadows and planning attacks on other national icons such as the space shuttle. A shuttle on the pad was vulnerable to attack from either the air or from the sea, and it wouldn't take a large airliner to cause a disaster. A light airplane flown by a single suicide pilot would get the job done. We had a lot of workers at the pad as we prepared the shuttle for launch. I worried about how to protect them so that they could focus on the critical work they were doing.

I worked with the air force, our security contractor, and the state to strengthen our defensive posture. We eventually had armed helicopters and flights of air force fighters to protect the shuttle during critical portions of the countdown and launch, as well as a much more intense security screening posture at all times and a more structured launch viewing procedure rather than just letting hundreds of cars enter the Center and park on the causeway. Fortunately, although the air force did have to force down several intruding aircraft as a precaution, these all proved to be non-terrorist intrusions, and there were no casualties as a result.

I had guns installed on our helicopters and trained the crews. After the shuttle rolled out, they flew the helicopter out to the launch pad, landed in an open area near the shuttle, and stayed on alert. The idea was that they would act like a hockey goalie and position themselves between an incoming aircraft and the pad. Shots would be fired only if the plane continued to fly directly toward the shuttle.

The NASA Administrator was furious when he learned about my armed helicopters. He called me at home one evening. He yelled at me so loudly that Benita could hear him from the other room. He was worried that we would shoot down some innocent person. When I finally could get a word in edgewise, I said, "Dan, we had to do something to protect our workers at the pad. I didn't ask your permission because I wanted you to have plausible deniability." He let me continue with our protective measure.

Tragedy: family

There was a family tragedy as well. In October 2002, as I arrived home from work, our daughter, Tanya Egan, called us. Benita and I were both on the phone when she explained that she had just been diagnosed with non-Hodgkin's lymphoma, stage 4, and was on her way to the UCLA Medical Center, where she would be met in the emergency room by some of her medical doctor friends.

This was totally unexpected and devastating. Benita and I were stunned. Our idyllic life was suddenly in the ditch. We had a tough night dealing with our emotions and trying to fathom why this was happening and how we could help. Benita made plans to fly to California immediately to help with our young granddaughters while Tanya was being treated in the hospital.

Tragedy: Columbia

There was a professional tragedy, too. On February 1, 2003, as I was escorting the NASA Administrator and other visitors at the Shuttle Landing Facility to witness the landing of STS-107, which was the 113th flight of the program, we heard the Mission Control Center calling Columbia several times to establish radio contact. At the time for Columbia to arrive over the field and announce her arrival with the signature double sonic booms, there was only silence. I knew immediately that Columbia was lost, as the shuttle is never late to arrive unless the worst imaginable accident has occurred. I knew in my heart that seven people had just died.

I told the NASA Administrator that we had had a bad day and needed to adjourn quickly to a secure facility to investigate the situation and take appropriate actions. He agreed.

Back in the Launch Control Facility, we saw that reporters on TV were showing strange sightings of flaming debris raining down over east Texas. Clearly, this was the worst-imaginable accident that I had feared.

After assuring that the crew families were secure and briefed on the accident, we began what would be a multi-month effort to recover Columbia and her crew and return them to KSC. Teams were dispatched to Texas and Louisiana to organize this mammoth undertaking, supported by teams from many other federal and state government agencies.

We also supported the Accident Investigation Board, looking into the cause of the accident and corrective actions that we would need to take before flying again. There were funerals and memorial services to plan and attend.

The details of bringing Columbia home are well presented in the book *Bringing Columbia Home* by Shuttle Launch Director Michael D. Leinbach and Jonathan H. Ward. The team was exceptional; despite the hardships of the job, they persisted, day after day. Walking through the briars of East Texas, finding all these little pieces of the shuttle—it was traumatic, to say the least. They were sleeping in tents, in these stables that they use for rodeos. The Forest Service moved in a lot of their infrastructure: tractor trailers—one would have showers in it, and another one would have food service—and things like that to serve these people, month on month on month.

Michael Leinbach was one of the key leaders of this team, and they stayed the course. They wouldn't let anything get in their way. They kept plowing through until we'd recovered all the essential pieces—all of the crew stuff, which we put into a special area because that's all sensitive; of course the bodies; and then the pieces of the shuttle that would help us confirm exactly what had happened.

We were able to lay out the remains of Columbia in a hangar at the Shuttle Landing Facility. The recovery of those remains was critical to confirming that a piece of foam from the shuttle external tank had fallen off the tank and hit a critical area in the leading edge of the wing. The resulting hole allowed superheated plasma to enter the wing during shuttle reentry and caused structural failure.

We planned the memorial service for Columbia and her crew to take place on the runway at KSC where she was supposed to land. I was involved in a critical decision on the morning of the event. We wanted to position the audience in the open on the runway to let them get the full effect of the ceremony, but bad weather threatened. It was cloudy, and rain was possible. After consulting with my weather officer, John Maduro, the world's best weather forecaster, I elected to position the guests on the runway, out in the open.

As the ceremony started, I found myself sitting opposite the Florida governor, Jeb Bush. He was on the stage and I was in the front row of the audience. I was startled by a large raindrop hitting me on my head as the ceremony started. I saw that the governor had noticed my flinch, and I just raised my hands, palms up in resignation. It would be what it would be; we were committed. He smiled.

The ceremony continued without any serious rain interference. At the conclusion and at the exact time of day that Columbia should have landed, a low-level flight of four T-38 jets appeared out of the fog heading down the runway. As they passed they executed the missing man formation. One of the jets pulled up into the sky and disappeared into the clouds.

It was a dramatic conclusion. I had trouble keeping my composure.

There were many people grieving at the organizations supporting NASA and the space shuttle program. I toured the shops at KSC, like the shop that sewed heat-resistant quilts for the shuttle. Everyone at that shop and many others worried that something that they may have done had caused the mishap.

We kept up a lot of communications during this time to reassure people that we would get to the bottom of this tragedy and explain the causes to them. These communications and the publication of the accident report eventually helped them to realize that, while we all shared in our collective failure to keep Columbia and her crew safe, none of the actions by members of the KSC workforce were implicated in the cause of this accident.

At the end of the investigation, we organized a tour for the entire workforce of the hangar where Columbia's remains were laid out on the floor. We took them out on buses and allowed them to walk the floor to see the results.

We obtained permission to organize and properly store the remains in the Vehicle Assembly Building so that we could support research efforts to improve our spacecraft of the future.

The Roy D. Bridges Bridge

After the accident report was published, I got a call from the NASA Administrator. He said, "I am going to reassign your Deputy Director, Jim Kennedy, as the Center Director at the Langley Research Center to set up a NASA Engineering and Safety Center (NESC) as a key action to prevent future accidents."

I protested. I said, "My background is aeronautical research as an engineering test pilot and former space shuttle astronaut. Jim does not have that type of experience.

"Also," I added, "he would be great as the future Center Director of KSC."

The Administrator agreed and ordered me to get ready to report to Langley.

I could have kept quiet and ended my NASA career at KSC, which was my true personal desire. But I felt that would not be best for all concerned. So off to Langley and another adventure.

There were going-away parties for Benita and me to thank us for our contributions at KSC. One gift that started out as a joke by Jim Kennedy still exists. Jim declared that the Banana River Bridge would be named the Roy D. Bridges Bridge, and a sign was erected. This was to signify that the JBOSC contract had "bridged" the waters separating KSC and Cape Canaveral Air Force Station. Many people have since commented that they had traveled over "my bridge."

Christmas Letters from 1997–2002

1997: Dearest friends and family,

I've been trying to write everyone a personal note/letter this year, and so far I've only gotten to the Hs, so thought I'd best type a quick note and get our new address off to you. I know we have really made a mess of your address book.

1998: Although we're much too young, we're now grandparents and thrilled about it.

The other big family news this year is that Brian and Jennifer have announced their engagement. They sprang the news during a spring vacation with us here in Florida.

We've adjusted well to Florida and condo living on the beach. Benita plays tennis often during the week and beats Roy regularly when we play on weekends. We have really enjoyed the sea views, and it's a great place to watch rocket launches.

1999: The big news was Brian and Jennifer's wedding on 6-27 in a beautiful setting in the Black Forest near Colorado Springs, with Pike's Peak as a backdrop for a romantic and spiritual ceremony. For Christmas, Kynna, our 23-month-old granddaughter, came for a visit with her parents. We had a grand time but were worn out after five days of trying to keep up with her at the Magic Kingdom, the zoo, and the beach. She's a blue-eyed beauty, and she moves fast from wake-up till bedtime.

Shuttle launches were few and far between, but the three we launched were all very significant missions—one to visit the new space station for outfitting and maintenance in May; the launch of the Chandra Xray Telescope and NASA's first female commander, Eileen Collins, in July; and the repair mission to the Hubble Telescope in December. We had a lot of unmanned launches, too, including a mission to catch some stardust from a comet and return it to Earth.

Roy went to Alaska in the summer and caught a really big salmon.

2000: We did a lot of traveling this year, so maybe that's why it seemed so short...a first-time cruise on the Disney Magic...Roy's work trip to Colorado + weekend visit with Brian and Jennifer... Roy went to Russia to witness the launch of the Zvezda to the space station (that was a once-in-a-lifetime adventure—Baikonur is a hard place to get to)...California to visit Tom, Tanya, and Kynna (how much Kynna has grown!), in conjunction with a rocket launch at Vandenburg for Roy and Arizona for Benita... Purdue University, where Roy gave a lecture to the engineering schools and we watched Purdue beat Ohio State...drive to Gainesville, GA on several long weekends to visit Roy's folks and sisters, and lots of visits with friends in Florida.

At work, Roy's team launched 5 shuttle missions and 6 unmanned rockets. There was a lot of behind-the-scenes preparation for seven space station construction missions planned for next year.

The beach is a great place to live. We walk and run on it often and enjoy watching the shore birds and the other wildlife (some two-legged) in the area.

2002: Our daughter Tanya was diagnosed with Non-Hodgkins Lymphoma in October. She has marvelous faith, a tremendously positive attitude, and high energy (she needs it to keep up with Kynna and Kiley!) She has tolerated the treatment regime well. We appreciate Tom, her friends in CA, and the wonderful team of doctors at UCLA. Together, they have provided a wonderful support structure as Tanya challenged this dangerous disease with grace and courage.

Brian and Jen continue to live and work in Colorado. Brian built a patio on their new home, and they have been remodeling the interior as they have time between work and hiking and snowboarding trips into the beautiful CO mountains.

Roy continues as Director of the Kennedy Space Center. His team's big project, the International Space Station, (ISS) is nearing a big milestone...We now know that there is much evidence of water below the surface of Mars as a result of more extensive surveys over the past two years from orbiting space-craft, which means that we may someday discover evidence of microbial life there. That will be an incredible discovery...it would indicate that life is pervasive in the Universe—where there is water and energy.

We are still having fun living on the beach and launching rockets to explore this amazing universe that God created for us.

Chapter 41: Historic Williamsburg and NASA Langley Research Center
August 2003–December 2005

Had I not been selected as an astronaut, I could have been a test pilot for the rest of my career, I was that enamored with the profession. Embarking on every new job in the rest of my career was like my going through parachute training at Fort Benning, standing in the door of an airplane, on a dark night, jumping into the unknown. I've never been there. I don't know the people. I don't know the stakeholders. Maybe I've got a clue about some of the challenges.

I was given only a few months to get up to Langley Research Center and set up the NESC. In addition, I was directed to show up at Langley without letting anyone know that I was coming. On my first day, I showed up on stage at the auditorium and was introduced to the workforce by the NASA Administrator.

During our house-hunting trip earlier, Benita and I had to be careful not to spill the beans. Unfortunately, we didn't find a house that we could afford, and that led to a mistake in judgment. I upped the price range and looked at some additional houses with my realtor without Benita in attendance. She was again tied up caring for our ill daughter in California, who was being treated with several rounds of chemotherapy and radiation treatments. I found what I thought was the perfect house, took a lot of pictures, and gave Benita a virtual tour with them. I thought that she was also "sold" and made an offer on the house. It was accepted, and I was relieved.

Later, I learned that she didn't appreciate my selection, but we both eventually came to enjoy our new home. It was in a gated community in historic Williamsburg, Virginia, on one of the golf courses in the Kingsmill Resort. From our upstairs window, we could see the James River at the end of the tenth fairway. We enjoyed walking and running on the cart paths around the course.

We also enjoyed exploring the many historic sites within a few miles. Jamestown, Williamsburg, and Yorktown were all examples of life in the early Colonial period and were fun to visit. We could travel between them on the historic Colonial Parkway through the woods that was free of commercial development. We were only a couple of miles from the Busch Gardens theme park, one of the most beautifully landscaped parks in the nation.

I drove to Williamsburg in one of our cars to close on the house, and Benita stayed in Cocoa Beach to deal with some scheduled medical procedures and the moving company. I stayed in the visiting quarters at Langley AFB for a few days while waiting for the house to close.

When it did in August, I purchased a queen sleeper couch to have somewhere to sleep until my wife arrived, and we had time to select and purchase some new furniture. We had decided to keep our condo in Cocoa Beach for the time being. When the items that we did move from Cocoa Beach arrived, I found myself hiding behind the boxes as Hurricane Isabel battered the house and yard.

I had installed a new roof before moving in, so we didn't experience any significant water damage inside the house. The yard was a different matter. We lost several trees, and I picked up 75 large bags of debris. Plus, the water from my neighbors' yards all ran under my deck on its way to the creek on the other side of our house and almost washed out the pilings. I had to contract with a landscaping company to grade the backyard to channel the water away from the deck and install some large flowerbeds to assist as barriers to the previous water flow channels. These were attractive and improved the appearance of our home.

We experienced some considerable damage to some of the older facilities on parts of Langley near the water. Several of the local communities where our workforce lived were heavily damaged. I sought and obtained permission to open the facility's gates to family members so that they could shower in our gym and eat in our cafeterias, newer buildings that were not near the waterfront. This was much appreciated.

One of the smartest early decisions that I made in planning for Langley was to invite Ralph and Lesa Roe to join me as key members of my staff. Ralph was previously the head engineer for the Shuttle Program at KSC and was currently working in the Shuttle Program Office at JSC. I wanted him to be the Director of the new NASA Engineering and Safety Center. Lesa would initially be in charge of our business operations as a direct report to me. After I completed a reorganization of the Center, she became my Deputy Director. Both proved to be excellent choices. Ralph did a great job in setting up the NESC and making it effective. Lesa was an excellent deputy in all ways.

Hints of trouble

I had been a friend of the former Director of Langley before he retired. People had a lot of respect for him and described Langley as the best-managed center in NASA. When I parachuted into Langley, I thought that my main challenge would be helping Ralph set up the NESC. I was terribly wrong.

The first hint of trouble brewing was President Bush's announcement in January 2004 of the new Vision for Space Exploration. It was a response to the Columbia accident to regain public enthusiasm for space exploration. The plan was to send humans back to the moon by 2020 in preparation for the human exploration of Mars. I was excited about it.

The NASA Administrator told me to talk to our congresswoman to get her support and to begin a campaign of public engagement. He assured me that the project would be funded with more top-line budget for NASA. Our aeronautical research budget would not be cut because of it.

The plan called for the International Space Station to be completed by 2010 and the space shuttle retired in the same year. A new capsule, Orion, would be built along with investments in a lot of new technology.

A month later, when the president's budget was announced, Langley's budget was cut by $100 million from the previous year's $800 million. Several major projects were canceled. My congresswoman was angry with NASA and me because I had unknowingly communicated a lie to her about Langley's budget not being a target to fund the president's new program. She had already promoted it to her constituents. But, to her constituents, budget cuts in their district because of the program felt like she was not supporting and advocating for them.

Reinvigorating the workforce

My workforce was extremely upset. I learned that they felt entitled to their top-line budget and projects. They had been protected through the years. They could not see a way forward.

I needed to help them adjust to this new reality and get them engaged in the new work. After all, Langley managed the Viking spacecraft, which were the first to touch down on Mars. The human space program with the Mercury astronauts resided at Langley until JSC was established in 1961 as the Manned Spacecraft Center.

We needed to reconnect to our legacy.

One of our first efforts to engage was to deploy a senior manager to JSC, where he embedded himself in the Shuttle Program Office. He helped them to understand how we could help with the return-to-flight projects. Langley picked up a lot of work as a result.

We also worked hard to bring new technology projects to the Center, which were focused on the return-to-the-Moon-and-on-to-Mars program. These were great additions. We soon found enough work to survive the first budget cut.

I knew that we weren't out of the woods yet. I needed to do a lot more to make us nimble enough to not just survive, but thrive.

I was successful at KSC by approaching challenges strategically. At our first leadership retreat at Langley, we all got on the same page about our strengths and areas where we needed to improve. We began to build a road map to achieve future successes.

Reorganizing the Center

The leadership team decided that we needed to reorganize the Center to focus on our strengths and the new direction for NASA. I realized that our most senior leaders needed a dose of new blood. Those at the highest rank, Senior Executive Service (SES), acted like they had jobs for life. I needed them to feel some of the pain that people working for them were feeling.

I convened a meeting with them in September 2004 and told them they would have to compete for an SES position in the new organization, and there would be fewer slots than we currently had. Each of them would be allowed to compete for three of the new positions.

I invited the Office of Personnel Management to approve our selection process. I also asked them to set up a leadership assessment exercise to score each applicant on their leadership capabilities.

In addition to the selection board, I interviewed each of them for a different reason. I asked them to tell me which positions at the next level under SES they would like if they weren't successful in winning one of the SES positions. No one would lose pay, just prestige.

We stood up the new organization and announced the winners of the SES competition in October 2004 at a senior leadership retreat.

Quite a few people were upset with me.

Leadership development

We hit bottom in February 2005 when the president's new budget was announced. We were cut by another $150 million. Such a drastic cut would most likely require a reduction in force.

Now people were really scared.

We held another senior leadership retreat to create the Center Transformation Project to address the budget cuts. The NASA Administrator gave it his gold star award when I briefed him.

We also started a major leadership development project that was instrumental in the eventual success of our transformation.

I stumbled into this leadership development training when the head of our research organization, who reported to me directly, asked permission to take his seven direct reports to a leadership training program in California for 10 days in November 2003. He said that they weren't working well as a team, and he had talked to someone who had attended this training, Learning as Leadership, with great results. Despite the time and expense, I gave my approval. When they returned, I interviewed the participants. All but one described the training as life-changing. The other one refused to go to the remaining three seminars because he described it as a cult religion.

I decided to attend the next offering in March 2004 to see for myself. It fell into the category of life-changing. Despite my years of leadership training and experiences during my air force and NASA careers, I discovered that my leadership style, which had been effective in those operational organizations, was not as effective in a research organization like Langley. In an operational organization, people expected the leader to be direct. At Langley, I joked that you could tell the extroverted scientists because they looked at my feet when they were talking to me instead of their own feet.

To say that they were inhibited by my direct style was a gross understatement. The training helped me to recognize my behaviors that were not effective and to reinvent my leadership style to be effective in a research organization. I also had the advantage of frequent coaching calls that kept me informed of what others were seeing in my behaviors so that I could correct any issues immediately.

We expanded the group of attendees to include all of those who reported directly to me. Over the course of the four seminars during the year, we jelled as a team and were able to select and fully engage with effective long-term strategies that proved to be highly successful.

Our leadership team became a team of entrepreneurs. The Kick-Start Teams that we had created developed into effective marketing organizations and began to bring new work to the Center.

The new NASA Administrator who arrived in 2005 made a wise decision to have healthy NASA centers as opposed to paying for the new Constellation Program, an early part of the Vision for Space Exploration, out of the aeronautical research centers' budgets. Both the Constellation Program and the Vision for Space Exploration were eventually cancelled or reformulated.

In creating the healthy centers, by redistributing other work to more fairly spread work among the centers, the Administrator basically reversed the cutting of our budget to the degree that it had been done under the Bush administration and restored a lot of that money. This removed the threat of large-scale layoffs at Langley that were on the near horizon. So we did not have to have these draconian workforce reduction programs that it looked like we were going to have to get into. We picked up a lot of new work for the exploration program, just as we had done to help the space shuttle program Return to Flight. Things began to improve rapidly.

The future looked bright.

Christmas 2003

> We're about as far behind as the federal government was with this year's appropriation bills. Not a pretty situation!
>
> Big changes and challenges were the order of the year:
>
> Roy became Director of the Langley Research Center in August. We do miss "living on the beach and launching rockets for a living." But this part of Virginia is new and exciting: historic, scenic, lovely tree and wildlife, friendly & smart people.
>
> Tanya was diagnosed with non-Hodgkin's lymphoma in Oct. 2002—was in guarded remission by summer—and now back at UCLA Medical Center getting ready for a bone marrow

transplant. She has red curly hair versus straight after last year's chemo. Tanya has a great attitude and appreciates all of your prayers as we do.

Columbia lost. Recovery of the debris from East Texas and solving the riddle of the mishap were priorities. We're working hard to return to flight and continue to explore—what we know the crew would want as a legacy.

Launching 2 rovers to Mars. Opportunity's launch was Roy's last at KSC.

Thanksgiving with Roy Sr. and Elizabeth in GA—both doing good—Pappy won the Senior Olympics Silver Medal for Pool Shooting at 91!

Chapter 42: Family Tragedy
2005

On top of the challenges at work, Tanya was battling cancer, and Benita and I had to help so that her husband could continue working to provide good health insurance. After a lot of chemotherapy and radiation treatments, she went into a brief remission. Tanya and her husband and two daughters visited us for the holidays in Williamsburg in December 2003 and we had a great time.

The good times didn't last long. The cancer returned with a vengeance.

In May 2004, Tanya had a bone marrow transplant. Benita spent three months in California caring for her. This was tough on Benita, who had to undergo a heart catheterization to correct an issue when she returned home.

The transplant initially appeared to do the trick. Tanya and her two girls joined us at our Florida condo in August 2004 for a wonderful vacation.

At Thanksgiving 2004, the entire family gathered at Tanya and Tom's home in California for a family reunion. Clouding the festivities was the news that the cancer was back. She needed another bone marrow transplant. While there we were all tested to see if one of us could be a bone marrow donor. None of us were a match.

She had her second transplant in March 2005 with bone marrow from an anonymous donor. Benita again spent three months in California caring for her as she prepared for and recovered from the transplant. I went out during the kids' spring break to keep them occupied with fun activities in the Los Angeles area. They also got to visit their mom in the hospital.

We decided to put our Florida condominium on sale in early 2005. Taking care of a second home, given everything else that was happening, was just too much. Prices of beachfront property were going crazy. My property taxes were skyrocketing, since I no longer had a homestead exemption. I summarized the situation by saying, "Prices are going crazy, the shuttle is retiring, and the seas are rising. Time to get off the beach."

We sold it in June 2005. The new owner wanted immediate occupancy. Benita and I traveled to Florida to move our household goods to Virginia.

While we were there, Tanya called. She'd had a setback and was being admitted to UCLA Hospital. Benita immediately boarded an airplane to California.

I completed packing our goods and drove back to Virginia to receive them. I planned a trip in early July to visit with Tanya and Benita at UCLA. I was supposed to fly out on a Saturday afternoon. I talked to Tanya, and she was upbeat. I was behind on some things that I needed to complete before the trip. She talked me into delaying my trip to Sunday.

A few hours later, Benita called and said, "Tanya coded and is on the way to ICU." I hastily packed while rebooking my Saturday flight.

By the time I arrived, Tanya was in a medically induced coma while being treated for sepsis. Benita and I took turns sitting in the ICU for the next couple of days. Tanya never regained consciousness.

The doctor met with us and said that they could not do anything else to help her. Her organs were beginning to shut down.

After that meeting, we went to a nearby restaurant for a meal. We were starving. The hospital called and told us to get back to the ICU, as her condition was rapidly deteriorating. We left our meal uneaten.

Benita and I, along with a priest, family, and friends, were holding her limbs as she passed.

Amazingly, she played music on the instruments in her hospital room—after she died, after they were unplugged. Her doctor friend, who was in attendance, confirmed the miracle. Being there and witnessing that helped us to grieve well and be able to step in to assure that her two beautiful daughters could enjoy the rest of their childhood, as our daughter would have wanted.

Yes, it was tough losing her, but we didn't lose our faith over that event. It made us stronger. This is not to say that we didn't fervently wish for a different outcome and pray daily for that. What it does say is that we all have to go someday, in some way, since we are biological creatures with a finite life span. Our strong faith helped us live life fully and confidently after this tragedy, as God intended.

We worked with Tom to plan a Celebration of Life and a Catholic funeral Mass for Tanya. As the funeral director opened the doors of the hearse so that we could take Tanya's casket into the church, a butterfly flew out. Afterwards, when Benita or I would be walking or jogging, we often had a Tanya sighting.

A few months later, many friends and family members took a ferry to Catalina Island, one of Tanya's favorite places. A Catholic priest led a communion and prayer service. Then we rented kayaks and paddled a couple of miles to a distinctive shoreline feature named Frog's Rock. We spread her ashes in the Pacific Ocean there.

Benita and I spent a lot of time on our deck—and later, when it was cold, in front of our fireplace—supporting each other as we grieved her passing. She would never let us be anything but optimistic as we supported her during her almost three years in treatment. We thought that she would eventually recover. That made her sudden relapse and death more shocking.

Mutual parting of the ways

For me personally, I needed more time to spend with my wife and family. My interactions with some of the headquarters staff deteriorated as they engaged with me on our plans to re-structure the Center to respond to the budget challenges. They wanted me to move on, so that is what I did. In October of 2005, I again announced my retirement. I was asked to stay on to do a study for the headquarters for a couple of months, but I relin-quished the front office to my deputy, Lesa Roe, immediately, and retired from NASA at the end of the calendar year.

From: Roy Bridges
Date: Friday, Sep 16, 2005

To all Langley civil service and contractor employees:

After thoughtful deliberation, I have asked the Adminis-trator to allow me to retire in January 2006. I have agreed to stay on as Center Director until a successor is named.

This decision was not an easy one for me. After much soul-searching, I have reached the conclusion that my decision is in the best interest of the NASA family and my family. The causes of this turn of events are not simple, as life is not simple for any of us. While not a direct cause, the death of my daughter this summer, after a valiant three-year fight against cancer, had a deep personal im-pact on me. I owe it to those who have given their all, especially the Challenger and Columbia crews, to give not just my best, but my complete focus at all times. I feel that taking myself out of a very demanding leadership role is something that I need to do right now because I am not 100 percent focused. I believe this is the best way that I can honor my "all in" commitment to you with integrity.

Rest assured, I will remain a staunch supporter and advocate for the NASA team. The contributions that we have made in Discovery's Return to Flight, the record-setting flights of the X-43A, and the landings of Spirit and Opportunity on Mars have been phenomenal. I am proud of you as well as the larger NASA team of dedicated civil servants and contractors it took to succeed.

Leading first the Kennedy Space Center and then the Langley Research Center teams over the last eight-and-a-half years has been a career high point for my family and me. You are truly inspirational for what you do for the Nation and the world. I look forward to cheering on the NASA team as you continue to achieve extraordinary accomplishments. It is truly a high honor and pleasure to serve with you.

Sincerely,

Roy

Without mincing words, I got fired, but I was ready to go. I regarded the award of several NASA Outstanding Leadership Medals and one Meritorious Rank Award as good evidence of the success of my service during my NASA tours as Center Director at Langley and Kennedy.

I was invited to speak at the tenth anniversary of the founding of the NASA Engineering and Safety Center (NESC) at Langley. I learned that in the ten years since its creation, they had completed over 500 in-depth, technical studies of potential safety issues that had been nominated by the chief engineers at NASA's centers.

If only we'd had the vision to set up the NESC after Challenger, we might have prevented the Columbia tragedy.

The essence of the leadership skills I had learned was timeless, priceless, and would serve me well in the next phase of my life.

How to parachute into a new organization and quickly learn what is working and what isn't.

Listening, and learning the best voices to take to heart: Who do you listen to?

Getting a broad understanding of the challenges confronting your organization that require a transformation.

Understanding the current organizational culture and what needs to change. For example, the culture between NASA KSC and NASA Langley were like night and day: What worked at one place was completely foreign to the other.

Developing consensus on the plan for transformation.

Advocating the way forward to stakeholders. At KSC, that almost got me fired.

At Langley, eventually, it did.

October 9, 2005

Dear family and friends,

This year we decided to write to you all now instead of waiting for the holidays. Things that we need to communicate are better said sooner rather than later in the event you haven't heard about them.

Many of you know that we lost our daughter, Tanya, to cancer on July 11. She fought the battle well for almost three years. Tanya lived her life with great joy and optimism. She was never a victim of the disease and never gave in to it. We are all better for having known her and loved her. We miss her very much.

Some of you may have heard that Roy has decided to retire from NASA at the end of the year. This was a difficult decision. Roy has been Center Director for almost nine years—six and a half at Kennedy Space Center and the rest here at Langley. Although we had been thinking that next summer would be the optimal time to leave, Roy decided to move that up. He gave the reins of the Center to his deputy, Lesa Roe, on October 3.

We don't know what is next for us. Eventually, we would like to migrate west to be closer to our kids and grandkids. Being here on the East Coast does facilitate visits with Roy's mom and dad, who continue to do well, and Roy's sisters and their families. We visit often. "Pappy" is still winning pool tournaments at 93. Mom is having some mobility problems but gets around well with her walker. They still beat us at penny poker, too!

Our faith, our family, and our friends sustained us this year. Thanks for being there for us. We love you.

Tanya Marie Egan
1970–2005
"Those who dwell among the beauties and mysteries of the earth
are never alone or weary of life."
Rachel Carson

Section 3: Northrop Grumman

Chapter 43: Business Unit Director
February 2006–March 2015

As my NASA retirement date approached, I began to get feelers from some surprising corners of academia and industry about what I could/should do next. One of the more interesting ones was from Northrop Grumman (NG).

I visited the NASA Langley Legal Office to make sure that it was okay to talk to them. They made sure that I had recused myself from all government business decisions and approved me to discuss future employment opportunities with them.

I was invited to NG headquarters in Herndon, Virginia, for an interview. I had an interesting discussion with their president, and he offered me a position to take effect after my retirement from NASA.

Parental care

In January I traveled to Gainesville, Georgia, to help my parents move out of their home—the home of my high school years, near the lakefront—to an independent living apartment in Birmingham, Alabama, near where my sister Nancy lives.

Mom had worked as a nurse until she could collect retirement and then joined my dad in his picture framing business, where she worked with him for seven or eight years. She took over the counter and customer duties, while Dad, whose hearing was getting worse, focused on the artistic design and construction of the frames—and changed the name of his business to "Frames by Liz & Roy." Eventually they sold the shop.

By then, Mom's health was declining. Among other difficulties, neuropathy made it painful to walk. Their laundry facilities were in the basement, and nevertheless, she continued to do the laundry even though she had to go up and down the stairs on her bottom—and that just wasn't going to work. She and Dad moved into an independent living facility in 2006.

An ice storm had caused a large tree limb to fall on their roof over their front guest bedroom, which caused roof and wall damage. I helped them get that repaired. I also sold their car, which they did not need. The assisted living facility provided a van to take Dad to the grocery store and drugstore when needed.

After the successful move was completed, my two sisters, their husbands, and I held an estate sale to clear their home of the things that they didn't need in their apartment. Afterwards, we put the house on the market for sale.

After the estate sale was completed, I stayed in their house overnight to stage my departure to Virginia the next day. About 9:00 p.m., after I had settled down for the evening, the front-yard intruder lights came on and startled me. I received a phone call from the neighbors about strange activity in the front yard.

A gang of people was rummaging through the large, roll-on trash bin where we had placed items that did not sell and remaining items that my parents had collected over the years and didn't want to keep. One of the gang members came to the front door and peered into the small window on the door.

"We are here for the sale!" he yelled.

He looked scary. I didn't open the door. "The sale is over," I yelled back through the closed door.

"Can we go through the items in the bin?"

"Okay," I said. "And take what you want."

They did!

Failing retirement

In early February, I got a cute greeting card from my wife. It showed a duck on a diving board, leaning forward over a small pan of water. The card said, "What are you waiting for? Jump in!" With that encouragement, I agreed to start work on February 13, 2006.

I had failed retirement again.

When parachuting into unknown new employment territory, there is both a thrill and a little bit of fear that goes with it. These organizations are doing important things. All of a sudden you're in charge, for better or worse. And not only does your career depend on doing well, but ... if you don't, you're done.

By accepting their offer, I violated all the rules of negotiating a new job. I didn't know for sure what my job duties were or who my supervisor would be. They had offered me a nice salary and working conditions with the promise that they would vector me into a responsible position after my orientation period.

One of the best perks was that I could work remotely—I wouldn't have to move from our home in Williamsburg to their headquarters in Herndon, Virginia. What that meant initially was that I would drive to Herndon after rush hour on Monday and back to Williamsburg before rush hour on Friday. They agreed to pay for my commuting and hotel expenses. Eventually, my work for them took me all over the world.

I was assigned to a team that was completing the stand-up of NG's newest sector. Northrop Grumman Technical Services (NGTS) was formally established on January 1, 2006—roughly six weeks before I parachuted in. The president of the legacy sector who had offered me a job was now running the Government Services Division in the new sector. I would work in his division.

I was assigned temporarily to the transition team. The team visited the other NG sectors to assess and advocate the transfer of many government services contracts to NGTS. This gave me an excellent view of the bigger Northrop Grumman as a whole and got me acquainted with many of the new contracts that we inherited.

One of my colleagues there was Major General USAF (retired) Mike Butchko. Mike and I had known each other since attending ARPS at Edwards AFB. He had also been Northrop Grumman's program manager for the Joint Base Operational Support Contract at KSC while I was the Center Director. He did a great job for us there.

Mike was serving as the Operations Director for the Government Services Division at NGTS. I became an understudy to him in that position when I wasn't assisting with the transition team.

A few months after I arrived, Northrop Grumman won the contract to operate the Nevada Test Site for the Department of Energy's National Nuclear Security Administration. Mike had been bid as the vice president for National Security

Technologies, LLC (NSTec), the company that had been established to run the Nevada Test Site.

One day Mike came to me and said, "WKYAGBG—Well, kiss your ass goodbye, General. I am out of here."

That was his humorous way of telling me that I was now the Operations Director as he departed the scene for Nevada to begin the transition.

Operations Director

As the Operations Director, I was responsible for the management of a suite of contracts performing a variety of services for government agencies. The program manager for each of the contracts reported to me. I was responsible to assure that they delivered excellent services and had good customer relations.

That meant a lot of travel all over the country and overseas. I started and ended the travels from my home in Williamsburg most of the time. Since my travels out of the small and wonderful Williamsburg Airport or the nearby Norfolk Airport invariably connected through the hub in Atlanta, I quickly became one of Delta Airline's high-mileage flyers. I also became one of Marriott's Platinum members.

I commuted by car to my office in Herndon during weeks when I wasn't doing customer or program personal visits. I wanted to get to know the functional directors and managers well, as I often needed their help to keep our contracts running well. These employees managed functions such as contracts, business management, business development, legal, human relations, and supply chain management, to name a few. The personal relationships that I developed with them over the first few years helped me to be successful over the long haul.

Operating Unit Director

After my first year there, the president visited me in my office
and said, "We are reorganizing and want you to become an
Operating Unit Director instead of Operations Director." That
meant that I would now also be responsible for profit and loss
of my portfolio of contracts in addition to my previous duties as
Operations Director. I had never had to worry about profit and
loss during my years in the government, so I had a lot to learn
to be successful over the long term.

Although the set of contracts changed over the years that
I ran operating and business units (consisting of more than
one operating unit) for NGTS, as we won and lost contracts, I
always had a diverse set. NGTS was the managing partner for
the Joint Base Operational Support Contract, which operated
the infrastructure for NASA KSC and the USAF's Cape Canaveral Air Force Station. Since I was the source selection official
for this NASA contract, I had a legal lifetime restriction: I could
not approach any NASA official about anything in this contract
over its ten-year life. I could work behind the scenes to help the
program manager at JBOSC with issues; I did that often.

A PORTFOLIO OF CONTRACTS

Other contracts that were in the portfolio included the
following:

Maintenance depot for the US Postal Service in Topeka,
Kansas

Support services for the USAF's Civil Engineering Center at
Tyndall AFB, Florida

Operation of the USAF's surveillance system for detecting
orbiting satellites as well as space debris at several locations including the islands of Diego Garcia and Maui and a continental
site in Socorro, New Mexico. The program manager was located
at Peterson AFB, Colorado.

Operation of the NASA Sounding Rocket Program from their facility at Wallops Island, Virginia. We launched rockets at many ranges in the US and overseas.

Operation of service and infrastructure contracts at overseas locations for the DOD in Qatar, Turkey, and Egypt

Transportation services for the army at Redstone Arsenal, Alabama

Launch support services for the USAF at Vandenberg AFB, California

Range support services for the army at White Sands Missile Range, New Mexico, and Ft. Huachuca, Arizona

Operation of the navy's test and training ranges across the country

Support services for the Missile Defense Agency's Ground Based Missile Defense System, which had a headquarters in Huntsville, Alabama, with operations support at Vandenberg AFB, California, and launch sites in Alaska

Engineering support services to NASA's Langley Research Center, Virginia

Payload processing services for the International Space Station at the NASA Glenn Research Center, Ohio

Independent software safety support to the Minuteman III ICBM program

These contracts were re-competed every five to ten years and often the customer changed the characteristics of the job when it was re-competed. This kept us busy.

I also served as the chairman of the Parent Organization Oversight Committee, which conducted four to six independent technical and safety deep-dive reviews each year at the Nevada Test Site. Results were reported to the NSTec leadership and the NGTS chaired board of managers. Later, I became a voting member of the board of managers.

Competing for contracts

We bid on some contracts, which were interesting even when we lost. For example, we bid to operate the Lawrence Livermore National Laboratory, California. I was bid as the chief operating officer, the number-two leadership position, which required me to learn a lot about the laboratory so that I could be successful in the orals competition that was one of the more important factors to be scored by the government. We convened on weekends in Las Vegas to practice in the early days.

We relocated to the actual site of the orals competition at a hotel in Albuquerque, New Mexico, as the date for the orals approached. We went so far as renting all the conference rooms at the hotel to assure that we would have unrestricted access to the actual site of the competition. We talked the hotel management into letting us use the service hallways and elevators to get to and from our practices to avoid giving "spies" from the competition information about our team. All of our bosses up to the chairman/CEO of NG were in the audience, supporting us for the finals. That was a lot of visibility on our performance. We did well.

I felt confident that we would win, so Benita and I took a Thanksgiving vacation to Lake Tahoe, one of our favorite places. While there, we made some side trips to visit the laboratory in California and the surrounding area. We were excited about our potential new home.

Alas, we didn't win after all, but it was a great experience.

NGTS continued to try to win another big National Nuclear Security Administration contract since it would be a good fit for our business model as well as a good fit given the company's national security focus. We joined one of the incumbents, the managing partner, Babcock & Wilcox, operating the Y-12 and

Pantex plants in Oak Ridge, Tennessee, and Amarillo, Texas, which were to be consolidated into one contract for the re-compete. The proposal was complex and difficult to prepare, but we did a great job. The Source Evaluation Board graded our proposal higher than any other in all categories.

Unfortunately, during the competition, Y-12 endured an embarrassing security incident.

An 82-year-old nun and two other anti-nuclear protestors slipped past security before dawn in July 2012 and defaced a nuclear material storage building with animal blood.

That was embarrassing to the National Nuclear Security Administration, and they decided not to award it to the incumbent on our team, given that, as managing partner, their name was on the front gate at the time. And the managing partner should make sure that the security contractor is doing their job right.

The source selection official raised the score of one of the other bidders in three of the five categories and then found a slight edge in those to give them the win. This was a heartbreaking loss. We protested twice but still could not get the award.

Since 2010, I had worked to field a team to bid on operating the Sandia National Laboratories in Albuquerque, New Mexico, and Livermore, California, the design authority for our nuclear weapons program. This is the jewel of the National Laboratories. After many delays in the re-compete schedule, our team won the job in 2017.

Persistence does pay off!

Holding family close

We continued to make Williamsburg our home from 2003 until 2013. After the death of our daughter, we invited our granddaughters to spend their summer vacations with us to give their dad a little break—plus, we really enjoyed their company.

I bought summer passes to the nearby Busch Gardens theme park and an associated water park. I took them to one or the other many afternoons after finishing my work from my home office. We also had swimming pools in our gated community and both kids took swimming lessons and learned to swim well. They attended our United Methodist church with us and attended Vacation Bible School.

We took many mini-vacations to regional attractions. For example, we visited Luray Caverns in Virginia, which is a magical place for young and older people. We visited the sites and museums in our national capital. While there we went to Wolf Trap for a performance of *The Wizard of Oz*, with the musical score performed live by the National Symphony Orchestra.

My favorite trip was one to Florida. We viewed the last space shuttle launch with our granddaughters.

Benita and I also made many Christmas holiday and spring break trips to see them and our son and his family. Many of these were ski vacations at one of Colorado's great ski resorts—Steamboat Springs, Breckenridge, Copper Mountain, Crested Butte, or Telluride. All of the family, including the four grandchildren, learned to ski, but after several incidents early in Benita's skiing career, she opted out of skiing. She still enjoyed being in the mountains with the family.

Revelation

Our grandkids were growing up. The girls would be in college soon, and we couldn't spend as much time as we wanted to with the boys, who were younger. In January 2013, one day the strongest feeling came over me in the form of a question:

What are we doing here in Williamsburg?

I told Benita that I had a premonition that we should move soon to be closer to our family. It took some convincing—we'd moved so many times. It was tough to pull up and move again. I think the fact that it came to me as a strong premonition really helped her decide.

I checked with my boss, and he was okay with me continuing to run my business unit as a telecommuter from wherever we decided to move. We talked over the pros and cons of a California location, a Colorado location, or somewhere in between. We finally settled on a move to the Colorado Springs area because our grandsons were still in elementary school, and we would have more time to interact with them locally. Our granddaughters were in high school and would be leaving for college in the near future. We made a house-hunting trip and found and purchased a home in Monument, which is just a few miles north of Colorado Springs.

We worked hard to get our Williamsburg house on the market and successfully sold it without too much difficulty. We had a large collection of things that we had accumulated over the years that we needed to downsize to make the move more affordable.

My "professional papers," collected over the many years in the air force and NASA, was one of those large collections. The air force had shipped these for free for me through all my military moves. I worked with the Purdue University Library, which had started a special collection of astronaut papers, to find mine a new home. I catalogued my items and shipped more than a dozen large cartons to them. We also downsized our other possessions. This was of some benefit to local charitable stores, where many on them were put on sale.

Fire and snow

We moved in late April. The day the moving truck arrived at our new home to unload, our driveway was completely covered with about three inches of snow that had fallen overnight. I thought they might leave and return on a better day, but they seemed unfazed. They just scraped the driveway and walkway to the front door and proceeded with unloading our stuff. I guessed this situation was common in the spring in Colorado.

After moving, I continued to travel to Herndon for business that could not be done virtually. While there, I kept an eye on the small repairs to our home that the new owner had demanded after his inspection.

Just a few days before closing, I got a call from my realtor. There had been a freak windstorm overnight and my neighbor's tree was now lying across my driveway. This was on a Thursday. Closing was scheduled for Monday. The same day I heard from Benita that she was voluntarily evacuating from our new home in Colorado because wildfires were threatening.

My realtor and I were able to locate a company to remove the tree and clean up the debris so that by Sunday night all was okay in Williamsburg. Fortunately, the wildfires stayed away from our new home as well.

NGTS reorganized again effective January 1, 2014. My new boss wanted me to set up my office in the NG facility near the Colorado Springs Airport. I would now have an administrative assistant and a large office with a great view of Pikes Peak.

The only downside was that I now had a 30–40 minute commute each way, depending on traffic. I had intentionally picked a home on the north side of the city to put me closer to the Denver Airport, which was where most of my business trips needed to originate to have a reasonable selection of flights and prices.

Oh, well, we can't always predict what is coming in the future.

On our spring break ski trip to Steamboat Springs in 2014, I made a bad choice. I skied down a slope that was a little too steep and icy. I hit a chunk of ice with my left ski, which caused the binding to release my ski. When the toe of my boot hit the slope, it catapulted my left shoulder into the hard, icy surface. My shoulder was completely dislocated and my upper arm was broken.

The ski patrol did a great job of getting me down the mountain and into an ambulance. The local hospital sees a lot of ski injuries and made short work of resetting my shoulder and bone. With a little Motrin for the pain and inflammation for a few days and a lot of physical therapy over the next few weeks, I recovered and was as good as new. This was my second broken-bone skiing accident. A few years earlier, I put on my ski poles the wrong way, fell, and broke a thumb, so I am well known now at the Steamboat Hospital emergency room.

Christmas Letters 2006-2013

2006: Roy retired from NASA on Dec. 31, 2005. After over 40 years with the government, it was time to get a real job!

We helped Roy's sisters and brothers-in-law move Mom and Dad Bridges to a very nice independent living apartment in Birmingham, Alabama. Roy was all alone in the house when the dumpster divers visited after the "estate" sale. It was right out of the movie *Deliverance*, but he managed to survive.

Dad turned 94 in October and still beats Roy at pool and gets his exercise every day. Mom is still getting around at 87.

In March, we gathered with family and many friends at Catalina Island to scatter Tanya's ashes. She loved the island. It will always be a lovely spot for Tom, the girls, and all of us to return to when we want to be nearer to Tanya in spirit.

Father's Day weekend, Brian called to say that Jennifer is expecting (a boy) in January.

Tom brought the girls to stay with us for two weeks in July. It was hard to let them go home.

2007: January: first grandson, Luke, born to Jennifer and Brian

Roy's mom developed mobility problems and moved next door to a nursing home. Dad is doing well and can walk over to visit. Dad's 95th birthday and their 66th anniversary.

Granddaughters for three weeks in July

Week with Brian, Jennifer, and Luke in October. Luke gave everyone the stomach flu, but it was still a wonderful visit

Roy's mom passed away in December, and we traveled to be at her funeral service

2009: We took the whole family to Steamboat Springs for skiing to begin the year. Roy took a tumble and broke his left thumb (he's a dummy for holding his ski poles the wrong way!)

Biggest event of the year: safe arrival of Levi Dylan Bridges on Good Friday

2012: In October, we celebrated Roy Senior's 100th birthday with a family reunion at Oak Mountain State Park

2013: We moved to Monument, Colorado.

Chapter 44: National Security Technologies (NSTec)
April 2015–November 2017
Northrop Grumman, short-term projects January 2019

I continued my work running my business unit and chairing the Parent Organization Oversight Committee for our site in Nevada. In the spring and summer of 2014, our company in Nevada, NSTec, experienced several minor safety incidents and one major incident with injuries to a worker. My boss asked me to lead a team to do a deep dive and develop a plan to eliminate the root causes.

Nevada

I formed an eight-person team, and we traveled to North Las Vegas, set up shop in a spacious conference room, and began work. Over the next two months, we dug up the underlying root causes and created a long-term get-well plan to achieve and sustain a culture of operational excellence. After out-briefing the company leadership and our board of managers, I returned to Colorado and resumed my day job.

Unfortunately, during subsequent trips by a smaller team and me to observe progress, we concluded that the company was moving far too slowly in implementing the changes that we had recommended. My boss was extremely concerned, as we were on the verge of re-competing the ten-year contract. He decided to create a new position, Vice President for Strategic Management, and asked me to commute to Nevada to fill the position and get the company moving in the right direction faster.

Initially, the NSTec leadership was a little wary of my role in the company and me. They soon warmed up to me, and we began to make real progress. I thought that I would be able to return to my day job after a few months, but, alas, that wasn't to be. Near the end of 2015, the president of NSTec retired, and we began a leadership shuffle. I was asked to become the Vice President for Operations, which would also include my duties from my previous position as Vice President for Strategic Management.

Over the next two years, the company made rapid improvements and achieved the highest award fee score in the complex during our last performance period. I convinced all the company's top leaders to attend the leadership training at the same company that I had used at NASA Langley. I was even able to convince the federal customer leaders to attend. After training the senior leaders, we had the company bring training on-site for the next level of company and federal management. The improvement in leadership resulted in an impressive increase in employee engagement, measured by annual surveys.

We fielded a strong team for the competition of the contract and wrote a good proposal.

We didn't win.

Perhaps we asked for too much fee. Our contract ended on November 30, 2017. The good news was that I could stop commuting to Las Vegas every other week and spend more time at home.

Clearly the new contractor inherited a strong leadership team at all levels. The NNSA Administrator awarded me his highest award, the Distinguished Service Gold Medal. I had to lead the transition to the new contract and team, and our people did a great job. We finished strong.

I expected to be laid off by NGTS after completing the Nevada transition, but, surprisingly, they asked me to stay and assist our program manager at Sandia with several improvement projects. We did well on those. After another NGTS reorganization that was effective on January 1, 2019, I was finally laid off.

Retirement. No, really.

For the third time, I started my retirement on February 1, 2019. Except for some short-term consulting jobs for NGTS as a part-time contractor, I didn't expect to sign up for more work in the future. At seventy-five-and-a-half, I was ready to make this retirement a success.

When I got the news of my layoff, Benita was in a rehabilitation facility, recovering from a broken right leg and arm, both of which required surgery. The bones were broken because she'd had a low-blood-pressure event when she stood up from her chair to go to bed. She fainted and fell hard. I had already gone to bed but heard the crash and rushed to her side. I was able to get her into bed but had to call 911 the next morning when it became clear that she could not put weight on her leg.

She rapidly regained her strength during her stay at the rehab facility and came home in mid-February.

We began planning a road trip to California to attend our youngest granddaughter's high school graduation. We visited with friends and family in New Mexico and Arizona on the way and ate at several of our favorite restaurants along the southern interstate, as we had traveled that road many times before.

Kiley's high school graduation was great, and we hosted a celebration dinner at a nearby restaurant for all who attended. Then we headed off to Mission Bay Beach near San Diego for a weeklong family vacation with our son and his family and Kiley and her father and sister.

We were sure that Tanya was smiling from heaven about how well her girls had done.

Retirement was turning out to be wonderful.

Christmas Letters 2015–2018

2015: On March 31, we lost Pappy. He and my mother were married for 66 years. During his long life, Dad had almost died twice, lost an eye playing football in college, and was nearly deaf, but he lived to the age of 102 1/2, and left us a little more than seven years after Mom died in 2007, one month before her 89th birthday.

We organized a family reunion at Jekyll Island as a Celebration of Life for him. All of his children and grandchildren and their families, as well as many cousins and relatives, helped to celebrate his life and scatter the ashes of Roy and Elizabeth in the Roberson cemetery in Screven, GA.

2016: Kiley is a sophomore and a softball pitcher. Kynna is now attending Chaminade University in Hawaii and pursuing a degree in Forensic Sciences. Levi and Luke are in second and fourth grades; Levi played football this fall, and Luke is taking piano lessons.

2018: Roy was invited to be Grand Marshall for Monument's Fourth of July parade this year. His one condition was that the boys be in the parade with him. One of the boys sported a hat labeled "From the Earth to the Moon" and the other had a hat inscribed "Next Stop Mars."

Epilogue

My wife and I continue to enjoy our retirement in Colorado in a nice home with a view of the USAFA, which was so helpful to me in pursuing my chosen career, the Rampart Range of the Rocky Mountains, and the top of Pikes Peak. I sometimes joke that I can see the USAFA cemetery from my deck, which will minimize the logistics when the time comes for me to take up residence there.

Our son has a great job in the area, which helps us have frequent visits with him and his family. Our daughter-in-law is a real blessing to us. Our two older grandsons are doing well in school and in after-school sports. We were all pleasantly surprised with the birth of a new grandson in March 2020. He is a real delight, although our visitations have declined because of the pandemic, which, now that everyone is getting vaccinated, will be in our rear-view mirror soon.

Our son-in-law still lives in California, but he and our two granddaughters visit often when they have a break from school. The oldest graduated from college with a Bachelor of Science degree in Forensic Science from Chaminade University in Honolulu, Hawaii. We all were getting excited about attending her graduation. Alas, it turned into a virtual event after the pandemic interrupted travel. What a disappointment to miss that. The youngest is in her third year at University of California, Davis, and doing well. We believe that our daughter would be very proud of these two, as we are.

Following my astronaut adventures, I had the privilege of leading a lot of great people who were engaged in challenging work to advance our national security and continue our exploration of aeronautics and space. I will always be deeply grateful for the opportunity to serve our nation leading these endeavors.

I refined my leadership style by pursuing training that helped me to identify things that I did in supporting my workforce and the mission that were problematic. With coaching and feedback, I changed so that I could be a more effective leader. I recommend every leader follow a path like I did, as it can have such a positive impact on many people as well as improve mission performance.

I was recently surprised when the Gainesville City Council voted to name a street after me. My classmates and teachers were certainly key to my success in getting into the Air Force Academy. It is a great honor to be remembered by them in this special way.

Finally, I thank God for protecting me so many times over the years as I encountered dangerous situations. My confidence in His protection helped me face each one calmly so that I could make wise decisions on the courses of action to resolve the crises.

I recommend to all who read this book to imagine the best life that you could have and then go for it. Surely, experiment as you complete your formal education and begin work to refine your dreams, but don't let anyone tell you that you can't or shouldn't go for it. You will have setbacks, as I did, but learn from them and try again until you get it right.

As the title of this book suggests, I pursued a path of adventure and service with an improbable chance of achieving my dream of participating in our nation's space program as an astronaut. I shared it with a loving wife and family.

The results exceeded my wildest expectations.

Acknowledgments

Completion of this book would have been impossible without the expert assistance of my editors, Lori Brown and Jennifer Windrow, and my publisher, Lisa Norman.

There are many members of my family and circle of friends, classmates, teachers, mentors, leaders, and colleagues cited in this book who provided enormous help to me during my life. Achieving my dreams would not have been possible without their support and guidance. I am grateful for everyone who touched my life in such positive ways.

I owe my life to those aviators with whom I flew in peacetime and combat through the air and space. I would especially like to mention my expert crewmembers of mission STS-51F who performed magnificently and those in Misty. I also owe my life to the expert Mission Control Team for my space flight.

Most of all, I thank my wife of 54+ years for her loving support despite frequent hardships along the way. In our time of service to the nation, the deal was two for one. The nation and I got her full devotion every step of the way.

List of Abbreviations

AAA—Anti-Aircraft Artillery
AF—Air Force
AFB—Air Force Base
AFMC—Air Force Materiel Command
AFSC—Air Force Systems Command
AFSPC—Air Force Space Command
AOC—Air Officers Commanding
APU—Auxiliary Power Unit
ARPS—Aerospace Research Pilot School
ATO—Abort to Orbit
BDA—Battle Damage Assessment
BOQ—Bachelor Officers' Quarters
CAPCOM—Capsule Communicator
CTF—Combined Test Force
DOD—Department of Defense
DCS—Deputy Chief of Staff
ESMC—Eastern Space and Missile Center
FAA—Federal Aviation Administration
IP—Instructor Pilot
JBOSC—Joint Base Operational Support Contract
JSC—Johnson Space Center
KSC—Kennedy Space Center

LaRC—Langley Research Center

MECO—Main Engine Cutoff

NASA—National Aeronautics and Space

NESC —NASA Engineering and Safety Center

NGTS—Northrop Grumman Technical Services

NNSA—National Nuclear Security Administration

NSTec—National Security Technologies

OSHA—Occupational Safety and Health Administration

PDP—Plasma Diagnostics Package

PEM—Program Element Monitor

R&D—Research and Development

R&R—Rest and Relaxation

ROTC—Reserve Officer Training Corps

RTLS—Return to Launch Site abort

SES—Senior Executive Service

SMC—Space and Missile Center

SRB—Solid Rocket Boosters

STS—Space Transportation System

UPT—Undergraduate Pilot Training

USAF —United States Air Force

USAFA—United States Air Force Academy

UTTR—Utah Test and Training Range